# FRIENDS OF PROMISE

———

## CYRIL CONNOLLY
## AND THE WORLD OF HORIZON

# FRIENDS OF PROMISE

## CYRIL CONNOLLY
## AND THE WORLD OF HORIZON

BY
MICHAEL SHELDEN

HAMISH HAMILTON
LONDON

HAMISH HAMILTON LTD

Published by the Penguin Group
27 Wrights Lane, London w8 5TZ, England
Viking Penguin Inc, 40 West 23rd Street, New York, New York 10010, U.S.A.
Penguin Books Australia Ltd, Ringwood, Victoria, Australia
Penguin Books Canada Ltd, 2801 John Street, Markham, Ontario, Canada L3R 1B4
Penguin Books (N.Z.) Ltd, 182–190 Wairau Road, Auckland 10, New Zealand

Penguin Books Ltd, Registered Offices: Harmondsworth, Middlesex, England

First published in Great Britain 1989 by
Hamish Hamilton Ltd

Copyright © 1989 by Michael Shelden

1 3 5 7 9 10 8 6 4 2

British Library Cataloguing in Publication Data

Shelden, Michael
Friends of promise.
1. English literature. 1900–1945—Critical
studies   2. English literature. Connolly,
Cyril, 1903–1974, to 1922. Biographies
I. Title
820.9′00912

ISBN 0–241–12647–9

Typeset by Richard Clay Ltd,
Bungay, Suffolk
Printed in Great Britain by
Butler and Tanner Ltd, Frome

FOR
SUE, SARAH, AND VANESSA

# CONTENTS

# ILLUSTRATIONS

CYRIL CONNOLLY and STEPHEN SPENDER at a party, in
the 1930s, with Dick Wyndham and Tom Driberg.
(Photo: Joan Leigh-Fermor)

PETER WATSON, mid-1930s
(Photo: Cecil Beaton)

WEDDING PARTY for Stephen and Natasha Spender at
Drayton Gardens, 1941
(Photo: Cecil Beaton)

LYS LUBBOCK, 1941
(Photo: Lee Miller)

CYRIL CONNOLLY, 1942
(Photo: Howard Coster, Courtesy National Portrait Gallery)

LAURENCE VAIL and JEAN CONNOLLY, 1945
(Photo: James Stern)

WALDEMAR HANSEN with Lucian Freud, 1947
(Photo: Waldemar Hansen)

NORMAN FOWLER with Peter Watson
(Photo: Waldemar Hansen)

PETER WATSON, mid 1940s
(Photo: Cecil Beaton)

CONNOLLY at 53 Bedford Square, London WC1,
HORIZON'S LAST ADDRESS, 1948.
(Photo: Courtesy of Deirdre Levi)

SONIA BROWNELL and LYS CONNOLLY at 53 Bedford
Square, 1948.
(Photo: Orwell Archive)

Two views of Horizon, 1940 and 1947

CONNOLLY mugshots, 1950
(Photo: Lys Koch)

PETER WATSON, 1947
(Photo: Waldemar Hansen)

TWILIGHT: CONNOLLY in his late sixties
(Photo: Cecil Beaton)

# ACKNOWLEDGEMENTS

I could not have written this book without the generous assistance of many people and institutions on both sides of the Atlantic. My first debt of gratitude is to Cyril Connolly's widow, Deirdre (now Mrs Peter Levi), who kindly allowed me to examine Cyril Connolly's papers and to quote from them. I have also benefited from conversations with her, and am deeply grateful to her for giving me so much of her time, and for supporting this project from the beginning.

I have been helped by several people who were important figures in the world of *Horizon*. Lys Koch invited me to spend a weekend at her home and patiently spent much of that time answering my questions about her life with Cyril Connolly in the 1940s. She also allowed me to read her many letters from Connolly, most of which are now held at the Lilly Library of Indiana University. She helped me to locate Waldemar Hansen, who gave me several interviews and access to an invaluable collection of correspondence, including scores of letters from Peter Watson. I very much appreciate his openness, and am grateful for the encouragement he gave me at various stages of my work.

I owe a special debt to Sir Stephen Spender for discussing the *Horizon* years with me. For other interviews and letters I am indebted to the following: John Craxton, Michael Dixon, Charles Henri Ford, Ruth Ford, Lady Glenconner, Clement Greenberg, Derek Hill, the late John Lehmann, Lady Caroline Lowell, Mary McCarthy, Margaret Mellis, Howard Nemerov, Janetta Parladé, Peter Quennell, Priaulx Rainier, Ricki Riker, Edouard Roditi, Lady Watson, and Anne Wollheim.

Among librarians I must thank first the staff of the Rare Books and Special Collections Department of the McFarlin Library, University of Tulsa, where Cyril Connolly's library and papers are now located. It is an enormous collection, but working with it was made less difficult because of the courteous help I received from Sid Huttner, Bonnie Mitchell, and Caroline Swinson.

I want also to thank Penny Baker of the Institute of Contemporary Arts; Bernard R. Crystal of the Butler Library, Columbia University;

Lilace Hatayama of the University Library, University of California, Los Angeles; Madeleine G. Gosselin of the Houghton Library, Harvard University; Cathy Henderson of the Harry Ransom Humanities Research Center, University of Texas; Sara S. Hodson of the Huntington Library; Michael Meredith of the Eton College Library; Janet Ness of the University of Washington Library; Sigrid P. Perry of the Northwestern University Library; C. G. Petter of the University of Victoria Library; Jean F. Preston of the Princeton University Library; Judith A. Schiff of the Yale University Library; Lola Szladits of the New York Public Library; Saundra Taylor of the Lilly Library, Indiana University; and Jennifer Wood of the Imperial War Museum.

I particularly want to acknowledge the help and encouragement of Ian Angus, formerly the Librarian of King's College, London, and co-editor of *The Collected Essays, Journalism and Letters of George Orwell*. He was an indispensable guide to the world of *Horizon* when I was beginning my study and introduced me to a number of important sources. He was always quick to respond to my requests for assistance, and was unfailingly generous with his time. I greatly value his support.

David Pryce-Jones's *Cyril Connolly: Journal and Memoir* (Collins, 1983) was immensely helpful as a source of information on Connolly's early years, and I want to acknowledge its influence on my own efforts to describe that period.

For permission to quote from letters I would like to thank the following: Hon. David Astor, Edward Mendelson, Laurence Pollinger Ltd, the Peters, Fraser & Dunlop Group Ltd, and Sir Angus Wilson. For permission to quote from the published works of Cyril Connolly I want to acknowledge Rogers, Coleridge and White Ltd. Publishers of works quoted in this book are acknowledged in the Notes and the Select Bibliography. If I have failed to acknowledge the proper copyright owners, I apologise and promise that due acknowledgement will be made in any future reprints.

For assistance in bringing this book to publication I want to thank Mark Hamilton of A. M. Heath; and Christopher Sinclair-Stevenson and Peter Straus of Hamish Hamilton.

For special favours and assistance I am grateful to Tom Derrick, Mary Ann Duncan, Sue Martin, Cecil Nelson, Jack Rollins, Stuart and Sophie Sperry, and Hugo Vickers.

The University Research Committee of Indiana State University must also be acknowledged for its generous help.

Finally, I want to thank my wife, Sue, for her constant support and understanding.

# INTRODUCTION

When the first monthly number of *Horizon* went on sale in London during the Christmas season of 1939, there was every reason to think that this new 'Review of Literature and Art', as it called itself, was destined for a short life. Even in the best of times little magazines tend to die young, but in the dark days at the close of the 1930s the odds against a new magazine were overwhelming. War had been declared in September, and throughout Britain cultural life was in a slump. The future for literature seemed bleak: writers were faced with the threat of military service; publishers were hampered by paper shortages; and established magazines were disappearing at an alarming rate, victims of declining sales and rising costs. Among the magazines which ceased publication in 1939 were *Cornhill*; T. S. Eliot's *Criterion*; *London Mercury*; Geoffrey Grigson's *New Verse*; and Julian Symons's *Twentieth Century Verse*. Even though the war had barely begun – the terrors of the blitz were several months away – literature was in retreat.

Remarkably, *Horizon* defied the odds; it not only survived this confused and uncertain period but flourished in it. Slim, compact, and moderately priced at a shilling, the first issue sold out within a week of publication. In a few months the circulation reached 8000, an impressive figure for a small review, especially when one considers that *Criterion*'s average circulation was barely 500. The contents of the new magazine were brilliantly eclectic. In the first six numbers there were poems by W. H. Auden, John Betjeman, William Empson, Louis MacNeice, and Dylan Thomas; critical essays by George Orwell, Herbert Read, and Stephen Spender; and short stories by H. E. Bates, Elizabeth Bowen, Julian Maclaren-Ross, and V. S. Pritchett. Throughout the war years the magazine appeared each month with amazing regularity, overcoming difficulties created by the air attacks on London and by the general disruptions and scarcities of life on the home front. The quality of the contributions remained high in these years, and the

I

magazine was praised for helping to keep the flame of literary culture burning brightly. By the end of the fighting in 1945, *Horizon* was generally regarded as the best and most influential literary review of its time.

The magazine was the creation of three talented friends, all still in their thirties when the first issue appeared: Cyril Connolly, principal editor and the oldest of the trio, was thirty-six; Peter Watson, publisher and art editor, was thirty-one; and Stephen Spender, associate editor, was thirty. None of them had worked on the editorial staff of a literary monthly before, and when they started *Horizon* they knew almost nothing about the complexities of printing and distributing a new periodical in wartime. Their enthusiasm and determination helped to compensate for their inexperience, and it took them only ten weeks to get out the first issue; in that short period they managed to assemble everything from scratch and to put the finished product on sale in bookshops all over London. They received some outside advice and assistance, but for the most part they plunged ahead on their own, improvising as they went along. For an office they used Spender's two-room flat in Bloomsbury, moving books and furniture aside to make room for piles of manuscripts and subscription forms. They chose a small London printing firm run by a friend, and for publicity they sent out several hundred circulars and placed a few quarter-page advertisements in the *New Statesman* and other papers. 'The aim of *Horizon*,' one such advertisement proclaimed confidently, 'is to provide readers with enjoyment and writers with opportunity, and to maintain a high literary standard during the war.'

From the beginning Connolly was the central figure at *Horizon*. The idea of establishing a new review was his, and everyone understood that he would have overall control of editorial matters. In addition, it was his responsibility to write the 'Comment' which normally began each number. Very often the editor's column in little magazines is nothing more than an occasion for routine reflections on art, life, and the contents of the current number; in *Horizon* the editorials sparkled with elegant prose and witty, perceptive insights into the cultural life of the times. Connolly was a gifted essayist with a sharp eye for detail and a rare talent for turning a phrase. Within the relatively short, essay-like format of 'Comment', he was able to put his skills to good use. Indeed, *Horizon*'s high literary standards were nowhere more apparent than in the carefully crafted prose of Connolly's editorials. He was expert at swiftly dissecting a subject into its most important parts and then summing up his views in one or two memorable sentences.

A King's Scholar at Eton and a Brackenbury Scholar at Balliol College, Oxford, Connolly had begun his writing career as a critic for the *New Statesman* in the late 1920s. His first book – a novel titled *The Rock Pool* – came out in 1936, but it was not until the appearance in 1938 of his second book – *Enemies of Promise* – that he began to attract widespread attention. This shrewd analysis of modern writers and modern literary life revealed a first-rate critical intelligence, and readers were intrigued by the book's unconventional mixture of criticism, autobiography, and candid literary shoptalk. When *Horizon* was launched a year later, its success confirmed that the author of *Enemies of Promise* was among his generation's most talented men of letters.

Given his interest in literary life and his background as a critic of modern literature, it was perhaps inevitable that Connolly would want to edit a little magazine. But the idea might have taken root as early as 1922, his last year at Eton. Two boys at the school – Harold Acton and Brian Howard – created a minor literary sensation when they published a magazine of astonishing quality and sophistication: the *Eton Candle*. Stylishly bound in bright pink cardboard covers, with canary yellow endpapers, the magazine featured stories, poems, and essays which perfectly captured the avant-garde spirit of the early Twenties. Praised by Edith Sitwell and Sir Edmund Gosse, *Eton Candle* caught the attention of the London literary world, and was even given a review in the *Times Literary Supplement*. Its success made a lasting impression on many of the boys at the school, including Cyril Connolly. Sixteen years later he could still vividly recall, in *Enemies of Promise*, the intriguing appearance of that 'strange pink album'.

Connolly came of age when little magazines were enjoying their period of greatest success. Between 1914 and 1922, *Criterion*, *Dial*, *Egoist*, the *Little Review*, and *Poetry* became famous as showcases for the latest works of Eliot, Joyce, Lawrence, Pound, and Yeats. For anyone who wanted to keep up with modern literature, the little magazines were essential reading. The sense of excitement Connolly felt when he discovered them in his teens and early twenties stayed with him for the rest of his life, and the idea of publishing his own magazine had become fixed in his mind by the time he was in his early thirties. 'Favourite daydream – edit a monthly magazine entirely subsidised by self', he wrote in his private journal in 1934. 'No advertisements. Harmless title, deleterious contents.' He even had a title picked out for it: 'Meridian'.[1]

The only thing that prevented this fantasy from becoming a reality before 1939 was money. Although he lived comfortably in the 1930s,

Connolly could never have afforded the costs of starting a monthly review. What made *Horizon* possible was the generosity of Peter Watson, who agreed to underwrite the expenses. Watson was the younger son of a millionaire baronet, and he enjoyed a handsome allowance from a family trust, which gave him the freedom to cultivate his interests in modern art, music, and literature. In the late 1930s he acquired a large apartment in Paris and filled it with a dazzling collection of paintings and sculpture by such artists as De Chirico, Gris, Klee, Miró, and Picasso. He became friends with many artists whose works he collected and, though he had little creative talent himself, his taste and judgment as a collector were valued among his artist friends. In the summer of 1939 he was planning to sponsor an art magazine in France, but when the war broke out he left Paris and settled in London, where Connolly – who had been a close friend since 1937 – promptly persuaded him to devote his time and money to establishing a new magazine in Britain. On 18 October 1939, *Horizon* was officially born when Watson, in his capacity as publisher, signed a printing contract for the first four monthly issues.

Connolly could not have found a better patron than Watson. Although there was occasional friction between them, Watson respected Connolly's editorial freedom, and usually accepted his decisions without question. For the most part he also paid the magazine's debts without question, spending at least a thousand pounds a year to subsidise production costs and payments to contributors and staff. Reserved and rather shy, he preferred to stay in the background at *Horizon*, but he was by no means a passive benefactor. He took his job as art editor seriously, going to great lengths to obtain knowledgeable essays on modern art and to find illustrations to accompany them. He also played an active part in the practical, day-to-day operations of the office, especially in the early stages. Of his importance to *Horizon* the art critic Roland Penrose has written: 'Patient and faithful, Peter was willing to accept responsibilities and give his support generously to the exacting task of editing *Horizon*. Peter provided the springboard which was essential not only for Cyril's flights into the worlds of the imagination but also for his return to earth, a union of complementary opposites.'[2]

Both Connolly and Watson wanted Stephen Spender, a mutual friend, to help with their new venture and, after a few days of discussion with him, it was agreed that he would become the associate editor. Already the author of nine books, Spender at thirty was a well-established literary figure – a playwright and critic as well as a prominent poet of the 'Auden generation'. His presence on the staff enhanced the credibility and prestige of the magazine and attracted important contributors. For his part, Spender welcomed the chance not only to help edit the new review but to contribute some of his own work, especially articles on the war and politics. One of the most important contributions in the early issues was the three-part serialisation of 'September Journal' – Spender's daily record of his reflections on the first month of the war.

Spender's time at *Horizon* was cut short, however, when his call-up papers arrived in 1941, sending him off to join a unit of the National Fire Service. From that point, the magazine was in the hands of Connolly and Watson, who ran it with the help of a few dedicated assistants and secretaries. Because his position at *Horizon* was deemed a 'reserved occupation', Connolly did not have to perform any military or government service, and was able to remain at his editorial job throughout the war. (For health reasons Watson was also exempt from service.)

Connolly regarded *Horizon* as his 'war work', and was defiant of philistine critics who dismissed the reading and writing of 'highbrow' literature as frivolous, escapist pursuits in a nation at war. In 'Comment' he insisted that whatever demands the war imposed on the country, it was vital for writers and artists to continue producing art in order 'to make our culture into something worth fighting for'.[3] Art was a necessity, not a luxury, he argued, and could not simply be pushed aside until the war was over. 'Art occupies in society,' he wrote in 1940, 'the equivalent of one of those glands the size of a pea on which the proper functioning of the body depends, and whose removal is as easy as it is fatal.'[4] At *Horizon* it was Connolly's self-appointed duty to remind the country that the survival of its culture was threatened as much by philistines at home as by hostile armies overseas.

To promote the cultural interests of the country as broadly as possible, Connolly kept the magazine open to contributors of all types. As long as the writing was lively and intelligent, he gave serious consideration to almost any submission, regardless of the author's style, reputation, or point of view. What he wanted to encourage most was individual talent, not particular literary groups or movements. 'If literature is an art,' he wrote in his second 'Comment', 'then a literary magazine should encourage the artists, whether they are Left or Right, known or unknown, old or young.' His eye for recognising new talent was sharp. Among the writers he 'discovered' were Julian Maclaren-Ross, William Sansom, Denton Welch, and Angus Wilson. Other writers who were given important exposure in *Horizon* early in their careers were Patrick Kavanagh, Arthur Koestler, Laurie Lee, Alun Lewis (Connolly was the first to publish 'All Day It Has Rained', Lewis's magnificent war poem), W. R. Rodgers, Philip Toynbee, and Vernon Watkins.

Connolly was on close terms with many talented writers of his generation, and often turned to them when he needed new material for *Horizon*. During the war he earned a reputation for throwing the best literary parties in London, and he sometimes used these gatherings to recruit a new contributor or to persuade an old friend to send him a recent piece of work. Connolly's critics sometimes complained that too much material in the magazine came from the editor's friends. To be sure, Connolly was guilty of publishing work he might have rejected had he not known the contributor. The same can be said of many editors, but his wealth of literary friendships produced some remarkable dividends for *Horizon*. Auden, Orwell, and Dylan Thomas, all longtime friends, brought him several of the magazine's most distinguished contributions – works which are now among the classics of twentieth-century literature: Auden's 'In Praise of Limestone'; Orwell's 'Politics and the English Language'; and Thomas's 'Fern Hill' and 'A Refusal to Mourn the Death, by Fire, of a Child in London'. Friendship also encouraged Connolly to take risks on brilliantly eccentric contributions which other literary editors might have balked at publishing; for example, Orwell's early essays on popular culture: 'Boys' Weeklies' and 'The Art of Donald McGill'. But whether contributors were known to him or not, Connolly often imagined that his position as their editor created some personal link between him and them. As Stephen Spender once observed, Connolly took 'a vicarious pleasure in the work of his best authors, as though they were his editorial creation'.[5]

As one might expect, the success of *Horizon* gave a great boost to Connolly's career. Publishers began offering him book contracts. The BBC invited him to take part in cultural broadcasts. And from May 1942 to September 1943 Lord Astor employed him as the literary editor of the *Observer*, a job he undertook in addition to his normal work at *Horizon*. His confidence in his writing grew and, in the year that followed his departure from the *Observer*, he completed his extraordinary wartime journal, *The Unquiet Grave*. Published at the end of 1944, the book received instant critical acclaim. Writing in the *New Statesman*, Raymond Mortimer hailed it as a 'twentieth-century classic', and in the *New Yorker* Edmund Wilson wrote: 'This small volume – a scant hundred and fifty pages – is one of the books that has interested me most, as it is certainly one of the best written, that have come out of wartime England.'[6] Within a year Connolly followed the success of *The Unquiet Grave* with another important book, *The Condemned Playground*, his first collection of essays and reviews. Representing nearly twenty years of work in literary journalism, the book gave ample proof of the versatility and richness of his talent. It featured astute critical pieces on other writers, autobiographical sketches, travel essays, cultural criticism, and some of the funniest literary parodies and satires in the English language ('Where Engels Fears to Tread' is perhaps the best known).

With the return of peace to Europe, there was renewed appreciation for *Horizon*'s importance as a champion of British culture during the isolation of the war years. Connolly earned widespread praise for his part in keeping the magazine alive and dynamic throughout that time. He suddenly became a literary celebrity. Early in 1946 *Time* ran a long, flattering story about him, complete with a photograph of the editor at work in his London office, his pen poised above the pages of a manuscript. Later that year the American *Saturday Review* featured a cover portrait of him, and when he visited the United States at the end of 1946 he was lionised in New York literary society. Back in London at the beginning of 1947, he learned that the French government had decided to award him the Legion of Honour, in recognition of the encouragement *Horizon* had given to French wartime writers. In the wake of all these developments *Horizon*'s circulation rose to more than 10,000.

Ironically, this success eventually proved *Horizon*'s undoing. For with his own career going so well, Connolly began to lose interest in serving other people's talents as an editor. He began to complain that editing was an 'unwholesome' influence on his creativity, draining his energies and corrupting his artistic sensibility. 'An editor frays away his true personality in the banalities of good mixing,' he lamented in the late 1940s; 'he washes his mind in other people's bath-water, he sacrifices his inner voice to his engagement book.'[7] After the war he began taking occasional breaks from *Horizon*, leaving the editorial chores to Watson or to the magazine's small staff while he stayed away for as long as a month or two at a time. He wanted the freedom to concentrate on his own work, to produce a new book which would meet the uncompromisingly high standards he had set for himself. In the memorable opening sentence of *The Unquiet Grave*, he declared, 'The more books we read, the clearer it becomes that the true function of a writer is to produce a masterpiece and that no other task is of any consequence.'

In the post-war period Connolly toyed with several ideas for a novel, but was unable to turn any into a finished book. As the decade came to a close, he decided that what he needed was not just a few short periods away from the magazine but an entire year's 'sabbatical'. He was determined to make an all-out effort to write a masterpiece. The magazine could continue in his absence for a short time, but there was not much point in trying to maintain it without him for as long as a year, because *Horizon* was too closely identified with him. So, in his 'Comment' for November 1949, he announced that the magazine would suspend publication for one full year. The tone of his statement suggested, however, that *Horizon* would probably be laid quietly to rest and not reappear. The next issue was indeed the last. At the end of the Forties, after a run of 121 issues and more than 10,000 pages, the magazine closed with the publication of 'a special number to commemorate the tenth year of our existence', as Connolly ironically described it in 'Comment'.

Nearly 9000 readers were still buying copies each month during the final year. If Connolly had been inclined to stay on, he might have held *Horizon* together for at least another decade. Without too much effort he could have kept most of the subscribers for several more years, giving them a pleasing menu of familiar names from the Forties and enough new writers to add variety and spice. But the Fifties could not provide Connolly with the kind of excitement and sense of purpose which had inspired him to work on *Horizon* in the first place. Surveying the literary scene at the end of 1949, he concluded that four years of post-war austerity had left literature in a dull and dismal state, and cited a dramatic decline in the quality of work contributed to *Horizon* as a major factor in his decision to give up editing. Established writers, he complained, were no longer willing to send their best work to a small review when more lucrative deals could be struck in the growing American market, and talented young writers were increasingly hard to find. 'In normal times,' he observed in his penultimate editorial, 'the slow desiccation of middle-aged writers would be balanced by the emergence of younger ones, but in the world of cold war and conscription this has not proved to be the case.'

A new generation was, of course, emerging from the post-war period – Amis, Larkin, Wain, and the other writers of the 'Movement' were only a few years away from making their mark on the literary world, in part at the expense of 'highbrow' men of letters like Connolly. But whatever the future held, Connolly no longer had the patience to wait for it at *Horizon*. His magazine had survived much longer than anyone had expected, and he felt that after ten long and difficult years the time had come to put it behind him and move on. As he joked in an essay written much later, 'Ten years for a little magazine is about the same as for a dog, i.e., a lifetime.'[8]

When *Horizon* closed, Connolly still had twenty-four years to live. Unfortunately, as a writer, he would find these years disappointing. He retired briefly to a cottage in Kent to work on a novel, but did not get far before he put it aside and became a regular reviewer for the London *Sunday Times*, where he remained for the rest of his life, commenting on other people's books while he struggled, unsuccessfully, to write his masterpiece. The few books he published after 1950 were made up mostly of reprinted pieces from his columns in *Horizon* and the *Sunday Times*. When he died in November 1974 at the age of seventy-one, the obituary writers were full of praise for his accomplishments of the Thirties and Forties, but lamented that, despite his obvious brilliance, he had never fulfilled the promise of those earlier decades.

Connolly had anticipated 'failure', and had spent a good part of his adult life apologising for not doing more with his talent. In *Enemies of Promise* he admitted many of his major weaknesses, confessing that he was too lazy to discipline his art, too fond of worldly pleasures to finish what he began, and too keen on conversation to save his ideas and witty remarks for his books.

A less obvious but perhaps more important problem – and one Connolly never fully acknowledged – was his difficulty with literary form. He could never make up his mind whether his talent was best employed in fiction, criticism, informal essays, or autobiography. Elements of each can be seen struggling against the others in almost all his books. He liked to think that his destiny was to write a great masterpiece of fiction, but as his only published novel – *The Rock Pool* – demonstrates, he lacked the skilful novelist's ability to develop a range of strong characters and a compelling plot. At his death his personal papers (now at the University of Tulsa) contained the manuscripts of at least half a dozen unfinished novels: hundreds of pages of material which defied his attempts to work them into shape. Despite his reputation for avoiding hard work, Connolly often put enormous effort into his writing, especially in the Forties; but, in spending so much of his time trying to write novels, he was going against the grain of his talent, which was essentially that of an essayist and autobiographer, not a novelist. Moreover, because he placed so much emphasis on writing fiction, he disparaged his work in other forms, dismissing some of his best essays as hack journalism.

These problems should not obscure the fact that he was a superb

9

stylist in whatever form he worked. He is a writer whom other writers love to quote; as Philip Larkin – one of Connolly's great admirers – has pointed out, there are no less than fifty-five entries for Connolly in the *Penguin Dictionary of Modern Quotations* (for comparison's sake, E. M. Forster has twenty-six, one of which is about Connolly). Though he failed to complete a unified, major work, the entire body of Connolly's writing, published and unpublished, is overflowing with splendid fragments worthy of inclusion in any anthology of English prose. The special, 'fragmented' quality of his work has perhaps been described best by an anonymous reviewer in the *Times Literary Supplement*, who observed in 1954:

> It may well be that Mr Connolly's ultimate achievement will be fragmentary, informal and occasional – using those terms as descriptive and not pejorative. It will not be a row of Collected Editions, but perhaps a kind of screen, each panel of which is filled with odd but conclusive sentences, novels of one paragraph, poems a phrase long and images as bright and arresting as a child's scrap-book.[9]

Cyril Connolly has often been written about since his death. He figures prominently in the biographies, autobiographies, and published letters and diaries of his contemporaries. In 1983 he was the subject of a long biographical essay by David Pryce-Jones, who used it as a supplement to his edition of Connolly's journal of 1928–1937. Pryce-Jones's work, however, has little to say about *Horizon* or Connolly's career after the Thirties. Until now the history of *Horizon* has remained largely untold, as has the eventful story of Connolly's life in the *Horizon* years – the most productive time of his career. My purpose in this book is to give these stories the sustained and detailed attention they deserve, and to do so in a way which blends literary history with criticism and biography. It is impossible to understand *Horizon* without taking into consideration the cultural and intellectual currents which swirled around it or the personal lives of those who steered it through the decade. Cyril Connolly's life and art will be at the forefront of this study, but ample space will be given to the lives of the many other 'friends of promise' who, in a variety of ways, contributed to the magazine's success. The most important figure in this supporting cast is Peter Watson, whose name has fallen into unjust obscurity since his death in 1956.

In the story of *Horizon*, art and life are inextricably linked, and this book will move back and forth freely between the two.

# ONE

# A MAN OF PROMISE

## I

In 1940 Cyril Connolly's father, a retired major of the King's Own Yorkshire Light Infantry, sent his son a thank-you note for the latest issue of *Horizon*, the first he had enjoyed reading. 'In my uneducated opinion, though not, I suppose, in that of your high-brow clientele,' his father wrote, 'it is far the best No. you have given us, for the reason that all is written in plain English and I can understand every word of it. Many of [the previous issues], even when I would have enjoyed the matter, have been written in such high-flown jargon that I've not understood a word.'

Matthew Connolly could never figure out why his son wasted so much time on 'highbrow' literature. Names like Auden, Eliot, and Joyce meant little to this practical military man trained at Sandhurst in the last years of Queen Victoria's reign. To him, a real writer was someone like Kipling, a hearty fellow who could put into 'plain English' the sentiments and desires of the common people. The issue of *Horizon* he praised contained a long review of a new book on Kipling. The review was hardly flattering to Kipling, calling him 'a nervous misanthropic artist', but that mattered not at all to Major Connolly, who so enjoyed reading the reviewer's quotations from Kipling that he was overwhelmed by a wave of nostalgia for the golden age of the Empire. 'I like the article on Kipling,' he told his son, 'which brings back the good old days of the Nineties, which were *not* naughty but very proper and over-chaperoned, but there was plenty of money, and cheap living, and country house life of an almost defunct splendour.'[1] Out of a sense of duty Connolly regularly sent copies of *Horizon* to his father, but he knew that most of the magazine's contents would be lost on the old soldier, a man so schooled in the conventions of the past that he signed even personal letters to friends and family 'M. Connolly, Major'.

Although Cyril was an only child, he and his father had never been close, and certainly by the time *Horizon* began the two had little in common. The major lived at the Naval and Military Hotel, a rambling old building in South Kensington occupied by dozens of retired captains and majors living on modest pensions in small, drab rooms. Around the corner was busy Cromwell Road, on the other side of which stood the Natural History Museum – almost a second home to Matthew Connolly. He spent many hours there each week as an unofficial scientific worker in the Department of Zoology, where he was without peer in the arcane study of non-marine *Mollusca*, or snails, as they are commonly known. He had developed a passion for collecting snail shells during a tour of duty in South Africa and, after his retirement from the army at the end of the First World War, he devoted his energies to expanding his collection. Hundreds of shells, neatly tucked inside pill-boxes lined with cotton, were labelled and filed in wooden cabinets along every wall of his hotel room. Adding to the clutter were stacks of conchological journals from around the world and several piles of the major's painstakingly typed research notes and scientific papers. A heavy bookcase was filled with assorted volumes about shells, including a massive 660-page monograph on South African snail shells written by Matthew Connolly. Published in 1939, when he was sixty-seven, this work was the apogee of his second career. Cyril Connolly took a disdainful view of his father's obsession with snails: 'It made me a conchophobe,' he once wrote, 'and I came to dread the names of colleagues – Pilsbry ... Tomlin, "Old Ponsonby" – and his latest exchanges with them.'[2]

Apparently, Connolly's mother too was unimpressed with her husband's devotion to snails for, within a few years of the major's separation from the army, she separated from him. They had been married in 1900, shortly after Matthew Connolly's promotion to captain, and over the next dozen years Muriel Maud Vernon Connolly dutifully followed her husband from one outpost to another, including Capetown and Hong Kong. It soon became clear that their marriage was not bringing either of them much happiness. Maud, as she was called by her friends and family, grew up in a prosperous and well-connected Anglo-Irish family. Her father had an estate of a thousand acres on the outskirts of Dublin, and her aunt was the Dowager Countess of Kingston. Maud was attractive and graceful, with a romantic fondness for birds, landscapes, and poetry. But her sensitive nature was wasted on a husband accustomed to the routine of army life and the analytical methods of science. She fell in love with one of her husband's commanding officers – General Christopher Brooke, a dashing hero in the Boer War and the First World War. Maud never divorced Major Connolly, but by the early 1920s she had settled into her own flat in London and was continuing her relationship with General Brooke. In the 1930s she and the general retired to South Africa, where they spent the rest of their lives.

Maud gave birth to her only child early in the marriage. On 10 September 1903, Cyril Vernon Connolly was born in Coventry, where his father was serving as the adjutant of a local battalion. A small but energetic boy, Connolly grew up deeply attached to his mother, rarely venturing out of her sight during his first six years. He shared her sensitive nature, and in later years would often attribute to her influence his love of art and natural beauty. The highlight of his childhood was his family's move to South Africa when he was five. The lush, Mediterranean landscape of the Cape Colony excited his youthful imagination and instilled a lifelong love of sunny climates. His parents provided him with a pony and several smaller pets, and took him on frequent excursions to the sparkling white beaches. In *Enemies of Promise* he fondly recalled 'the walk to the sea through clumps of rushes and over white sand feathered with the tracks of lizard and all around me an indescribable irradiation of sun and wind and space and salt'.

Shortly before he turned seven, this idyllic beauty was abruptly taken away. His father was sent to a new post in Hong Kong, and his parents agreed that Cyril should return to England rather than accompany them to such a distant and exotic place. The separation from his mother was heartbreaking, and he was never quite able to forgive her for leaving him behind. 'Insecurity and the only child's imagined need for love' took hold of his character, he later wrote, and for the rest of his life he was haunted by the fear of desertion.[3]

Back in England, Connolly was cared for by his father's mother, who lived in Bath. He went to school there as a day boy until his parents returned from the Far East and put him in a private boarding school, St Cyprian's, on the Sussex coast. He was barely eleven when he began his first term and, except for the holiday breaks, the school was his home for the next three and a half years. The fees were high, but St Cyprian's had a reputation for preparing boys for scholarships at top public schools, particularly Eton and Harrow. With the seventy-five other boys at the school, Connolly studied primarily languages and history and, under the stern supervision of the headmaster and his wife – Mr and Mrs Wilkes, he spent gruelling sessions translating Greek and Latin texts or memorising interminable lists of names, places, and dates. The school attracted a number of boys from prominent families; judging by a letter Connolly sent his mother in 1916, St Cyprian's was home to a mixed collection of noble sons. 'This term,' he wrote, 'we have an awful lot of Nobility . . . 1 Siamese prince, the grandson of the Earl of Chelmsford, the son of Viscount Malden . . . who is the son of the Earl of Essex, another grandson of a lord and the nephew of the bishop of London.'[4]

Young Connolly was clearly impressed by all these titles, but his closest friend at the school was neither aristocratic nor rich – he was an awkward, introspective boy who had been taken on by the school at reduced fees because his family could not afford to pay the full expense. He was the son of a retired bureaucrat of minor standing in the colonial service; his name was Eric Arthur Blair, known today by his adult pseudonym – George Orwell. The establishment of his lifelong friendship with Connolly was one of Orwell's few happy experiences at St Cyprian's; he detested the school's strict regimen and snobbish atmosphere. Thirty years later he was still venting his anger in a bitter account of his schooldays titled, ironically, 'Such, Such Were the Joys'. By contrast, Connolly's criticism of the school in *Enemies of Promise* is restrained and mild. In Orwell's account the headmaster and his wife are nothing less than monstrous; in Connolly's memoir they are merely vulgar and ridiculous. Orwell speaks painfully of his 'hatred' and 'loathing' of the place, but Connolly is content to show his disapproval in satirical asides: 'Though Spartan, the death-rate was low.'

In 1917, Connolly took the scholarship exams at Eton, Charterhouse, and Wellington, and won acceptance at all three. There was no doubt about Eton being his first choice, and in the summer of 1918 he took on an impressive new identity: C. V. Connolly, Esq., K.S. [King's Scholar], New Buildings, Eton College, Windsor. His first year at Eton was not a happy one. The senior boys of the Sixth Form had the privilege of administering discipline, and Connolly was frequently singled out for punishment. Summoned before the Sixth Form, he would kneel on the seat of a chair and hold tightly to its back legs while one of the older boys thrashed him. To be beaten by the Sixth Form and bullied by other boys was simply part of the normal initiation into life at Eton then, but Connolly came in for more than his fair share because he was not good at games and because many of the boys simply did not like his looks.

He was not handsome: he had a spotty complexion, a thick brow, and a short, flat nose. He was slender but clumsy and sometimes slow. Several boys teased him for being 'ugly', and one joked that Connolly's pug nose made him look as though he had been 'kicked in the face by a mule'.[5] He had attractive features – a delicate mouth; a soft, intelligent voice; and a pair of bright, playful blue eyes – but he became convinced that he was 'ugly' and to compensate for his lack of physical charm he tried to win friends by flattery and wit. Gradually, those who bullied and beat him were seduced into liking him. He learned how to divert them by making fun of himself and by parodying the misfortunes of other boys like him. In his words, 'I made them laugh at the expense of their victims and my sarcasm became useful.'

He also sought refuge in books, keeping out of sight in the School Library instead of submitting himself to the humiliating rough-and-tumble of the playing fields. He read voraciously, finding escape in the dreamy worlds of romantic poets – especially the early Yeats – and in the remote histories of ancient and medieval civilisations. Long hours of escapist reading gave way to long hours of serious study, and he began to make his mark as a promising scholar. He had to take care not to seem too ambitious about his work because, in the opinion of many Etonians, intellectual seriousness was as much a social handicap as physical ugliness. 'Intelligence was a deformity which must be concealed,' Connolly observed, and he made a point of studying in secret as much as possible, doing some of his reading 'illicitly at night by candle'. Yearning for acceptance, he cultivated the image of a 'brilliant idler', someone who could consistently score high marks without appearing to make much effort. The ruse worked. He won popularity as a sort of school jester, an irreverent wit incapable of taking anything seriously. All the while his scholastic record continued to improve, as if by magic.

The pinnacle of his success at the school came in 1922. Early that year, his fourth and final one at Eton, he travelled to Oxford to take the scholarship examinations for Balliol, and in March he learned that he had earned the Brackenbury History Scholarship. This honour was followed in April by a more surprising triumph: his election to Pop, the Eton Society. Pop was a self-elected group of the two dozen most popular boys, most of them handsome young gods of the playing fields, who were allowed considerable independence and authority. They formed the ruling élite of the school, and in Connolly's day included such grand names as Antony Knebworth, the Earl of Lytton's accomplished son, and Alec Dunglass (later Sir Alec Douglas-Home). It was heady company for Cyril Connolly, who at eighteen was still unhandsome and hopelessly unathletic. Amazed at his good fortune, he speculated that his election to Pop had been a token gesture to show that its members 'appreciated intellectual worth and could not be accused of athleticism'.

Near the end of his time at Eton, Connolly was teased about his achievements by a friend who joked, 'Well, you've got a Balliol scholarship and you've got into Pop – you know, I shouldn't be at all surprised if you never did anything else the rest of your life.' It would have been easy to laugh this off and forget it, but Connolly was unable to put it out of his mind. Even at the height of his success at school, disillusionment began to set in. He began to worry that he had come too far too fast, and that reality would catch up with him and never again bring him anything to compare with his honours at Eton. He dreaded becoming one of those old boys whose life turns into a long steady decline after schoolboy victories. Even his honours began to appear as a potential drag on his future, for they had established him as a young man of promise, and that burden threatened to become more than he could bear. 'Early laurels weigh like lead,' he later lamented.

To maintain his balance, he sought to avoid adding further laurels to his crown. He began to neglect his study of history; shortly after winning the Brackenbury, he decided that he 'hated' history because 'it stank of success'. He passed his time reading French poetry and Pater's *Marius the Epicurean*, adopting 'aestheticism' as his new creed. He discovered Aldous Huxley's *Crome Yellow* and monitored, from a distance, the intriguing activities of the Eton Society of Arts – the small group of boys who, under the leadership of Harold Acton and Brian Howard, put together the *Eton Candle* magazine. In his final weeks at school, he began wearing grey flannel trousers with a black dinner-jacket and a panama hat, and during 'the lime-flowered summer evenings' he took to haunting the banks of the Thames in search of 'golden moments'.

In October 1922 Connolly went up to Balliol but, after the disillusionment of his final weeks at Eton, he could not take his studies seriously. His time at Oxford became, in his phrase, 'a three-year day-dream'.[6] He avoided lectures, skimped on preparations for his weekly tutorials, and scorned competitions and prizes. Surrounded by a few well-chosen friends – among them Kenneth Clark and Peter Quennell – he lived more or less as he pleased. In later years he joked that his only exercise at Oxford was 'running up bills'.[7] He enjoyed dining out and drinking with his friends, staying up late talking about 'life' and 'art' at parties, playing bridge, or going sightseeing with undergraduates who, like Kenneth Clark, owned motorcars. Anything was preferable to studying.

But while he was busy enjoying himself, his time at Oxford raced swiftly to its conclusion, and in the summer of 1925 he found himself faced with final examinations. Not surprisingly, he performed poorly. He obtained only a Third Class degree, hardly what was expected from a Brackenbury scholar. His parents and many of his friends were deeply disappointed, but he took it in his stride. Academic honours were not all that important, he claimed, and would not help much in the literary career he had begun imagining for himself during his last year at Oxford.

In the meantime, his prospects of finding a good job were dim, and the easy credit of his undergraduate years quickly dried up. His parents, now separated, reluctantly provided him with a little money while he looked for a permanent job. Finally, in June 1926, he found a position which seemed to fit his needs perfectly. The American-born writer Logan Pearsall Smith, son of a prosperous Quaker family from Philadelphia, wanted a bright young man with literary ambitions who could serve as his secretary and whose career he could encourage by providing a stable income and ample free time for writing. When Connolly offered himself for the job, Pearsall Smith hired him on the spot.

The fact that Connolly had recently come down from Balliol weighed in his favour, for Pearsall Smith was also a Balliol graduate, and still felt a strong sentimental attachment to the college. He was sixty years old when Connolly first met him, and was known primarily for his two collections of aphorisms – *Trivia* (1918) and *More Trivia* (1922) – and for a popular linguistic study, *The English Language* (1912). He was a slow, fastidious writer who thought nothing of spending several days perfecting a single sentence. His family had left him a comfortable sum to live on, so he did not have to worry about making his literary work pay. 'All my days are Sundays,' he liked to boast.[8] A lifelong bachelor, he owned a house in Chelsea and a quaint Tudor farmhouse in Hampshire overlooking Southampton Water.

As Pearsall Smith's new secretary, Connolly was given a few minor tasks: correcting proofs of magazine articles or tracking down bits of scholarly information, but for the most part he was left alone to pursue his literary interests. Although Pearsall Smith could sometimes be stuffy and pretentious, Connolly found him an understanding and tolerant companion, and soon came to regard him as a 'father-figure' – a sympathetic older man with the education, taste, and income Major Connolly so obviously lacked. Pearsall Smith enjoyed playing this part, having no children of his own. He liked dispensing fatherly advice about friends, money, and art, and it amused him to sponsor the literary plans of a younger man.

Pearsall Smith introduced Connolly to one of the most influential men of letters in London – the literary editor of the *New Statesman*, Desmond MacCarthy. He became well-acquainted with MacCarthy and his wife, Molly, when they visited Pearsall Smith at his country home in the summer of 1926. Connolly's first impression of MacCarthy was that he was 'a very good man indeed – wise, humorous and kindly', and over the next few months that impression deepened as MacCarthy repeatedly went out of his way to help Connolly establish a literary career.[9] He began by allowing him to do a few unsigned reviews for the *New Statesman*; when these efforts proved worthy, he gave him his first signed appearance in print with a review of a new seven-volume collection of the works of Laurence Sterne. It was not an easy assignment for an inexperienced young writer, but Connolly handled it skilfully, revealing an extraordinary command of style and critical judgment for someone only twenty-three years old. In later years Connolly frequently gave MacCarthy credit for helping him to develop his skills as a literary journalist, recalling once that working under the editor was like taking a 'tutorial seminar' in writing. MacCarthy, he said, 'gave free lessons on how to express yourself. He often praised you and you'd be very pleased, then suddenly he'd say, "This is bosh!" and bosh it was as a rule.'[10]

Shortly after Connolly wrote his review of Sterne's works, Mac-Carthy offered him a fortnightly column in which to review novels for the *New Statesman*. He accepted the job enthusiastically, and his first signed column appeared on 3 September 1927. Over the next year and a half he reviewed several important works – Gide's *The Counterfeiters*, Hemingway's short-story collection *Men Without Women*, Mann's *Death in Venice*, and Evelyn Waugh's *Decline and Fall* – but, predictably, he had to spend most of his time writing about 'the worthy second-rate', and repeated exposure to such work killed his enthusiasm for regular reviewing. In addition, when MacCarthy left the paper to join the *Sunday Times* in August 1928, Connolly felt much less at home at the *New Statesman*. He did not get on well with the chief editor, Clifford Sharp, a bad-tempered alcoholic whose knowledge of contemporary literature was embarrassingly weak. After submitting the manuscript of his column one day, Connolly was stunned to hear Sharp complain of it, 'For Christ sake! Who's this woman Valéry? Why can't you keep Valéry out of this? You might be having a wonderful affair with her, but we don't want to hear about it.'[11]

By the end of 1928 Connolly had decided to give up his job with the paper and go back to living on a modest allowance from Pearsall Smith.

In his last column in February 1929, he seized the opportunity to blast the earnest writers and publishers who had helped to encourage 'a whole school of second-rate English fiction'. What infuriated him most, he declared, was the glut of pretentious, self-consciously 'literary' novels by grave young men and women who had 'read too well and loved unwisely' – books with titles like *Polished Corners* and *Our Daily Bread*. 'Perhaps anyone who writes a novel can make a hundred pounds,' Connolly wrote, 'but if this is the motive of their authors, why not write a pot-boiler and make a thousand? All this washy and sophisticated worthy slop degrades the novel as a form of art while in no way justifying it as a form of income.'

Connolly aspired to write a novel which would show the right way to do the job. Indeed, he was trying to write at least two novels when he gave up his column, both strongly autobiographical and neither very good. The title of one of them, *Green Endings*, sounds like the titles he enjoyed ridiculing in his column. Such ironies did not escape him, because his criticism of others was in part aimed against himself – against his 'worthy second-rate' efforts to write fiction. When he finished criticising others in his column, he subjected his own work to the same close scrutiny, which is one reason why he found it so hard to complete a novel. Ultimately, it was impossible to keep his fundamental weaknesses as a novelist hidden from his sharp critic's eye, but he was prodded along by a passionate desire to join the ranks of the great novelists. When he finished his last column, he packed his bags and headed for Spain, hoping to find a quiet, sunny place where he could live cheaply while he worked on one of his novels.

## II

Connolly did not travel to Spain alone. He was accompanied by a young American student, Jean Bakewell, whom he had met on an earlier visit to Paris. She was only eighteen years old, but for more than a year she had been living in Paris, more or less on her own. She was there, ostensibly, to study art, but much of her time was taken up by the social life of the Latin Quarter. Sophisticated and well-read, she was mature beyond her years, and moved easily in the company of artists, writers, and intellectuals. She came from a wealthy family in Baltimore, Maryland, and carried herself with the assurance of one who was used to getting what she wanted.

Connolly described Jean as tall and slender with 'short dark hair, green eyes and high cheekbones'. She had a 'lovely boy's body', and there was a natural, uninhibited look about her, which was reflected in her fondness for casual, bohemian fashion – a typical outfit was 'Low shoes, blue skirt, blue sailor's sweater, spotted handkerchief and beret'.[12] He was immediately attracted to her, captivated by her American freshness and spontaneity. 'She suits me perfectly,' he told a friend in England; 'she is affectionate rather than passionate, fond of good food, good books, good films, good talk, good places . . . she has a natural taste for the first rate rather than any restless intellectual pretensions.'[13]

Although his trip to Spain did not bring him significantly closer to completing a novel, his affair with Jean prospered, and within a year they were married. The two travelled to Baltimore for the ceremony, staying with Jean's family. Connolly was overwhelmed by the family's affluence, and was amazed to find that their house had 'more bathrooms than bedrooms and more cars than there are people, 6 cars for a family of 5'.[14] The couple received several expensive wedding gifts, including a set of diamond studs for Connolly, and Jean's mother agreed to give her daughter an allowance of at least a thousand pounds a year – enough to enable the couple to live comfortably without either having to work. On the passage back to Europe they had their own stateroom, and in the summer of 1930 they rented a small house in the South of France, among the hills between Toulon and Marseille. In this cosy Mediterranean retreat, surrounded by tall pines and palm trees, the first year of their marriage was spent 'living for beauty'.

Thanks to Jean's money, Connolly was able to enjoy an independent literary life in the manner of Logan Pearsall Smith, and, when they established a permanent residence in London in the early Thirties they settled in Chelsea, not far from Pearsall Smith's house. Over the next few years Connolly and his former patron were often in each other's company, playing chess or haunting secondhand bookshops together in search of first editions. In 'leafy tranquil cultivated' Chelsea, as Connolly described it, life imposed few demands: he and Jean had a spacious flat in the King's Road, two servants to cook and clean, and a car for quick escapes to the country.[15] They entertained often, giving dinner parties for literary friends such as John Betjeman, Elizabeth Bowen, Nancy Mitford, Anthony Powell, Peter Quennell, and Evelyn Waugh. (Visitors were sometimes taken aback by the Connollys' fondness for eccentric house pets, which included ferrets, lemurs, and an African genet.) The days were free for writing, but, without the pressure of deadlines or financial need, Connolly found it all too easy to put off working. He could afford to wait until he was in just the right mood for work and, like Pearsall Smith, he fussed over a sentence until he was satisfied that it was 'perfect'. He continued to write occasional reviews, but with the satisfaction of knowing that he did not have to do it for the money.

In the spring of 1934 he finally managed to finish a novel. The work was, in his own description, 'very short, lyrical, and seedy'. Because of its 'uncommercial' length and 'sordid' subject matter, it was not published until 1936, and then only in Paris and New York.[16] *The Rock Pool* still seems awkwardly short today, but its cast of decadent expatriates in the South of France are rather tame by current moral standards and few modern readers would find the story shocking. But in the Thirties no English publisher wanted anything to do with a book which features, in its first chapter, two lesbians dancing together (one of them wearing a man's tweed suit and an 'apache cap') in a French bar full of odd-looking artists and writers. After Faber & Faber and another London firm turned the novel down, Connolly gave up trying to find an English publisher, telling his friend Sylvia Beach, proprietor of Shakespeare and Company in Paris: 'Alas my little novel The Rock Pool is smut-bound . . . I think that I must try and have it done in America, or else it will have to appear in an under the counter way, like the Obelisks.'[17]

Eventually the book was accepted by Jack Kahane's Obelisk Press in Paris, as well as by the more 'respectable' firm of Scribner's, in New York, but by then Connolly was so disheartened by his inability to secure an English publisher that he dismissed the book as a failure. He told his friend George Orwell that the novel was 'lousy', and that the best thing in it was the Preface, which is concerned in part with criticising the publishers who had rejected his work. His attack on these cautious gentlemen reaches its climax in this wonderful sentence: 'I know there is a theory that a book, if it is any good, will always find a publisher, that talent cannot be stifled, that it even proves itself by thriving on disappointment, but I have never subscribed to it; we do not expect spring flowers to bloom in a black frost, and I think the chill wind that blows from English publishers, with their black suits and thin umbrellas, and their habit of beginning every sentence with "We are afraid", has nipped off more promising buds than it has strength-ened.'[18]

He could snipe at the publishers for rejecting his work on moral grounds, but had their rejections been based on artistic considerations he would have had less room for argument. Naylor, the young English hero of the novel, never really comes to life. He merely articulates certain ideas and attitudes which Connolly wants to examine in the novel – the snobbery of English society, the corruption of artistic sensibility by material and social pressures, and the conflict between the life of the mind and the demands of the flesh. Connolly is clumsy in dealing with these subjects, while trying to manage dialogue, plot, and setting. He is sometimes so distracted by the mechanics of constructing a novel that he writes appallingly bad sentences. It is difficult to imagine that he would have let this sentence stand had he been writing non-fiction: 'Beneath the blouse, with its Russian collar, the small firm breasts seemed made with halves of broken tennis balls.'

A few months before *The Rock Pool* was published, he conceived the idea of writing an autobiographical sketch of life at Eton. The idea came to him after he had reviewed a book about the short but glamorous life of Antony Knebworth, his friend when they had been members of Pop. Lord Knebworth had died at the age of twenty-nine in a plane crash, a few years after he had begun a promising political career. In the aftermath of his death, his father wrote a memoir of his son titled, simply, *Antony*. In reviewing it for the *New Statesman* at the end of 1935, Connolly gave some of his own impressions of the world he and Lord Knebworth had known at Eton – a world which already seemed to Connolly to belong to a very distant past. These impressions proved so intense that they continued to occupy his thoughts long after the review was finished, and he resolved to write about them at greater length. Two and a half years later his account of his life at school appeared as the third and final section of *Enemies of Promise*.

In contrast with his experience with *The Rock Pool*, he found writing *Enemies of Promise* relatively easy, and a major London publisher, Routledge, brought it out. After ten years of struggle to create plausible characters in fiction, he chose in *Enemies of Promise* to write about himself. This gives the book a more interesting and complex protagonist than any he could invent. The whole book is dominated by Connolly's personality, although only Part III, 'A Georgian Boyhood', is straight autobiography. When he writes about modern novelists in Part I, he discusses their works not as an objective critic but as a disappointed novelist who passionately wants to understand how to write good fiction. When he considers, in Part II, how ambition, reputation, and the marketplace affect the ways in which writers work, he speaks poignantly of the failures and frustrations of a literary career, describing them in sharp detail, as one who has experienced them personally. The entire book is an experiment in what he calls 'ideology-autobiography', a work 'in which an author looks back on himself in relation to the ideas of his time'.

The experiment produced some impressive results. Connolly makes general literary arguments come to life with vivid autobiographical insights or dramatic details. When he writes of the insidious influence of journalism on literary style, he illustrates his point by introducing the semi-autobiographical character of Walter Savage Shelleyblake, whose career becomes bogged down in the swamps of journalism, where he writes reviews with titles like 'Swansong at Lichfield' and 'Expatriate from Auchinleck'. Like Connolly at the *New Statesman*, Shelleyblake finds himself 'promoted to reviewing novels ... If he is complimentary and quotable, he will be immortalised on the dust-wrapper and find his name in print in the advertisements. And eight to ten novels a fortnight, sold as review copies, add to his wage.'

Flashes of autobiography are scattered throughout the first two sections of the book, and it is through such detail that Connolly establishes his hold on the reader's imagination. His ideas about literature are almost always instructive, but what sets them apart is his rare ability to illuminate the pragmatic, human side of any literary question. His approach is intimate and dynamic, and seldom strays into the realm of pure theory. He never loses sight of the fact that reading and writing are individual acts carried out against the backdrop of everyday life, and this special focus gives his literary speculations and observations uncommon immediacy and liveliness.

In November 1938, shortly after *Enemies of Promise* was published, W. H. Auden wrote to him:

> I think *E. of P.* is the best English book of criticism since the war, and more than Eliot or [Edmund] Wilson you really write about writing in the only way which is interesting to anyone except academics, as a real occupation like banking or fucking with all its attendant egotism, boredom, excitement and terror. I do congratulate you on a brilliant but also solid and moving book.[19]

Although Connolly's book received several good reviews, it did not make much money; its appearance was overshadowed by the Munich crisis, and sales were disappointing.

Perhaps the most famous remark in *Enemies of Promise* is Connolly's warning, 'There is no more sombre enemy of good art than the pram in the hall.' Unlike so many of his observations in the book, this bit of wisdom was not arrived at by experience, for he had discovered early in his marriage that Jean was unable to have children. Unless they adopted a child, there would never be a 'pram in the hall' to disrupt their lives, but by 1938 his life with Jean was threatened by complications of another kind. Although his wife had done everything within her power to help his career, he had come to blame some of his failures on the carefree existence she had helped to create for him, a life he took for granted but increasingly resented. It had made him, he thought, too dependent and easygoing, reinforcing all his worst faults. He believed that during his marriage his talent had gone 'off the boil', to use his phrase, and he wanted to hold Jean partly responsible. In more rational moments he knew very well that it was unfair to blame her for giving him exactly what he had wanted, but he could not help seeing her money as a curse as well as a blessing. Writing in his journal in 1934, he had added 'too much leisure' to his private list of 'enemies of promise'. 'With so much leisure,' he wrote, 'one leans too hard on everyone and everything and most of them give way.'[20] He convinced himself that for the sake of his art he needed to be less dependent on Jean, though what he had in mind at first was simply breaking some of his emotional, not his material, ties to her.

Jean proved amazingly tolerant of his almost childlike need to rebel against her, patiently standing by while he indulged in a series of short affairs with other women. But late in 1937 he fell in love with a young woman who established a hold on his imagination as powerful as that exercised by Jean in Paris eight years earlier. Like Jean in 1929, she was a bright, attractive student with boundless curiosity about anything connected with the arts. She was twenty-two, twelve years younger than Connolly, and when he met her she was preparing to enter the Chelsea School of Art as a student of painting. Her name was Diana, and she came from a conservative, upper-middle-class English family which had operated a printing firm in London for many years. She had been brought up at her parents' country home in Hampshire and had received a conventional education at a fashionable boarding school in Kent. Connolly was charmed not only by her beauty and intelligence but by her innocent enthusiasm for art. Her dream of becoming a painter inspired him to think of her as both a muse and a fellow artist with whom he could share his life. He was soon excitedly telling her that one day he would find a large studio somewhere in London, where they could paint and write together, two kindred spirits devoted to 'Art'.[21]

By the time that *Enemies of Promise* appeared, Connolly had become deeply involved with Diana, but he was still living in the King's Road flat with Jean. Although their marriage was barely intact, Jean hoped that her husband would eventually turn his attention back to her. It was clear that he still valued her affection, and on more than one occasion he had vowed to stop seeing Diana, but he could never bring himself to make a firm decision. Despite the fact that Diana repeatedly urged him to go back to Jean, he could neither give up his new love nor break with his old, insisting that both women were, in their separate ways, essential to his happiness. Exasperated, Jean began spending more of her time away from London, travelling to France and Italy for extended visits and finally, in the spring of 1939, her patience ran out. The lease on their flat had expired, and she decided not to renew it, telling Connolly that she was separating from him and intended to move to France. Within days, she had packed her bags, closed the flat, and departed for Paris, leaving her dejected husband in a hotel room in Sloane Square.

## III

Jean had several friends in Paris, some of whom had known her since her student days, but her two closest friends in the city were a wealthy young Englishman and his American companion, both of whom she had met through Connolly. The Englishman was Peter Watson, and the American was Denham Fouts – Watson's lover – a strikingly handsome young man who had grown up in a small town in Florida.

Watson was an Old Etonian whose first year at school had coincided with Connolly's last year. As schoolboys, they had never been introduced – they were too far apart in age to have had much contact – but Watson knew who Connolly was in those early days, because he would have been caned for not recognising a member of Pop. After Eton they had remained in separate worlds until one summer day in 1937 when Watson and Fouts met Connolly and Jean in the Austrian resort town of Kitzbühel, where they were all spending several days relaxing in the mountains. The four quickly became friends, but Jean, in particular, found the company of Watson and Fouts appealing. She discovered that she had much in common with them; like Watson, she had been brought up in a wealthy family and was living on an independent income (though hers was far less than his) and, like Fouts, she was an American expatriate living with an Englishman whose social background and education were unlike anything known in the States. She found it easy to talk to both these new friends, and after their first meeting Jean often visited the two men in Paris, where they had taken an apartment in the Rue du Bac. When she arrived in France after separating from Connolly, she inevitably turned to Watson and Fouts for sympathy and companionship.

A delicate, gentle man, Watson was a good friend to several women during his life, though his interest in them never went beyond the bounds of friendship. He discovered his homosexuality early in his youth, and never had any sexual interest in women. When he was in his early twenties, however, there were a number of attractive young women who had their eyes on him as a potential husband, not least because his father was one of the richest men in England. Sir William George Watson's estate was valued at two million pounds when he died in July 1930, a few weeks before the twenty-second birthday of his youngest child, Peter. In the Depression an estate of that size represented wealth on a truly grand scale. Almost all the money had come from the business Sir William had founded before the turn of the century, and from which he had retired as chairman in 1926 – the Maypole Dairy Company, a firm which manufactured margarine and sold it in over a thousand company-owned shops throughout Britain. When butter was in short supply during the First World War, the company had reaped enormous profits from the increased demand for margarine, and Sir William had created a life of considerable luxury for himself and his family with this money. Peter Watson grew up in a large country house in Berkshire known informally as the 'White House' because it resembled the presidential mansion in Washington. Properly known as Sulhamstead House, it was on a hill overlooking the River Kennet, and had seventeen bedrooms. The family also had a house in Mayfair, and a chauffeured Daimler to carry them back and forth between town and country.

Although his father had invited him to join the family business, Watson did not find the idea appealing. His mother had encouraged him to take an interest in the arts – she was especially drawn to music and loved going to the opera – and she was not surprised when he showed more enthusiasm for literature, music, and painting than for the margarine trade. She made sure that he had a generous income from a family trust, and was content to see him live independently as an art connoisseur and collector, unfettered by business obligations. After his father's death he spent his time educating himself in museums, galleries, and concert halls throughout Europe and America. He sought out artistic friends, and soon became known in London, New York, and Paris as a cultivated, intelligent supporter of modern art. His friends in the Thirties included the composer Igor Markevitch, the stage designer Oliver Messel, and the painter Pavel Tchelitchew, who so much admired Watson that he painted a large portrait of him as a handsome knight in blue armour. Another friend was Cecil Beaton, who frequently accompanied Watson on trips abroad and who tried, without success, to become his lover.

Cyril Connolly was impressed with Watson's glamorous way of life, and appreciated his excellent taste not only in art but in wine, food, clothes, and countless other things. Whatever Watson wanted, he could afford to buy the best, whether it was Vuitton luggage or a Bentley motorcar. However, he made no show of it, and this understated elegance appealed to Connolly, who liked to imagine that he could live as well if he had been blessed with the means. Indeed, Watson's privileged existence seemed to embody many of Connolly's daydreams about a life of ease and independence and, in typical fashion, Connolly had come to think of Watson as his 'discovery'. But when Jean moved to Paris and began seeing a great deal of Watson, the thought that they were enjoying themselves together was almost more than Connolly could stand. He felt deserted not only by Jean but by Watson, especially when she indiscreetly wrote to him that Watson thought a long separation might be good for her marriage. Connolly wrote back angrily to warn her against listening to such 'destructive advice', and vowed, 'I don't think I ever want to see Peter Watson again, such counsel he gave to you.'[22]

During the summer of 1939 he wrote numerous letters imploring Jean to return, but he continued to want her to accept him as he was. 'If I gave up [Diana] I should feel you had bullied me,' he wrote, 'unless there were many things you would also give up.' He confessed that he was 'in guilt up to my eyes', but he also felt compelled to stir up feelings of guilt in her, telling her that without her support, 'I shall turn into a Desmond [MacCarthy], with perpetual London ill-health, much hack-work and little money, and that all the countries we were going to see, I never shall see, and that if there's a war the pound will be worth nothing, and writers earn no pounds.'[23] A few days later he tried a more conciliatory approach:

We must be serious. We must live as if the world were going to end – and we must see serious people, it's no good being serious over frivolous people, always cleverer or deeper than the company we keep. No more lemurs. I think we should go somewhere where we know nobody and make new friends – what about a kind of mass observation of USA à deux . . . Or Mexico, or Russia. I don't consider most of our friends worth the paper we don't write to them on.'[24]

These hopelessly unrealistic plans did nothing to change Jean's mind, and by the middle of the summer Connolly was desperate. Jean had generously continued sending him money from Paris, but after several months he feared that their separation was permanent, and that the day would arrive when she would cut all their ties.

In July and August he earned some extra money by taking on the kind of hack work he had wanted Jean to help him avoid; for five weeks he served as film critic of the *New Statesman* (edited by Kingsley Martin). The low point came during his last week when he found himself trying to think of something to say about *Tarzan Finds A Son*, starring Johnny Weissmuller. The best he could manage was that Mr Weissmuller 'is beginning to look old round the neck'.[25] In the middle of August he accepted an invitation to stay for a few weeks at the Ulster home of his friends Ran and Angela Antrim, and he wrote forlornly from there, 'Am pierced by memories of better days – the whortle-berries and pines of Kitzbühel when we were just getting to know Peter Watty.' Now, he complained, he had nothing: no wife, no house, no book to write, 'nothing in the world but 3 suitcases'. There was nothing to look forward to, 'no hope, only despair and longing for cessation of feeling, for engine running in closed garage, running one away to oblivion'.[26]

It is impossible to say whether he was serious about this threat of suicide, but it was enough to persuade Jean to see him again, and a meeting in Paris was arranged for the end of August. In addition, Peter Watson wrote to apologise for any misunderstandings arising from his conversations with Jean. He assured Connolly that he had no intention of interfering in their marriage, and that he did not want to see their separation become permanent. 'Please get it out of your head,' he wrote, 'that I want to see you and Jean separated. I do not and I should be very sorry if it happened and I only wish that a solution could be found and that you could be happy together, as I am fond of you both.' Watson even made an effort to show understanding for Connolly's concerns about work, telling him, 'I certainly do not think you should do journalism reviewing now that you hate it.'[27] Connolly was grateful to have this expression of sympathy and, as he travelled to Paris for his meeting with Jean, he decided that he should also meet Watson separately. He wanted not only to explain his troubles with Jean but to discuss a literary project he had been contemplating for most of the summer. He had decided that the time was right for bringing out a new review in London, and he wanted to edit it. He had long dreamed of having his own magazine, and he believed that Watson might be persuaded to help him, especially if his friend really did care about saving him from the grave of journalistic hack work.

The hastily arranged trip to Paris was not a success. Jean told him that the possibility of her returning to him was slight, and that she was determined to live her life as freely as possible, without any definite plans for the future. She wanted to continue living in France apart from him, though she was vague about whether she would stay in Paris or go elsewhere. Connolly had no better luck with Watson, who showed little enthusiasm for sponsoring a magazine in England. They met for lunch at a sidewalk café, and Connolly spent a good part of the afternoon trying to convince his friend that a new magazine was needed and that good contributors could readily be found for it. Several months later he tried to recapture the scene in a draft of a letter written to attract American subscribers to *Horizon*:

> Cyril Connolly, a literary critic on the English *New Statesman*, was trying to persuade his friend Peter Watson to come home and start a paper. Watson refused, he could not bear England, he said . . . [It] was a Victorian period piece, and he was already committing himself to an art paper in Paris. If he went anywhere, it would be to Arizona to buy an orange farm. Connolly argued that there were already too many art magazines in Paris, there were *Verve, Cahiers d'Art*, and *Minotaure* – it was in England, where *Criterion*, the *London Mercury*, and *New Verse* had all come to an end, that a new periodical was needed. Instead of hating England in Paris he should bring his hate to London, where it could do some good. He should leave the whale, like Jonah, and return to blast Nineveh. Watson was not convinced, he did not want to abandon his collection of Picasso and [De] Chirico, his sombre faubourg apartment with the eighteenth-century windows.[28]

Connolly had almost no chance to reflect on Watson's decision. The next day, 1 September 1939, war broke out in Europe, and the idea of starting a magazine seemed out of the question. Since there was widespread fear that fighting might spread quickly into France, Connolly had little difficulty persuading Jean to return with him to England. After their arrival in London, however, Jean decided to travel to Yorkshire, to stay with friends for at least a few weeks. She was still unwilling to go back to her old life with her husband.

A few days later Peter Watson also returned, travelling from Paris to Calais in a troop train, sharing his compartment with silent, brooding soldiers. (Denham Fouts had chosen to visit Finland shortly before war began, and his return to England was delayed for several days.) Watson left Paris in such haste that he did not even pack luggage for the trip. Almost everything that he owned was left behind in his apartment in the care of a Rumanian friend, who agreed to have his art collection safely stored until his return.

Although Jean was keeping her distance, Connolly felt relieved simply to have her back in England and, with war news occupying his attention, he no longer spent so much time thinking about his personal problems. 'My spirits are very high,' he wrote, 'and I spend most of my time cheering up Peter . . . and [Diana].' He added that he was even trying to land a steady job that would see him safely through the war, explaining that he had hopes of finding work either at the new Ministry of Information or at a daily newspaper in London. 'I am determined to get something, as it will be intolerable to be only pink cannon fodder by the time the days draw in – if we're all back at school one must be a prefect.'[29]

There was indeed a kind of schoolboy jauntiness about him in the early weeks of the war, a feeling that he could somehow find a way to survive whatever hardships were imposed on him. Thus when September came to a close and he still had no definite job, he did not panic. The war was settling into a period of inaction on both sides and, as it became clear that this waiting game might continue for some time, he began to think once more about starting a magazine. It had occurred to him that the war, regardless of how bad it might become, had nullified Watson's earlier excuses for not backing the magazine. If they were going to be confined to England for the foreseeable future, he reasoned, why not create their own 'war work' and occupy themselves in an interesting way? With Watson's help and the government's blessing, the idea might succeed.

One evening in the last week of September Connolly and Watson were invited to a party at Elizabeth Bowen's house in London, and during the evening Connolly again raised the proposed magazine. The arguments seemed to be all on his side and though Watson was still reluctant to support the idea he had trouble finding new reasons to reject it. Finally his resistance was overcome. War or no war, Cyril Connolly was determined to have his literary review, and this time his persistence paid off. This time Peter Watson said yes.

# TWO

# WAR OF WORDS
## 1939–1940

## I

Peter Watson knew enough about Cyril Connolly's private life to realise that some new crisis involving Jean or Diana might cause his friend to postpone work on their magazine or abandon it altogether. He also knew enough about his working habits to doubt whether his friend could keep up with the demands of a monthly deadline. Even if Watson had not known Connolly personally, a reading of *Enemies of Promise* would have produced similar doubts, because its author admits his faults so freely, confessing that he is 'a lazy, irresolute person, overvain and overmodest, unsure in my judgments and unable to finish what I have begun'. These are not the qualities to inspire confidence in a new editor, so Watson sought out another person to share the editorial duties and possibly take over if Connolly left abruptly.

He approached his friend Stephen Spender and asked whether he would be willing to serve as associate editor. 'Peter asked me specifically to help edit *Horizon* because he wasn't absolutely sure about Cyril,' Spender recalls. 'He wanted to have three editors, and then if Cyril didn't work out, I would be there to help Peter carry on.'[1] Although Connolly did not know the true motive behind Watson's offer, he was all in favour of Spender joining them because he thought that a poet and a critic might combine nicely to form 'a complete editorial character'.[2] He was also a friend of Spender's, and welcomed the chance to work with him.

Spender was willing to help, but he was reluctant to assume a formal editorial title. Another friend, John Lehmann, also wanted him as associate editor of *New Writing*, and Spender was troubled by the need to choose between the two magazines. He preferred to give informal, occasional assistance to both. But in the early autumn of 1939 it was not clear whether Lehmann's magazine, which had first appeared in 1936, would survive much longer; rather than wait to see whether its

31

prospects would improve, Spender decided he would quietly accept Peter Watson's offer, but, to avoid offending Lehmann, he insisted that no mention of his editorial post appear in *Horizon*. True to his wishes, it never did.

Watson and Spender had known each other for about two years. They had both been at Oxford in 1927–1928 – Watson at St John's College, and Spender at University College – but Watson had left after only one year, and Spender does not recall seeing him in Oxford. They were only a few months apart in age. Watson was born on 14 September 1908, and Spender on 28 February 1909. The son of a distinguished Liberal journalist, Spender was raised in Hampstead, where he attended day schools before going up to Oxford. At university he met Auden and Isherwood, and within a few years he and his two friends had become famous as the leading figures in a new 'school' of Left-wing writers and intellectuals. Spender's involvement with the Left was always vague and ambivalent, and certainly did not prevent him from establishing a close friendship with a man as rich as Peter Watson. Indeed, he was no more immune to the appeal of Watson's wealth than was Connolly. Recalling many years later a Swiss journey he had taken in 1938 with Watson, Spender wrote of his rich friend:

> When I think of him then, I think of his clothes which were beautiful, his general neatness and cleanness, which seemed almost those of a handsome young Bostonian, his Bentley and his chauffeur who had formerly been the chauffeur of the Prince of Wales, one wonderful meal we had in some village of the Savoie, and his knowing that the best food in Switzerland is often to be found at the buffets of railway stations.[3]

Travelling in Watson's enormous dark green Bentley, the two young Englishmen must have looked striking together, for both were tall and thin, with prominent eyes and long, angular features. Watson was able to disguise his awkward frame with exquisitely tailored suits, but Spender dressed more casually, and this served to accentuate his large, gangling build. Like almost everyone else who knew Watson, Spender was fascinated by the easy, unassuming way in which his friend was able to cultivate the art of living well:

> He had the characteristics of a self-made person. One felt that he had gained little from Eton and Oxford. Putting this another way, one might say that his education had all been through love: through love of beautiful works and through love of people in whom he saw beauty. He detested politics, officialdom, priggishness, pomposity and almost everything to do with public and bureaucratic life.[4]

In 1938 and 1939 Spender saw a good deal of his friend, usually visiting him in Paris at the apartment Watson shared with Denham Fouts; they always got on well, but Spender was less comfortable with Fouts, whose great physical attractiveness and 'Deep South' charm masked a volatile, sometimes nasty temper. There were rumours about his past and tales of erratic, dangerous behaviour. Once, when Spender was staying at the apartment, Fouts stormed out of a passionate argument with Watson, rushed downstairs into the courtyard, and began firing a revolver into the air. A few minutes later Fouts returned with a sullen look on his face, 'and flung the empty revolver on to a table'.[5] On another occasion Fouts is reported to have been so overcome by anger that he drove a car into the Seine, leaping out just before it crashed into the water. There was no predicting what he might do next; in sharp contrast with his thoughtful, reserved companion, he was incapable of disciplining his emotions.

Spender had become friendly with Connolly before he met Watson. Their initial meeting was uneasy due to unusual circumstances. In March 1935 Spender had published his first book of criticism, *The Destructive Element*, a work which explores the relation between literature and politics, and Connolly reviewed it for the *New Statesman*. A copy of the review reached Spender during a holiday abroad and he was angered by what he read. Among other things, Connolly complained that the book was 'often awkwardly written, arid, inconsequent and hard to follow'.[6] Spender promptly wrote to him to answer the criticism, and a private meeting was arranged between the two. They discovered that they were able to push their differences aside and find interest and pleasure in each other's company. It was the beginning of a friendship occasionally strained by indiscreet remarks on both sides, but it managed to survive these ups and downs, ending only with Connolly's death some forty years later.

Ironically, when Spender accepted Watson's offer to work on the new magazine, his personal life was in almost as much turmoil as Connolly's. Earlier in the summer of 1939, Inez Pearn, Spender's first wife, had left him and gone to live with the poet and sociologist Charles Madge. Spender had fallen in love with Inez in 1936 and had married her within a few weeks of their meeting, but by the beginning of 1939 it was obvious that the marriage was not working. Her departure was not unexpected, but Spender found her rejection difficult to face. At the end of the summer, he was still struggling to accept the failure of his marriage, a struggle intensified by his anxiety over the war. 'It so happens that the world has broken just at the moment when my own

33

life has broken,' he wrote in the journal he began early in September.[7] To ease his private sadness, he tried to lose himself in work. He wrote for long hours at a time in his journal, partly with the idea of publishing some of its less personal material, and he worked on his novel *The Backward Son* (which came out in 1940, with a dedication to Peter Watson). He contributed reviews to periodicals and wrote letters to friends, but these activities did not occupy him completely, and the idea of helping to start a magazine appealed to him, partly as another way to take his mind off his problems.

As soon as he agreed to join Watson and Connolly in their venture, he offered his flat as their first office. Good office space was not easy to find in London, and though his two rooms were modest in size they were in a good location. The flat was on the ground floor of a narrow Georgian house in Lansdowne Terrace, facing Coram's Fields – a children's playground in Bloomsbury. Here, at the beginning of October, Spender and Connolly decided on a name for the magazine. They had a difficult time making their choice. As Spender explains in his autobiography, *World Within World* (1951):

> Connolly thought first of 'Equinox', with the quotation from Marlowe, *Lente currite equi noctis*, on the title page. Yet 'Equinox' *seemed* unoriginal, and the quotation rather discouraging. For some time we weighed the claims of 'Orion'. As I remember . . . we chose 'Horizon' in a moment of despair, when I took a copy of Gide's *Journal* from the bookshelf, and my eye fell on the word 'horizon', which occurred rather frequently.

This story is a good one, but Spender admits that when he recounted it for Connolly a decade after the incident, his friend smiled and said, 'Think again, Stephen. If you think hard enough, you'll remember that you thought first of *everything*.' Spender does not say whether Connolly offered his own version of the event, but both of them liked the name right away, and there was never any hesitation about adopting it. Neither attached any special significance to the word – it simply had a pleasant sound and a connotation of renewal which reflected the spirit of the project.

As soon as they had agreed on a name, the two editors began looking for the right contributors to grace the pages of the first issue, and one of the first writers Spender approached was his publisher at Faber & Faber, T. S. Eliot. After talking informally with Eliot about the magazine, and asking for advice as well as a literary contribution, he received a letter in which Eliot gave one or two polite suggestions but no contribution, explaining that he simply had nothing on hand to offer. Although he made it clear that he wanted to give the magazine his support, he could not promise a contribution any time soon. The most interesting thing about this letter is a brief remark about a long poem which, Eliot said, he was currently debating whether he should write. He wanted the poem to be roughly the same length as 'Burnt Norton', and had been formulating plans for it over a long period.[8] What he was obviously referring to was 'East Coker', written during the following six months, which contains some of his most powerful poetry. It would have been a great triumph for a new magazine to publish such an important poem, but when it was finished in March 1940 Eliot sent it to the *New English Weekly*, a journal with which he had a close connection of long standing.

Spender did not have any better luck when he asked Virginia Woolf to send something to *Horizon*. He knew her well and at the time that he and Connolly were making their first efforts to find contributors she was staying, off and on, at her new London home in Mecklenburgh Square, a short walk from Spender's flat, at the opposite end of Coram's Fields. He visited her there and at her home in the country, and she was aware of the plans for *Horizon* almost from the beginning, but she carefully avoided being drawn into them. When Spender wrote formally inviting her to contribute on the subject of 'The Young', she declined politely. She was reluctant because her own Hogarth Press published John Lehmann's *New Writing* and, as she told Spender, she felt obligated to give Lehmann's struggling magazine 'any help I can'. In her diary she confessed that she turned down Spender's offer because 'if I write for glory, it's to be in our own paper.'[9]

When Lehmann learned of Spender's involvement in *Horizon*, he did not take the news well. He believed that Spender had made a firm commitment to be his editorial associate, and he feared that many of the prominent contributors to his magazine would begin sending their best work to *Horizon* instead. He also thought the new magazine might borrow some of the editorial ideas he had shared in 'frankest friendship' with Spender.[10] For several weeks the two men were caught up in a 'deadly feud', as Virginia Woolf called it at the time.[11] Lehmann was not appeased by Spender's efforts to keep his name from being mentioned in *Horizon* as one of its editors ('The year 1939, I should have realised, was no time for "appeasement",' Spender later remarked).[12] And Virginia Woolf and Lehmann were disturbed that Spender was not being completely frank about the extent of his involvement in *Horizon*. After a visit from Lehmann in late November, she wrote in her diary, 'John gets garrulous after wine. He can't make it up with Stephen. Stephen half lies about Horizon & his part in it mostly. Offers to bring it to the Hog. [Hogarth]. Steals young writers.'[13] Within a few months the dispute was resolved. It was agreed that Spender would continue contributing to *New Writing* and maintain a discreet editorial involvement in *Horizon*. Virginia Woolf remained on cordial terms with Spender until her death in the spring of 1941, but she contributed nothing to *Horizon*.

Despite the distraction of Lehmann's 'feud' with Spender, organisation of the new review went ahead rapidly. Spender's friend Tony Hyndman provided some temporary secretarial help; and the problem of finding a good, reliable printer was solved when another friend, Tony Witherby, offered to do the work at his family's printing firm, H. F. & G. Witherby Limited, located in High Holborn, less than a mile from Spender's flat. Stationery was printed and letters from both Connolly and Spender asked dozens of well-known writers to send in contributions.

A short letter also went to potential subscribers, from a list generously supplied to Connolly by the *New Statesman*. Dated 23 October 1939, the letter admitted that trying to start a new magazine in wartime was not going to be easy, 'but we have decided that the difficulties of production and distribution at the present time are not so serious as the absence of any periodical where the best creative work can be made available.'[14] The war and the demise of so many little magazines during the year gave a sense of urgency to *Horizon*'s subscription appeal. Advertisements, with subscription forms included, soon appeared in the major literary weeklies, and over the next few weeks hundreds of completed forms began to arrive in the post, including ten from Christopher Isherwood in distant Hollywood. Spender remembers days in his flat when 'I would be awakened in the morning by the envelopes which contained our filled-in subscription forms, and a cheque for 6s. 6d. falling on to the floor.'[15] Neither the new subscribers nor the editors knew exactly what kind of literary review *Horizon* would become, but there was so much uncertainty about the future that no one seemed to expect more than a vague promise that the magazine would give its readers the best that wartime conditions would allow. It was not the time for a lengthy, strictly defined manifesto. 'A magazine had to be eclectic to survive,' Connolly later wrote. 'It was the right moment to gather all the writers who could be preserved into the Ark.'[16]

## II

At the end of the first week of October, Connolly set out his basic view of literature in wartime in an article for the *New Statesman* called 'The Ivory Shelter'. Predictably, he complained about the difficulty of creating good literature when publishers were cutting back on new titles and when civilian life in general was under a cloud of gloom: 'As human beings artists are less free now than they have ever been; it is difficult for them to make money and impossible for them to leave the country. Lock-up is earlier every day, and they are concentrated indefinitely on an island from which the sun is hourly receding.' The only thing for writers to do, Connolly advised, was to forget about the outside world and concentrate on their writing; for public events were now far beyond the control of writers and intellectuals, and censorship might limit increasingly the chances to speak out. If a writer could manage to remain in civilian life, the isolation imposed by the war might give him, ironically, all the peace and solitude necessary for creating good art. 'War is a tin-can tied to the tail of civilisation,' Connolly concluded; 'it is also an opportunity for the artist to give us nothing but the best, and to stop his ears.'

This is a theme Connolly would return to repeatedly in *Horizon*. Of course, he found it impossible to remain indifferent to public events, but felt that he and other writers should be free to ignore the war if they wanted to. Otherwise magazines like *Horizon* would have nothing to offer the public except war stories, war essays, war poems, and war art. There had to remain opportunities for writers to create works which flowed freely from their imaginations, regardless of relevance to a particular time or place. In his own life he could certainly see some advantages to being 'locked up' in an England at war. It would force him, he thought, to settle down to serious work. He would put the easy life of the past behind him and devote his attention to his career. There would be no escapes to the South of France or other sunny retreats, but only the cold, damp English climate and the unreal darkness of London during the blackout. This would prove the final cure for his laziness and lack of concentration, or so he hoped.

Just two days after 'The Ivory Shelter' was published, however, he discovered that even a quiet life devoted to art was not free from danger. On 9 October he and Diana were on their way to lunch in a taxi when, not far from Sloane Square, a speeding army lorry slammed into them broadside. A few seconds before the crash, Diana relates,

37

I was telling Cyril to write to his mother in South Africa. He felt guilty about not doing it and wanted me to remind him about it by asking every so often, 'Have you written to your mother, Cyril?' I had just finished the question that day when I saw a pained look suddenly come into Cyril's face, which for a second I thought was a reaction to my question. And then, from my side of the taxi, I felt the impact of this horrible crash.[17]

Miraculously, he survived the accident without a scratch, but Diana was not as lucky. When the taxi came to a rest, she realised that she had almost no feeling below her waist. Her pelvis had been broken. She was rushed to St George's Hospital, at Hyde Park Corner, and spent nearly six weeks recovering from her injuries before being transferred to another hospital, just outside London, for four more weeks. It was almost Christmas before she was able to go home, and it took her another two months of rest to recover fully from the accident.

Connolly went to see her in St George's every day promptly at six, when the evening visiting hours began. Before the accident he had been looking forward to having her work with him at *Horizon*, but now he had to carry on without her, though on his daily visits he told her of the progress made. He was genuinely amazed that he had survived the accident without injury. Not long afterwards he scribbled on the back of a piece of paper, 'Is two weeks now since rendezvous with fate at fork of roads. He released, sorry a mistake, she crossexamined by death, handed over to pain for further questioning.'[18] Instead of being chastened by his brush with death, he became more confident that he could survive whatever terrors the war might bring to London. When he wrote to his mother, he was able to joke that the collision with the army lorry 'is all the war I have seen', and he told her confidently, 'Don't worry about me. I am the last person to be killed, much too old, adaptable, and lucky for that kind of thing.'[19]

A few days after the accident Jean returned to London to stay with Connolly for several weeks, more out of sympathy for his traumatic experience than from any change of heart about their marriage. Whatever her reason, he was grateful to have her back. Since the spring he had been living mainly in hotels but as soon as Jean was at his side again he persuaded her to help him rent a studio cottage in Knightsbridge. In the middle of October they moved into 26a Yeoman's Row, which was the same house he had shared with an Oxford friend in the late 1920s. Returning there after such a long period of time was perhaps a sentimental way of reverting to the beginning of his literary career in

London, when his expectations were high and his promise had not been dimmed by disappointments. He needed that sensation of making another fresh start, and he needed it in a palpable way, as though returning to a scene of his younger days would restore some of the vitality and excitement of that time. When he wrote to his mother on the fourteenth, he was preparing to move into Yeoman's Row, and he described enthusiastically how it had been improved in recent years. Despite all that had happened to him since the spring, his mood was beginning to steady. 'I have been through a very unhappy period the last few months,' he told her, 'but everything is all right at present.'[20]

Although Connolly's hopes for *Horizon* were high, Peter Watson was not so optimistic. Even with Spender working so hard, Watson remained dubious. He thought the magazine's chances of capturing the public's interest were low, and was afraid that even if it were a success, the war would take a turn for the worse and put an end to *Horizon*, one way or another. There was a cynical, world-weary side to his character, which kept him from showing too much enthusiasm for anything. In mid-October, when he wrote to an American friend, the film critic Parker Tyler (who lived in New York and was a close friend of Pavel Tchelitchew), he spoke of the plans for *Horizon* in the most reserved way. 'Perhaps we will bring out a sort of pamphlet in December,' he wrote, and almost apologetically he asked whether Tyler would help them find a distributor in New York 'because we would like to perhaps sell a few in the U.S.A.'.[21] The whole business was embarrassing for Watson, since he was essentially a private, unambitious man. He did not like to call attention to himself and, indeed, insisted that he not be identified in *Horizon* as its publisher or art editor. He did eventually allow his name to appear on the magazine's stationery, but only as 'V. W. Watson' (everyone knew him as 'Peter', but his legal name was Victor William Watson).

His initial agreement to underwrite *Horizon*'s expenses called for a mere thirty-three pounds a month, the cost of printing and distributing a thousand copies. This was a signed agreement with the Witherby printing firm, but he had obligated himself on an informal basis to pay much more, including salaries, contributors' fees (which were two guineas per thousand words for prose, and one guinea per page for poetry), stationery, postage, advertising, and other miscellaneous expenses. He expected to get some money back from subscriptions and bookshop sales, so his investment was still reasonable considering the extent of his means. Because his expectations for *Horizon* were meagre, he did not see any reason to spend lavishly on it. As far as he was concerned, it would be a success if the one thousand copies he had paid for were all sold. Although he was by nature a generous man, he could be unusually cautious about money, especially small sums. This tendency became more pronounced after the beginning of the war, when he suddenly became more serious about his finances. The poet Edouard Roditi has recalled one occasion when this side of Watson's character was revealed:

> I remember lunching with Watson in London in the fall of 1946. After lunch we strolled through the Burlington Arcade and I stopped before the window of a jewelry store. In the mass of objects displayed there, I spotted a jade and gold cigarette-case, Russian and obviously made by Fabergé. We went into the store together. They wanted only twenty-five pounds for it and I bought it on the spot. Peter was speechless. I explained to him why I had bought it, the store obviously had no idea what it was worth. Peter still felt I was a bit extravagant for a poet ... [he] was in some ways penny-wise and pound-foolish.'[22]

One reason for Watson's caution was that with the outbreak of war his finances had begun to suffer. A large part of his art collection was out of reach in Paris, as were other investments held in France; and at home various economic changes, including higher taxes, greatly reduced his trust income. He also had other causes to support besides *Horizon*. Throughout the Forties he gave financial support to several writers and artists.

It is impossible to say how large his income was in any given year, but in the Forties he became much less free with his money and lived in a simpler fashion than when Connolly and Spender first knew him. There were no more Bentleys or sets of Vuitton luggage. He still had large sums to spend on the things that mattered to him, but he became more conscious of waste and more determined to use his funds wisely. He stopped looking like a stylish young man of leisure, and began to take on a more practical, informal, and somewhat subdued – at times even sombre – appearance. The transformation did not come about overnight, but it had begun by the time of *Horizon*.

Many of his friends were mystified by this change. Connolly, in particular, could not understand why someone so well-off would want to watch so carefully how his wealth was spent. He thought such an attitude took all the fun out of having money. Frugality was not a virtue he could embrace. He was always inclined to live beyond his means, and if he had money to spend he was generous in sharing it with his friends. It was therefore impossible for him to hide his disappointment when he thought Watson was being tight with money. Diana notes that when the friendship between the two men was beginning, 'They were almost in love with each other – very flirty. But early in the war Cyril began to complain that Peter was becoming too austere, that he didn't live like a rich man should, and that he ought to spend more lavishly on meals, hotels, clothes, car, etc.'[23]

Because Watson initially had such mixed feelings about putting money into *Horizon*, he stayed in the background during the days in October and November when the first issue was being assembled. He worked for a few weeks as a clerk for the Red Cross in London, and he wrote a few letters on *Horizon*'s behalf, including one to an old friend in France – Gertrude Stein – asking for a literary contribution. He found such letters painful to write; he was not used to asking favours of other people, and was particularly disappointed when Stein sent in an unacceptable piece of work. Writing to Cecil Beaton, Watson complained that Stein had submitted '3 pages of the most arrant balderdash I have ever read, a poem-opera-play about Lucrezia Borgia. It sounds much funnier than it really is, so I don't know really what to do with it now . . . *She just wasn't trying.*'[24]

The deadline for contributions had been the end of November, and the first issue was ready to go to the public. Watson reported to Parker Tyler that the Ministry of Information had looked over the material and had given approval for publication. The last hurdle had been cleared and a release date was set for the middle of December. Again taking an apologetic tone, Watson wrote to Tyler, 'I hope we will not be too English for America, but then we *are* English.'[25]

### III

'Horizon out; small, trivial, dull. So I think from not reading it.' Thus Virginia Woolf, writing in her diary on 16 December, recorded her first impression of the new magazine. If this dismal view had been widely shared, Watson's fears about *Horizon*'s fate would soon have been realised. Fortunately, Woolf's opinion was not a common one.

Within days, the magazine benefited from positive notices in the daily and weekly press. Tom Driberg, writing as the gossip columnist 'William Hickey' in the *Daily Express*, was approving, as was E. M. Forster, who mentioned it during a broadcast for the BBC. At the *Sunday Times* Connolly's old friend Desmond MacCarthy gave his blessing in a glowing review, and a notice in the *New Statesman* concluded with this endorsement: 'A monthly magazine such as Mr Connolly can be trusted to produce is seriously needed, and we hope that the public will hasten to scan this new *Horizon*.'[26] Watson had been persuaded to increase the first printing from 1000 to 2500 and, to his great surprise, every copy was sold in a few days, necessitating a second printing of 1000, which also sold out quickly.

The unexpectedly high sales caused problems when bookshops ran out of copies; had this demand been anticipated in a larger first printing, sales might have been even higher, especially since the magazine came out during the Christmas rush. Writing to Diana, whose long hospital stay was finally coming to an end, Connolly explained that the magazine's success had caught everyone off guard: 'Forgot about 40 subscribers, who never got their copies, and we are just beginning to get cross letters from them, we are sold out, and have had to go round the shops buying back copies to send them, and now the shops are nearly all sold out!'[27] Although Watson complained privately that the first number 'was rather too full of vague political ramblings', its success lifted his spirits. In early January he reported to Parker Tyler, 'To begin with I was myself very underconfident, but we have had such a response this time that I am beginning to feel differently about it.'[28] He added that the next issue would have a printing of 5000, but 7000 were ordered and all were eventually sold, doubling the circulation of the first issue.

The 'vague political ramblings' which irked Watson were written by J. B. Priestley and Herbert Read. They were bland, conventional reflections on the war, but they probably contributed a great deal to the magazine's success: both the authors were 'big names', and at that stage of the 'phoney war' there was a real hunger for 'thoughtful' commentaries on the reasons for the war and the future of a post-war Britain. This was a time when the conflict was still largely one of words, and many people still thought it might be over within a year. Spender was especially eager to make *Horizon* a forum for analysing 'war aims' and understanding the social responsibilities of writers and intellectuals. If he had been in complete control of the journal, there would probably have been more articles like Read's, posing earnest questions such as 'Do the war aims of the Allies represent a body of truth to which the intellect can pledge its services?'

Connolly recognised that political articles had a place in *Horizon*, but he felt no real editorial commitment to anything except 'Art' in the broadest sense, and therefore had no consistent policy towards the war or any other political issue. He was usually out of his depth in serious politics, and was better off when he adhered to his ideal of the artist surveying the world from the high tower of imagination. Connolly was essentially apolitical; adjusting to this fact was not easy for Spender. In his autobiography he says of his involvement with *Horizon*: 'I, who started out with concern for planning post-war Britain, defending democracy, encouraging young writers, and so forth, was disconcerted to find myself with an editor who showed little sense of responsibility about these things. His editorial Comments were brilliant, wayward, inconsistent, sometimes petulant.'

In his first editorial Connolly tried to establish his basic position by declaring, 'Our standards are aesthetic, and our politics are in abeyance'; but he went on to say in the next sentence, 'This will not always be the case, because as events take shape the policy of artists and intellectuals will become clearer.' Instead of declaring bluntly that it was not necessary for *Horizon* to have a political policy, that the editors were free to publish whatever they liked, he kept the matter open for debate, at least for the time being, arguing that the uncertainty of the period made any sustained policy difficult. 'At the moment,' he wrote, 'civilisation is on the operating table and we sit in the waiting room.' Apparently he felt he had to say something about political policy, however tentative, because readers would expect it. Literary magazines, he believed, could not go back to the days when a journal such as 'the original *Life and Letters* which flourished ten years ago had no political aspect,' but the old *Life and Letters* was just the sort of apolitical magazine that suited his temperament best.

He was more successful at expressing his views in 'The Ant-Lion', the essay he wrote for the first number – the best thing in the issue. It begins with Connolly recalling a long summer stay in the South of France before the war. He remembers lying on the beach and noticing the anti-lion insects digging conical depressions in the sand. The intricately designed funnels are impressive works of 'insect art', but they are also clever traps. The dark hole where the ant-lion silently waits for its prey is both an intriguing example of natural beauty and an ugly chamber of death.

He finds a human parallel to this natural phenomenon in the French town of Albi, where he tours the Musée Toulouse-Lautrec. The dark world of the artist's paintings overwhelms him with a mixture of admiration and disgust. 'The world of the hunchback Count is nocturnal, gas-lit, racy, depraved and vicious.' At the end of the long gallery, a door opens to reveal a sunlit terrace which offers 'a lovely and healthy prospect, in which fields and cities of men blend everywhere into the earth and the sunshine.' Standing at this door, Connolly feels refreshed by the vision before him, but he is suddenly drawn back to the world in the dark gallery behind him:

> Deep in his lair the Ant-Lion is at work; the hunchback Count recalls us; the world of poverty, greed, bad air, consumption, and of those who never go to bed awaits, but there awaits also an artist's integration of it, a world in which all trace of sentiment or decadence is excluded by the realism of the painter, and the vitality of his line . . . The crowd who stand in their tall hats gaping at the blossoming Can-Can dancers are in the only place worth being.

Connolly uses Toulouse-Lautrec as an example of how powerful the pull of art can be. He may be tempted to go towards the sunlight on the terrace – to the 'healthy . . . fields and cities of men' – but ultimately the self-contained world of art attracts him more.

This is not the sort of policy statement readers might be expected to look for in a new magazine, but in its indirect, poetic way that is what it is. It establishes Connolly's 'stand': his passionate belief in the purity of aesthetic appeal, and his respect for the independent authority of artistic vision. This, at any rate, is his ideal position, but it is more realistic to see him poised at that doorway where life and art divide, standing between the 'real' world of cities and politics and wars, and the 'unreal' world of the artist's dream. On that borderline, 'attraction fights repulsion as in the cold wavering opposition between the like poles of a magnet.'

For the pleasure of reading 'The Ant-Lion' and Louis MacNeice's haunting poem 'Cushendun', and for the delight of studying a reproduction of Henry Moore's 'Reclining Figures', the first number of *Horizon* was well worth one shilling. The magazine also included poems by Auden, Betjeman, and Frederick Prokosch, and review essays by Geoffrey Grigson and Spender. Still, there were some critics who found little of appeal. In his second 'Comment' Connolly reviewed some of the complaints he had heard or read: 'The editorial is escapist and cagey, the poetry out of date . . . There are too many political articles, and, while full of dull things, the magazine is also much too short.' He was not really bothered by such remarks, all of which were to be expected, but he was disturbed by another line of attack, which admitted that the magazine was 'full of lovely things', but concluded with the questions, 'Should a magazine be just full of lovely things? Shouldn't it stand for something? Be animated by a serious purpose?'

Connolly did not refer such critics to 'The Ant-Lion', whose point would have been lost on them; instead he tried to explain his position in a short commentary on the departure of Auden and Isherwood to America a year earlier. This was not the best way to make his case. His remarks gave the impression that he approved of their unwillingness to return home to face the war, whereas he was not really concerned at all with whether they were right to leave or stay. What he saw in their self-imposed exile was an implicit admission that they had lost faith in art as a tool for social change. 'They have abandoned what they consider to be the sinking ship of European democracy, and by implication the aesthetic doctrine of social realism that has been prevailing there.' He welcomed their move as a sign that art was escaping fom the burden of having to demonstrate a social consciousness before it could be judged worthwhile. *Horizon*, he suggested, could help reawaken people to the fact that writing is 'an end in itself as well as a means to an end, and that good writing, like all art, is capable of producing a deep and satisfying emotion in the reader whether it is about Mozart, the fate of Austria, or the habits of bees.'

His position is clear enough, but he did not need Auden and Isherwood to help him make his point. Indeed, his point was soon lost when other writers began quoting, out of context, his statement that 'the departure of Auden and Isherwood to America a year ago is the most important literary event since the outbreak of the Spanish War.' This was used, unfairly, as evidence that he approved of their actions, but even Auden was not quite sure what Connolly was trying to say in the editorial. 'I think it meant to be friendly,' he later remarked.[29]

Editors may talk as much as they like about the kind of writing they want to encourage, but in the end they are judged by what they publish. At some point every great editor must find one great writer whose work he can serve. Connolly did not take long to find that great writer, and he did not have to look far to find him. In December 1939 George Orwell told him that he had just finished a book called *Inside the Whale*, which contained three long essays. Connolly asked whether he could publish part of it in *Horizon*. At that point the book had no publisher, and Orwell was not sure that he would find one. He was also uncertain that the essays were suitable for *Horizon*. The shortest of the three, 'Boys' Weeklies', was still rather long for magazine publication, and its subject hardly seemed appropriate for *Horizon*'s 'highbrow' readership. Why would sophisticated readers of a literary monthly want to read about popular boys' papers like the twopenny *Gem* and *Magnet*? Serious essays on popular culture are common today, but 'Boys' Weeklies' was the first important essay of its kind written in

45

England. Much to his credit, Connolly had the foresight to accept it, even though it took up nearly a third of the magazine.

This essay, which came out in March 1940, perfectly illustrates Connolly's argument that the artistry of good writing makes itself felt regardless of the subject or the political persuasion, if any, of the author. What matters about Orwell's piece is not so much the subject as the artistic vision focused on the subject. We are made to care about boys' papers because Orwell cares about them and conveys his interest in a forceful and imaginative way. The small world of their fictional stories is one Orwell knew intimately as a boy, and one he is able to bring to life with a novelist's skill, as in his description of the absurdly unrealistic 'mental atmosphere' in *Gem* and *Magnet*:

> There is a cosy fire in the study, and outside the wind is whistling. The ivy clusters thickly round the old grey stones. The King is on his throne and the pound is worth a pound. Over in Europe the comic foreigners are jabbering and gesticulating, but the grim grey battleships of the British Fleet are steaming up the Channel and at the outposts of Empire the monocled Englishmen are holding the niggers at bay.

This is the kind of inspired writing Connolly wanted in *Horizon*, and though Orwell's viewpoint is partly political – objecting to the conservative bias of the papers – no reader has to share his political opinions to enjoy the essay. (It sparked a bit of controversy, when the editor of *Magnet*, Frank Richards, composed a witty and spirited response to Orwell, which Connolly published in full, and which promoted lively discussions in literary circles when it came out in May.)

When 'Boys' Weeklies' first appeared, Connolly pointed out in 'Comment' that one of *Horizon*'s ambitions was 'to help free writers from journalism by welcoming unpopular forms and by encouraging those contributions which can be reprinted'. As one who had spent the better part of his career complaining about the burdens and limitations of literary journalism, he wanted to make his magazine a refuge for writers who were longing to escape 'the perpetual brightness, uniformity, brevity, and overproduction' demanded by journalistic work. 'These evils,' he wrote, 'a monthly review can do something to alleviate by encouraging authors to write on subjects about which their feelings are deepest, by asking for thought and imagination instead of the overwhelming brightness by which so many of us are dazzled, and by affording them as much space as possible.'

Over the next ten years many writers would benefit from this policy, but no one used it to better advantage than Orwell, who wrote half a dozen important essays for the magazine. He followed 'Boys' Weeklies' with 'The Ruling Class' (December 1940); 'Wells, Hitler and the World State' (August 1941); 'The Art of Donald McGill' (September 1941); 'Raffles and Miss Blandish' (October 1944); and 'Politics and the English Language' (April 1946). In addition, his best essay – 'Such, Such Were the Joys' – was written for *Horizon* in response to a request from Connolly, who, according to Orwell in 1947, 'asked me to write a reminiscence of the preparatory school we were at together'. When the piece was finished, however, Orwell withheld it 'because apart from being too long for a periodical I think it is really too libellous to print' (it remained unpublished until two years after his death).[30]

Connolly's decision to publish 'Boys' Weeklies' demonstrated that *Horizon* was not going to be a simple caretaker for literature during wartime. It would take risks and do the unpredictable, without much regard for what was happening in the war. When Orwell's essay was published, events were moving in a new and more dangerous direction – Norway and the Low Countries would soon be invaded – but Connolly had the audacity to think that his readers would be interested in a long article about *Gem* and *Magnet*. He was right, of course – the essay went over well because it was so engagingly different.

He tried to fill each issue with rich and surprising variety. In the March number Orwell's essay was followed by a story from a new younger writer named Philip Toynbee, and in the same issue there was a poem by Betjeman, an autobiographical sketch by William Plomer, a reproduction of Graham Sutherland's 'Association of Oaks', Spender's 'September Journal' and, as the lead contribution, Auden's moving tribute 'In Memory of Sigmund Freud'. Connolly may not have defined his editorial views clearly but he was making good his promise to print the best work available. His taste was more valuable to the magazine than any manifesto. As Spender later acknowledged, 'The strength of *Horizon* lay not in its having any defined cultural or political policy, but in the vitality and idiosyncrasy of the editor . . . Although Connolly was inconsistent, being energetic, enthusiastic, indolent, interested and bored by turns, he held his own views passionately and, on the whole, with judgment.'[31]


## IV

During its early months *Horizon* suffered some setbacks, most of them relatively minor. The magazine's first advertisements had promised that the third or fourth number would be devoted entirely to young British painters, complete with sixteen collotype plates, articles on individual artists, and an introduction by Kenneth Clark, the guest co-editor of the issue. At an early stage of the planning, Kenneth Clark had agreed to edit an art number, but he was suddenly appointed to an important position in the Ministry of Information, and by the end of January 1940 was so overwhelmed with work that he had to back out of his commitment. Peter Watson did not want to do the entire issue by himself, so the idea had to be dropped, which was a great disappointment to many readers.

Another advertised contribution which never appeared was an article on detective fiction by Somerset Maugham, though it reached galley proof stage before it was dropped. Maugham was one of the first invited to contribute and when he sent in his essay it was duly accepted; but after reading the galleys Connolly decided to reject it, though he knew that Maugham's name on the cover would undoubtedly help sales. 'I don't say this is a *bad article*,' he reportedly commented at the time. 'It's good enough to be accepted for *Horizon* but not quite good enough for me to publish.'[32]

In April 1940 the magazine faced the problem of finding a new printer. Tony Witherby went into the army and, with his departure from the family business, Connolly and Watson had to look for another firm. Now that *Horizon* was established and operating successfully, with sales far above the meagre 1000 anticipated in the beginning, Connolly persuaded Watson to enlist the services of the Curwen Press, where master craftsman and artist Oliver Simon presided over the most respected printing business in London. Simon, who had printed *Life and Letters* in the late Twenties and early Thirties, was also the editor of his own magazine: *Signature*, a journal of typography and the graphic arts. The chance to do *Horizon* appealed to him, and an agreement was quickly reached, but as this important matter was settled a major crisis erupted.

In late April, the government announced severe new restrictions on the supply of paper. The successful German invasion of Norway had cut off 80% of Britain's supply of wood pulp, and every periodical had to limit its use of paper. As a relatively new publication, *Horizon* was especially vulnerable – supplies were allocated according to pre-war levels of usage and any magazine started after September 1939 could not, technically, justify its claim to paper. (After May 1940 it became illegal to start a new magazine.) *Horizon* managed for a few months while Connolly and Watson negotiated with the Ministry of Information for a steady supply of paper. Eventually, this was granted, thanks largely to Connolly's friendship with Harold Nicolson, whom he had known since the Twenties, and who was Parliamentary Secretary at the Ministry at that time.

In the wake of *Horizon*'s early success, it had become obvious that a permanent office staff was needed to handle the accounts and the growing volume of editorial and business correspondence. With two or three hundred submissions pouring in during a single month, someone was needed just to sort the paper. In February a colourful young Scotsman named Bill Makins was hired as business manager and, with the help of a temporary typist, the office was soon put in order. Tall and bearded, Makins had worked in advertising, but he wanted to become a literary agent, and saw his job at *Horizon* as an opportunity to meet authors and to learn the business end of publishing. He was efficient and full of ideas for improving the management of the magazine and for attracting more advertisers. He stayed with *Horizon* for two years, then left to serve in the army. His character was brilliantly sketched by Julian Maclaren-Ross in *Memoirs of the Forties*, where he is described as looking like a 'Scottish tribal chieftain'. Makins met Maclaren-Ross in the spring of 1940, when *Horizon* published the latter's short story, 'A Bit of A Smash'.

In his memoirs Maclaren-Ross also provides a vivid portrait of Connolly at the time of their initial meeting, several weeks before his short story came out. Arriving at Lansdowne Terrace to introduce himself, he did not know whether he would recognise the editor, because the only photograph he had seen was one printed in a copy of *Enemies of Promise*, where Connolly appeared as a slender youth in an Eton suit and top hat. When the door of the *Horizon* office opened, he found himself confronted by a man in his mid-thirties who bore little resemblance to that picture. 'His face was round, plump and pale, his shoulders sloped from a short thick neck, and dark hair was fluffed thickly out behind the ears ... The housemaster's outfit affected by many writers of the Thirties – tweed jacket, woollen tie, grey flannels baggy at the knee – gave him an unbuttoned rather than an informal air.' Maclaren-Ross noticed that Connolly shuffled as he walked, and that he slumped when he sat down in an armchair. 'His movements like his voice were indolent, one had the impression that he should have been eating grapes, but at the same time his half-closed eyes missed nothing.' Connolly was amiable and courteous, but Maclaren-Ross also found him 'a formidable person' who was not 'amenable to direct questioning (though fond of it himself)'.

49

In the habit of sleeping late, Connolly was rarely at the office before noon, and he would often arrange to do his work during long lunches at the Café Royal in Regent Street or the White Tower in Percy Street. With his briefcase overflowing with books, manuscripts, and proofs, he established himself in a comfortable spot in the gallery of the Café Royal, and there conducted business as he ate and drank with writers, publishers, and friends. It was his equivalent of the eighteenth-century coffeehouse, because he often imagined himself as a man of letters in the Augustan Age, supported by an indulgent patron and entertained by witty and urbane literary friends.

This fantasy was not so far from reality as it might seem, because the war created a tighter sense of community among writers, and there was an intensity and focus to literary life, in many ways reminiscent of earlier times. Also, with so little competition from other magazines, Connolly was able to exercise an extraordinary degree of influence over the literary scene. His was the sort of prominence more typical of important men of letters in the previous two centuries than in ours. As his hair began to recede from his high forehead and his face grew rounder, he even began to look like some well-fed eighteenth-century arbiter of culture. Spender once remarked that it was easy to look at Connolly's large head and imagine it covered with 'a wig like the one worn by Gibbon in the engraving which is the frontispiece of many editions of *The Decline and Fall* – he could have been painted or caricatured seated in a coffee house with Dean Swift or Dr Johnson.'[33]

Editing was a social act for Connolly. He liked talking to writers about their work, or promoting the magazine on social occasions, but he did not have much patience for the labour of sorting through submissions and preparing copy for the printers. More often than not, he put off choosing contributions until the very last moment; and he was apt to delay writing 'Comment' until the final deadline. It is easy to say that he was lazy, and leave it at that, but he was also a perfectionist and often put off doing his work because his expectations for it were so high. The finished product was never as good as his imagination had anticipated. He would arrange and rearrange material, hoping to create just the right mix, and inevitably it would fall short of his hopes. Dreaming of what he might accomplish, or talking about it with others, was always more enjoyable than doing the work itself. In *The Unquiet Grave* he describes this weakness as part of a general pattern: 'In one lovely place always pining for another; with the perfect woman imagining one more perfect; with a bad book unfinished beginning a second.'

In the early spring of 1940 Diana was finally well enough to join the staff of *Horizon* as a reader. Her job was to read through new submissions and put them into piles for Connolly marked 'good', 'very good', 'borderline', and so on. (Connolly joked that the only problem with 'borderline' was that it never got any better than 'borderline'.) Diana worked a few hours each day, and Watson paid her a small weekly wage. Since her release from hospital in December, she had continued her relationship with Connolly, though neither had settled plans for their future together. Sometimes they talked of marriage, and sometimes they seemed on the verge of agreeing to part for good.

Jean had moved out of London again, going to Malvern Wells, in Worcester, to stay with friends. She too was undecided about the future. She was thinking of returning to America but, knowing that the war might keep her there for a long time, she began to have mixed feelings about leaving, and her attitude towards Connolly softened. 'Darling what are your plans?' she wrote late in February. 'Why don't you and Diana take a cottage in the country and I'll come and stay and we'll all be highminded and Bloomsbury and the best of friends. You can be Lorenzo and I'll be Frieda and she can be Brett, I think.'[34] This opening encouraged Connolly to think that their marriage might somehow be held together, and he began pressuring Jean to return to London. In March, however, realising how rash her talk of 'Bloomsbury' had been, she insisted that they should stand by an earlier agreement to continue their separation for another year. 'I thought we had agreed,' she wrote, 'to separate anyway for a year until I got over my phobia of living with you. If in that year you got over your desire to live with me, that would serve me right for indulging in phobias.'[35]

In May Jean heard that her mother was suffering from ill-health. With the war becoming more threatening almost by the hour, she decided that if she wanted to cross the Atlantic for a visit home she had better do it very soon. She booked passage on a ship sailing from neutral Ireland and on 9 May, the day before Hitler sent his troops racing across the Low Countries, she made out her will, fearing that her ship might be attacked. She sent a copy to Connolly, for she had decided to leave him all her assets and had stipulated, in addition, that he be given half her yearly allowance for the rest of his life. Her departure was set for mid-June and in the few weeks remaining, Connolly did his best to talk her out of leaving, but she was determined to go. She tried to pretend that her stay in America would last no more than a few months, but both knew that the war might keep them apart for years instead of months.

One week before her departure, Connolly travelled to Oxford on business. From the lobby of the Randolph Hotel, where he was staying for the weekend, he tried to place a trunk call to her in Malvern Wells, hoping to arrange another meeting. It was late in the evening and he was sitting nervously in the hotel lounge while he waited for the call to go through. The evacuation of British forces from Dunkirk had just been completed, and the telephone lines were clogged with calls, so he had a long wait. By a quarter past eleven he was alone in the lounge except for a small group of army officers, who had been talking among themselves about their recent escape from Dunkirk. One of the officers, a military policeman, became suspicious of Connolly's lonely vigil, and decided to ask him for his identity card. 'You seem very interested in our conversation,' the officer said, studying him carefully. When he learned that his suspect's name was 'Connolly', he said sharply, 'Irish, eh? How long have you been in this country?' From then on everything went quickly downhill for 'the Irishman', who proved not to have a current identity card, and who produced a British passport issued to him in Austria in 1937, which the officer quickly noted was 'a very short time before Hitler moved into Austria'. The hapless suspect, who had been innocently trying to call his wife, found himself back in his room surrounded by the officer, a local police inspector, and several constables, all of whom seemed certain that they were on the verge of capturing a Nazi spy. When the inspector came into his room, he looked at Connolly and said, 'Good evening, sir, I understand you are an Austrian.'

It took some doing but, as Connolly later explained in an angry letter to the *New Statesman*, he was finally able to convince his interrogators that he was the harmless son of a retired major in the British army, a graduate of Oxford, and the editor of a respectable literary magazine in London. He had retrieved from his luggage a copy of the latest *Horizon*, and proudly held it up as irrefutable evidence that he was in fact an Englishman of some importance, for the phrase 'Edited by Cyril Connolly' stood out in bold letters on the cover. But this grand gesture almost backfired when one of the policemen examined the contents of the magazine and noticed that it included a reproduction of a painting of nude males – 'Sleeping Knights' by Burne-Jones. 'Nude figures', the policeman informed his colleagues in an ominous voice. They might have discovered not only a dangerous spy but a pornographer. What ultimately saved Connolly was the admission that he had been not only to Oxford but to Eton. The inspector was impressed, and Connolly's responses to questions revealed that he was indeed a true Old Etonian. In those innocent days, that fact was enough to discount spy charges.

Connolly's letter protesting about his treatment appeared under the heading 'Spy-Mania' in the *New Statesman* on 15 June, the very day Jean had sailed from Ireland for America. (She was accompanied by Denham Fouts, who was also trying to get back home while it was relatively safe to travel.) Connolly and Jean had indeed met once again before her departure, and said their good-byes. When he returned to London, he was disconsolate. Her decision marked for him the end of their marriage and of the hopes he had associated with their early life together – their plans for travel, a home in the country, a bright social life, and a dazzling career for him as a novelist and critic of international renown. Those had all been daydreams but as long as Jean had remained in his life those dreams seemed to have some solid, magical core, and now that was gone. Knowing how much of his fantasies were caught up in his emotional attachment to her, Jean had tried to leave him with a little hope before she sailed. 'Darling darling heart, don't grieve,' she wrote. 'I love you and will write you every week and will come back to you.'[36]

# THREE

# PUBLISH OR PERISH
## 1940–1941

I

After Dunkirk, when air attacks against England became a threat, Peter Watson decided to leave London and spend the summer in a large rented cottage on the coast of Devon. He invited Spender, Connolly, and Diana to join him, suggesting that they do their *Horizon* work in the safety of his retreat. Everyone agreed and by the end of June they were all together in Thatched Cottage, Thurlestone Sands, at the southernmost tip of Devon. It was a beautiful but isolated spot: the nearest bus stop was two miles away, the nearest shops five miles. Because of petrol rationing Watson had not brought a car from London, though he occasionally hired one for day trips in Devon and Cornwall. For the most part, everyone had to rely on buses and bicycles. Watson hired a local woman to cook for them, and paid her salary and almost all the other expenses of their stay.

At first, Connolly was delighted with the idea of retreating to a sunny seaside cottage. It was a relief to escape from the greyness of London and the constant exposure to war news, almost all of it depressing. In Thurlestone, at the beginning of the summer, the war seemed far away, something talked about in news broadcasts. When he first arrived, he spent several afternoons enjoying himself on the beach. In jersey and shorts, he searched the rock pools for prawns, crabs, or lobsters, using a net and spade to trap his prey, loading it into a bucket, and then proudly taking his catch back to the cottage to show off to his friends. (When the cook arrived for her first day of work, she was under the impression that the muddy little man with the spade and bucket was 'Mr Watson's gardener'.)

Connolly also enjoyed organising trips into the surrounding countryside, mostly for the purpose of house-hunting. He would persuade Watson to hire a car, and off they would all go, driving over the hills of Devon and Cornwall in search of the perfect house with the perfect view to serve as a permanent wartime retreat. The war had brought down prices in the area, and some good houses were going for as little as one thousand pounds. Of course, the plan was that if they found the right house Watson would find the money for it. Nothing came of these expeditions, because Watson was never serious about buying any of the houses they inspected. He was merely humouring Connolly and passing time.

Spender had often spent summer holidays in that part of Devon when he was a boy, and he enjoyed exploring the coast again, going off by himself on a bicycle to Salcombe harbour, where he would rent a boat and spend an afternoon rowing. He invited several friends down to visit him, and sometimes the influx of guests would double the number of people at the cottage. For a while the atmosphere was almost like a pre-war summer holiday, but then in mid-summer German planes were spotted flying along the coast, and bombing raids were launched against Plymouth, about fifteen miles away. There were no attacks in the area around Thurlestone, but from the cliffs where the cottage stood the night raids on Plymouth could be observed. 'The black sky seemed a background to fires and bombs and shells,' Spender recalls, 'shaken like spangles out of it, and criss-crossed by the straight lines of searchlights.' [1] After seeing one of these night attacks, Spender wrote a short poem about it, and it was published in *Horizon* in September under the title 'The Air Raid Across the Bay'. The first stanza vividly recreates the spectacle of the distant battle in the air, where

> Searchlights push to the centre of sky
> Rubbing white rules through dull lead,
> Projecting enormous phantom
> Masts with swaying derricks,
> Sliding triangles and parallels
> Upon the abased wasted distances.

Even before the bombings of Plymouth began, Connolly had decided that he wanted to return to London. After his first week or two at the cottage, he had become bored. He complained that there was not enough to do, and that without a car he felt too isolated. 'Cyril was very unpleasant at times,' Diana says. 'He would sulk on his bed all day, complaining about the lack of things to eat and the general inconvenience of country life.' [2]

Writing to Tony Witherby in August, Connolly made it clear that life at Thurlestone had quickly lost its charm. 'I spend my time here reading French poetry and waiting for meals, oppressed with a general sense of deterioration.'[3] He was also brooding about Jean. He had learned early in July that she was safely settled in America, but after one or two cables from her there was a long silence. The suspense of wondering when he would hear from her again weighed heavily on him. And, in turn, his increasing irritability weighed on Diana and everyone else at the cottage. By the end of August, when the summer lease expired, no one was sorry to leave. According to Diana, 'We were all rather thankful to return to London.'[4]

Thurlestone was especially trying for Watson, who had been distressed not only by Connolly's moodiness and complaints but by the mounting costs of feeding, transporting, and entertaining everyone at the cottage, including visitors. 'Peter, paying for it all, became irritated and a bit cast down,' Diana explains. 'He was genuinely worried about his financial position and the constant drain.'[5] Since the fall of France in late June, his communication with Sherban Sidery, the Rumanian friend overseeing his property in Paris, had been cut, and he was deeply worried that the art collection on which he had lavished so much money and attention might be sold off or confiscated by the Nazis. He had managed to get a number of things out of Paris before the German invasion of France, and as a precaution against any future attack on England he had sent some of his larger pieces to America with Denham Fouts. By far the most valuable of these was an enormous oil painting – nearly six feet high and four feet wide – by Picasso, called 'Girl Writing', and it had been in Watson's collection since the mid-Thirties.

In sending this oil and other works to New York with Fouts, Watson knew that he was still running a risk of losing these treasures, and not merely because they might be lost at sea. The greatest risk was in relying on Fouts to care for them, for his friend's lack of self-control was complicated by another problem – drug addiction. Fouts had grown increasingly dependent on a drug habit he had picked up on a trip to Asia with a former lover. He had used Watson's money to sustain his habit and, although he received a regular allowance in America, it was quite conceivable that the paintings might be sold for cash in a moment of desperation. But Watson's fatalism made him accept that, if the paintings were going to be at risk anyway, the best thing was to entrust them to someone he loved and accept the consequences. Despite their different personalities, he and Fouts did indeed love each other.

At the heart of their relationship was a powerful passion. Normally a man of caution and reserve, Watson found the absence of those qualities in Fouts fascinating and attractive. The difference in their personalities and backgrounds was enormous. The son of a baker, Fouts had left his small, conservative hometown on the Gulf Coast of Florida when he was only sixteen. He had been expelled from high school at the age of fifteen for writing a provocative defence of socialism in the school newspaper, among other things. After several restless months working in his father's bakery, he had run off with a rich businessman travelling through Florida, and by the time he was nineteen he had made his way to Paris, supported by a series of wealthy lovers. Before he settled into his relationship with Watson in the mid-1930s, Fouts was notorious for his sexual adventures with various European millionaires and celebrities. One lover was a Prussian aristocrat, who had taken him to some Nazi rallies in Berlin, and another was Prince Paul (King Paul of Greece) who had entertained him on the royal yacht during a long Aegean cruise.

Not surprisingly, many of Watson's English friends were shocked when he became attached to this 'wild' American boy, who looked like a teenager in the late 1930s – though he was only five years younger than Watson. As Watson once admitted, there were several things about Fouts, most especially his drug habit, that 'horrified' him, but he was irresistibly drawn to him, playing the 'responsible parent' one moment and the indulgent lover the next.[6] He tried to break Fouts's dependence on drugs, sending him to clinics for special treatment and even hiring male nurses to stand watch over him day and night while he was going through withdrawal pains. But nothing seemed to work, and time after time Fouts would return to his habit, taking cocaine, smoking opium or – towards the end of his life – injecting dangerous amounts of heroin.

Truman Capote, who knew both Watson and his lover in the Forties, speculated that Fouts had 'used his drug addiction to sado-romantic advantage, for Watson, while forced to supply the money that supported a habit he deplored, was convinced that only his love and attention could rescue The Beloved from a cocaine grave.'[7] There may be some truth in this, but it is also true that Watson was the first person who showed Fouts real affection, not merely sexual attention, and the first person who tried to help him, not exploit him. Indeed, it was out of concern for Fouts's safety that Watson encouraged him to leave England. He also hoped, foolishly, that Fouts would find it easier to resist drugs and other dangers when the corrupting influence of the Old World was removed.

At the time when Watson was ending his stay at Thurlestone, Fouts was on his way from New York to Hollywood, where there were

certainly enough corrupting influences to match whatever Europe had
to offer. He spent the entire war period in Los Angeles, except for a
few months of service in a forestry camp as a conscientious objector. At
one point he did try to put his life on a new path, earning his high
school diploma through correspondence courses, and then gaining
admission to the University of California at Los Angeles. He took a
part-time job in a bookshop, rented an apartment near the ocean at
Santa Monica, and tried to settle into an ordinary routine. As a college
student he excelled in French, having spoken the language fluently
throughout the Thirties, but courses in chemistry, physics, and math-
ematics proved too much for him. The fact that he was more than ten
years older than most of his fellow freshmen did not make his studies
less difficult, and after only one year he dropped out. A woman friend
who knew him in college remembers that 'at first he was very serious
about his studies, saying that someday he wanted to go on to medical
school. But after living adventurously in Europe, he simply couldn't
settle into the college routine. He was really too restless, too independent for college and, I think, already too old to change.'[8] Gradually, he
slipped back into drugs. By the end of the war, he reached the stage
where his need for money was so great that he sold Watson's large
Picasso, and all the other works sent with him to America.

Jean Connolly visited Fouts in California not long after he first
arrived there, and the two of them spent some of their time in the
company of Christopher Isherwood. Many years later Isherwood gave
a sensationalised account of this period in his autobiographical novel
*Down There on a Visit*, portraying Jean as a bored, ageing rich girl who
had taken to drink and casual sex, and depicting Fouts as a fast-talking
hustler from Dixie fond of saying things like 'honey chile'. His treatment of Jean – whom he calls 'Ruthie' – is especially heavy-handed,
but there are some striking descriptions of Fouts (called 'Paul'), one of
which focuses on the effect of his unusually youthful appearance:

> He looked boyishly skinny; and he was dressed like a boy in his
> teens, with an exaggerated air of innocence which he seemed to be
> daring us to challenge . . . His dressing so young didn't strike me as
> ridiculous, because it went with his appearance. Yet, since I knew
> he was in his late twenties, this youthfulness itself had a slightly
> sinister effect, like something uncannily preserved.

Although Isherwood professed to like Jean, even claiming that he found
her sexy, his descriptions of 'Ruthie' are hardly flattering: 'She has
that cosy quality of a subhuman and therefore guiltless creature; she

might just have emerged from a warm burrow under a hill.' (In contrast, Jean once received the highest compliment imaginable from Auden, who told her that she was the only woman he knew who could keep him up all night.)[9]

Although Watson adjusted to life without Denham Fouts, Cyril Connolly found it almost impossible to stop thinking about his wife. Like Fouts, Jean remained in America throughout the war. She stayed only briefly in California before returning to New York, where she became involved in a circle associated with the New York art world. She was, for a time, close to Peggy Guggenheim, sharing an apartment with her in Manhattan for a year. And for six months in 1943 she was a regular contributor to the *Nation*, reviewing art exhibitions. She sent Connolly money and wrote to him occasionally, but she used her freedom in America to establish an independent life. When she left England, Connolly had suggested that she look up a new contributor to *Horizon* who lived in New York: a promising young art critic (and an editor of *Partisan Review*), Clement Greenberg. Much to his distress, Connolly learned a few months later that Jean and Greenberg had fallen in love. Their affair was passionate and complex, and lasted nearly two years, coming to an end only after Greenberg had gone off to the army in 1943. By that time it was clear that Jean was in America to stay, and that she had no desire to return to England. At first, she had meant to come back, she later confessed in a letter, 'But I enjoyed myself, too. I got tougher . . . You made me pretty unsure of myself.' And she added, with a gentle touch of sarcasm: 'Well, I loved you very much and I like you very much and I hope you will be happy with somebody managing and pliable and sweet and witty, pretty and much nicer than apeface Jeanie.'[10]

Connolly was not willing to forget or forgive. In his mind Jean was guilty of the ultimate crime – she had deserted him when he needed her. 'While I blame myself for the Diana business . . . I do blame you very much for everything since you went to the USA,' he wrote. 'I think you deserted me in the most cruel and horrible way at a time when life was most intolerable and desertion hurt all the more.'[11] Throughout the war he continued to be haunted by the past. In 1943 he wrote, 'Whatever I write or read or think about, if I persevere long enough, takes me back to the miseries of 1939; all ends in frustration, tears, and the sense of all-is-lost.'[12] Although his marriage was dead, his memories of it lay in an 'unquiet grave'.

## II

In July 1940, *Horizon* published Goronwy Rees's 'Letter from a Soldier'. Formerly on the staff of the *Spectator*, Rees was now a military officer, and he took exception to Connolly's belief that 'war is the enemy of creative activity, and writers and painters are right and wise to ignore it.' In a scolding tone Rees accused Connolly of denigrating the common soldier, who could not enjoy the luxury of ignoring the fighting, and who was expected to face death so that civilians like Connolly could remain free. Rees complained, 'You say, in effect, to the artists: let the British and French soldiers protect you, but ignore them while they die for you and wait till they have killed the ogre that threatens.' Despite the conviction of this attack, it distorts Connolly's position. Concentrating on art rather than war does not mean that one ignores the sacrifices made by soldiers on the battlefield.

It would have been easy for Connolly to ignore Rees, or to bury his attack in small type at the back of the magazine. Instead he printed it, with a prominent heading, at the front – in the space normally reserved for 'Comment' – and put his response to it among the back pages. Furthermore, he admitted there was some justice to Rees's charges. *Horizon*, he confessed, had not taken the war seriously enough, and Hitler's recent victories on the Continent had made it clear that 'we cannot afford the airy detachment of earlier numbers. We have walked through the tiger house, speculating on the power and ferocity of the beasts, and looked up to find the cage-doors open.' But, he countered, the problem was really one of tone, not of substance, for 'the fact remains that war *is* the enemy of creative activity ... The point which *Horizon* has made is that though this war is being fought for culture, the fighting of it will not create that culture.' His position was essentially a sound one and, though he sometimes undercut it by treating the war too lightly, his critics were often guilty of taking his views too seriously, analysing them as though they had been printed in a government white paper instead of a literary magazine.

In the next number (August 1940) Connolly could not resist having some fun at the expense of those who thought *Horizon* should give more attention to the war. Squeezed in among short stories, a poem by C. Day Lewis, and articles on Racine and ancient music, was a solemn essay on military tactics: 'Generalship Old and New' by Major-General J. F. C. Fuller. Connolly gave the piece top billing on the cover of the magazine, and no doubt some readers assumed that General Fuller and his article were invented. But the general was a retired officer of the Oxfordshire and Bucks Light Infantry and a leading authority on tanks. Except for a brief remark at the end of 'Comment', Connolly presented the article without introduction, as though it belonged perfectly with the rest of the 'highbrow' contributions. But its turgid, rambling discourse on 'the requirements of generalship' needed no introduction; its outrageously bad style is better than any parody:

> Originality, not conventionality, is one of the main pillars of generalship. To do something that the enemy does not expect, is not prepared for, something that will surprise and disarm him morally. To be always thinking ahead and to be always peeping round the corners. To spy out the soul of one's adversary, and to act in a manner which will astonish and bewilder him, that is generalship. To render the enemy's general ridiculous in the eyes of his men, that is the foundation of success.

Perhaps a few readers, including the general, did not see the joke, but thought that finally 'highbrows' like Connolly were showing an interest in subjects which really mattered. But for those who recognised the joke, the point was clear enough – what mattered in *Horizon* was literature. Earnest discussions of tank tactics old and new might serve the war effort and show that the magazine was not ignoring what was happening in the 'real' world, but would hardly serve the needs of literature.

Connolly enjoyed the joke so much that he wrote a parody of the general's article and published it at the end of August in the *New Statesman*, identifying himself as 'Rear-Colonel Connolly'. Titled 'What Will *He* Do Next?', it is almost as good as General Fuller's original. Like the general, 'Colonel Connolly' is a tank expert who has thought long and hard about the contributions 'a small highly mechanised strike force' can make to modern warfare. He has written specialised books on the subject, but he is not quite sure how to explain his views to the intellectuals who read the *New Statesman*. He does his best to put his theories into simplified form, though he is more successful at giving civilians advice on practical problems in the event of a German invasion, such as 'How to stop a tank':

> For a tank trap it is only necessary to remove the paving stones outside your house (borrow a wheelbarrow from the man next door) and dig a pit some forty feet wide by twenty deep. Place a sheet of wire netting over the road, cover it with cardboard or brown paper, and a top dressing of asphalt. Your trap is made.[13]

'What Will *He* Do Next?' was published as Connolly was returning to London from Thurlestone. Ironically, he had seen more German planes over 'peaceful' Devon than he would have spotted all summer long if he had stayed in London, which until the last week of August suffered only one significant raid.

There was considerable fear of invasion, and most Londoners assumed that large-scale air attacks were imminent. Indeed, early in the evening of 7 September the raids began, and for the next fifty-seven nights great waves of German bombers, averaging more than 150 planes each night, pounded London. On the first night Connolly and George Orwell were together at Athenaeum Court in Piccadilly, where Connolly had taken a furnished flat on the top floor. The worst bombing was in the East End, but from the rooftop of Athenaeum Court they saw the night sky ablaze over the river, where huge fires had engulfed the docks. Earlier, a few stray bombs had fallen near Piccadilly; Orwell had been forced to take cover from flying shrapnel. But it still seemed beyond belief, as though the explosions and fires were part of some imaginary spectacle. Feeling oddly detached, Orwell looked out over the scene from the rooftop and came away impressed 'by the size and beauty of the flames'.[14] The only consolation for them was that Athenaeum Court was a sturdy modern building of steel and concrete, and was thought to be relatively safe as long as the bombs did not fall too close to it. (Peter Watson was also living in the building and was helping to pay for Connolly's flat, which was small but not cheap.)

On the following night, the German attack spread into Bloomsbury, inflicting terrible damage on the district's elegant streets and squares. In Guilford Street, which ran next to Lansdowne Terrace, a bomb ruptured a gas main and set off a large fire, while another exploded in the playground opposite *Horizon*'s office. No one was hurt, and the only damage to the office was a broken window pane. Virginia Woolf's house in nearby Mecklenburgh Square was not so fortunate. It survived the initial attacks, but unexploded bombs in the square went off a few days later, and the ceilings collapsed, leaving it a shambles. For a fortnight the area around Lansdowne Terrace was cordoned off because of unexploded bombs, and *Horizon* was without an office for a good part of September. (Spender still had many of his books and other belongings stored there, but it had long ago completed its transformation from a flat into an office.) To add to *Horizon*'s problems, the Curwen Press was bombed at least three times. A raid in October destroyed two thousand copies of one issue. These were quickly replaced, but the printers had to work under a gaping hole in the roof of their building. In the December 'Comment' Connolly complained, 'The offices of *Horizon* would seem to be a military objective second in importance only to our printers.'

The same 'Comment' pointed out that the magazine's circulation had suffered a sharp decline since Dunkirk. After selling 8000 copies of the April number, *Horizon* had a sale of only 5000 at the end of 1940. Part of the problem was that fewer copies were being ordered by newsagents and booksellers. New restrictions designed to save paper prevented them from returning unsold copies of periodicals, so they ordered only what their shops were sure to sell. To keep its ration of paper secure, *Horizon* needed to build up its circulation by expanding its list of regular subscribers, but the blitz had made that difficult. The disruptions in the postal service had caused endless problems with the subscribers the magazine already had, and cancellations from those people made it hard to gain ground from new subscriptions. *Horizon* needed all the help its friends could give. 'We exist to provide good writing,' Connolly told his readers, 'and we must not forget it. But we barely exist, and those who wish us well can help by getting us more readers and more subscribers.' He was not above shaming people into subscribing, if that would do the trick. In 'Comment' he declared, 'If we can go on producing a magazine in these conditions, the least you can do is to read it. The money *Horizon* loses would provide you with, if not a Spitfire, at any rate a barrage balloon. If you would rather have that, say so.'[15]

Except for a short trip to Scotland in October, he stayed in London through the worst weeks of the blitz. It would have been easy to evacuate the magazine and its staff to a remote spot in the countryside; but after the first few nights of bombing Connolly – like so many Londoners – became accustomed to the raids and the dangers, and was determined to carry on as normally as possible. Even during heavy and close raids, he surprised friends by his calmness. Peter Quennell remembers an occasion when he and Connolly were caught in the street, and he could not persuade his friend to take cover in a public shelter nearby. 'Bombs were going off all around us, and Cyril simply stood inside a doorway calmly waiting for the raid to end. I was visibly frightened, thinking any minute a bomb might hit us, but when Cyril saw the expression on my face he just looked at me and said, "Be calm. Really, you know, we've all had interesting lives."'[16] (Much later, when the Germans began sending over the VI flying bombs, Connolly's composure broke down. He admitted that he was utterly terrified by the new weapon, which killed so suddenly and randomly.

When he spoke of his fear to Harold Nicolson, he was told that he ought to worry more about his 'dear ones' fighting in France, 'who are in far greater danger'. To which Connolly responded, 'That wouldn't work with me at all, Harold. In the first place, I have no dear ones at the front. And in the second place, I have observed that with me perfect fear casteth out love.') [17]

In Peter Watson's case the blitz brought one important change for the better: he acquired new respect and admiration for his country. He was deeply moved by the great courage ordinary people demonstrated every day in the streets of London, and gratified to see the unity of people of all classes in the face of the German attacks. He too remained in London during the grim autumn months of 1940, and did his best to ignore the dangers. His flat in Athenaeum Court might have been safer than most places, but it was still vulnerable to direct hits. He was resolved to accept all risks: 'I never go to a shelter,' he told Cecil Beaton. 'I would rather die in my sleep.' [18] Unlike Connolly, he was even willing to accept the risks of military service. His elder brother, Sir Norman Watson, was an RAF officer, and Peter was also prepared to serve the RAF if he were needed. While waiting to be called up, he declared in a letter to Parker Tyler: '[I] am no pacifist, one must fight for anything worth having and rightly so.' [19] His physical examination by RAF doctors in October showed, however, that he was seriously underweight and mildly jaundiced – he suffered from periodic attacks during much of his adult life – and he was therefore rejected.

As the blitz dragged on, Watson developed a keen sense of pride in *Horizon*'s ability to keep going despite the hardships involved in preparing, printing, and distributing each issue. He was pleased to be a part of it all, and began to look upon his work as a kind of patriotic service – a defiant gesture for British culture against the German threat. He was no longer apologetic about the magazine or doubtful of its value. When it was reported to him that Cecil Beaton had called *Horizon* 'cowardly', Watson wrote, 'I wish you would write and tell me exactly why. I imagined we had been really rather morally courageous.' In a rare show of anger, he complained to Beaton that some of their wealthy French friends had lately shown true cowardice by fleeing France and then secretly giving their support to Pétain's puppet régime in Vichy: 'How I despise those super-rich (some of whom you and I have known very well) who sent all their money to England and America . . . and are now living over here feeling very pro-Pétain, not daring to say so openly and afraid to return in case Pétain came in against England.' [20]

*Horizon*'s 'courage' did not go unrecognised by its readers. Despite

Goronwy Rees's complaints in July, it soon became clear that quite a few soldiers placed high value on the magazine's defence of culture. During the stay at Thurlestone, when the air war was just beginning, Spender recalls that 'we received letters from pilots fighting in the Battle of Britain, often saying they felt that so long as *Horizon* continued they had a cause to fight for. Such letters could only make us feel unworthy and ashamed. Yet for these young men, *Horizon*, *New Writing*, and one or two other literary reviews, were the means whereby they felt that they, as well as we, survived the war.'[21]

One young contributor to the June 1940 number, a pilot named Gully Mason, was shot down and killed just a short time after he visited the editors at Thurlestone during a brief leave. Later in the war the famous Spitfire pilot Richard Hillary, author of *The Last Enemy*, asked if he could contribute an article. His proposal was accepted, but he died in an air crash before it could be written. In 1942 *Horizon* published a story called 'The Pupil', submitted by a young fighter pilot stationed in Tunisia. Rollo Woolley, the author of the story, had been at Rugby and Oxford before joining the RAF, and his appearance in *Horizon* was warmly received. He placed another story in *New Writing*, but at the age of twenty-three he was killed in an air battle over North Africa. After his death, Connolly learned that a diary had been found in which Rollo Woolley had written in capital letters over a whole page: 'MY STORY ACCEPTED BY HORIZON!'[22]

Just after the beginning of the blitz, Spender decided to put aside his editorial work at *Horizon* for a few months. He had been offered a teaching job at Blundell's School in Devon and, though he had serious doubts about his suitability, he wanted to give it a try. Connolly was clearly in charge of the magazine, and was holding his own so well that there was no compelling reason for Spender to give anything more than occasional help. He decided to accept the teaching position, and returned to Devon to see whether life as a schoolmaster would agree with him. One term was enough to persuade him that he had made a mistake; he discovered not only that he disliked the school but that he missed being in the middle of things in London, despite the dangers.

Part of the attraction of going to Devon had been the prospect of finding more time and solitude for his work. Since the beginning of the war he had written a considerable amount, but too much of it had been done in a hurry and in response to events, without allowing time to reflect on the direction his work was taking. Although he thought it important to address the issues raised by the war, he did not want it to dominate his work, and he was anxious to establish a balance between the claims of art and those of social responsibility. In September he had written in *Horizon*, 'The artist cannot remain aloof from the short-term issues of his time, but his position is not to lose himself in them.'

At Blundell's School, however, he began to fear that he was becoming too remote from events. When Christopher Isherwood wrote to him from California and ended his letter with, 'This is where you should also be,' it occurred to Spender that in moving to Blundell's he had already come close to running away from the war. In an open letter to Isherwood published in the *New Statesman* on 16 November, he did not criticise his friend for leaving England, and admitted that his circumstances in Devon were not all that different from Isherwood's: 'I, living in the country, and with a reserved occupation, am in much the same position as yourself.' But Spender also reminded himself and Isherwood that 'you can't escape. If you try to do so, you are simply putting the clock back for yourself: using your freedom of movement to enable yourself to live still in pre-Munich England.' Isherwood, of course, did not see any need to leave California, but within two months Spender left Devon and returned to London, where he remained until the last months of the war.

At the end of his single term of teaching, Spender set aside his worries about the kind of writer he should be and concentrated long enough on the business of writing to complete his best poem about the war. Again, as with his earlier poem written at Thurlestone, the inspiration came from the air war. The poem is called simply 'Air Raid' (*Horizon* published it in February 1941); its focus is not on the distant battle in the skies but on the human tragedy of the victims below.

It begins with a calm, detached description of the ordinary lives of one family before their home is hit by a bomb. Even as the war rages around them, they try to keep up a normal existence and to sustain the illusion that their lives will remain orderly and routine. Spender captures as well as any poet of the time the unreal normality of civilian life during the blitz:

> They wear the right clothes, and acquire the safe ways,
> Hear the news, discuss golf, and fill out their days
> With work, and meals brought from the kitchen range.
> And no one sees anything empty or strange
>
> In all this. And perhaps that is right. Nothing is
> Until an unreasoning fury impinges
> From a different vision of life . . .

When their home is bombed, their private domestic world is shattered and exposed to the curious gaze of outsiders, the front wall having collapsed and opened the house's jumbled remains to public view: 'the inside made outside faces the street.' The scene was one repeated thousands of times during the blitz, and Spender concludes his description in an austere but moving tone:

> But the home has been cracked by metallic claws,
> Years of loving care ground to rubble in jaws,
> And the delicate squirming life thrown away
> By the high-flying purpose of a foreign day.

Just one month before 'Air Raid' appeared, *Horizon* had published Alun Lewis's 'All Day It Has Rained', the first major poem about the war written by a soldier. At the time he wrote it – early autumn 1940 – Lewis was serving with the Royal Engineers in Hampshire, and knew no more about the war than the average civilian. His poem is not concerned with armies storming across battlefields or other heroic deeds, but is a powerful evocation of the ordinary soldier's life, in which the greatest enemy is often boredom. The only combat in Lewis's poem is with 'the skirmishing fine rain' that lays siege to his camp all day, drenching the countryside and confining the 'moody' soldiers to their tents, where the hours of waiting for the sky to clear are restlessly endured.

Connolly was impressed with Lewis's ability to convey 'something of the sad monotony' of 'army life as it really is', and was delighted to publish the poem as an example of war poetry at its best. He made it the lead piece in the January 1941 number, placing it just ahead of Dylan Thomas's first war poem, 'Deaths and Entrances'. The popular press had been asking for months 'Where are the war poets?' and now Connolly was in a position to name at least two, though, as he acknowledged in 'Comment', neither of them would satisfy anyone looking for 'stirring' war poems from another Rupert Brooke. In any case, Connolly argued, 'war poets are not a new kind of being, they are only peace poets who have assimilated the material of the war.'

Alun Lewis's poem was an immediate success, and in the next five months two more works by the young soldier were published in *Horizon*. Eager to meet this talented contributor, Connolly asked him to come up to London, and Lewis gladly agreed. Later, the poet wrote to his mother about his introduction to 'the strange nervous *Horizon* gang': 'I felt as if my khaki were too rough and my boots much too heavy to be near them: Spender's long fingers and tall restless body and head high up in the air above his sloping shoulders he was like a mixture of hawk and dove. I don't think they'll ever lead the people to a new world. I feel satisfied that my work is sincerely valued by them, though; they were very thoughtful in speaking with me, not patronising or off-hand, and Connolly said he hopes to go on printing my work for a long time yet.'[23]

Partly as a result of his publication in the magazine, Lewis was offered a book contract by Allen and Unwin. Bill Makins, business manager of *Horizon*, was so taken with Lewis's work that he spoke directly to Philip Unwin about the poet, and in May 1941 Lewis received a letter from Unwin asking whether he had enough work available for book publication. Lewis sent a collection of his poetry, and in 1942 Unwin brought it out under the title *Raiders' Dawn*, which was advertised with the claim 'The War Poet has arrived at last!' The book proved so popular that it was reprinted six times in the next four years. But the 'War Poet' did not survive the war; in March 1944 Lewis died in Burma, apparently from a self-inflicted bullet wound. He was twenty-eight.

### III

While Connolly struggled to keep *Horizon* going during the blitz, troubles of a different sort were brewing in his personal life. His relationship with Diana had been strained since their last weeks at Thurlestone, when Connolly's moodiness and complaints had made him a difficult companion. Nevertheless, after their return from Thurlestone he had continued to raise with her the possibility of marriage, and had carried on with his ritual house-hunting, vaguely planning for a new life together in a place of their own. He found several places, but proved incapable of taking definite action, and he was still unable to consider filing for divorce from Jean. Diana was growing increasingly impatient and, after her experience at Thurlestone, had finally decided against any permanent romantic relationship with him. She had her own friends and her own life, and was disillusioned by his behaviour.

In late autumn 1940 Diana left London and went to stay in Oxford for several weeks; partly she wanted to escape the bombing in London, but she also wanted some time away from Connolly. Like Jean, however, she discovered that separating from Connolly was not easy. He pleaded with her to come back, writing letters like the ones he had sent to Jean in 1939, making extravagant promises and, in desperate moments, threatening suicide. Diana found it difficult and distressing to ignore these entreaties; as she was to write later: 'I wanted to get away from Cyril, but of course he was very good about persuading women to stay on, especially when he used threats of suicide, which he could deliver quite convincingly, or saying that his art would be ruined. Though suicide threats have to be taken seriously, I still find it amazing that I believed some of the things he told me, particularly on the occasions when I asked him, for everyone's sake, not to continue seeing me. However, he was much older than I was, and I was very young and credulous.'[24]

But this time Diana steadfastly refused to return to him. At Christmas she went home to Hampshire and stayed there until the end of January, when she returned to London to share a house with friends. Connolly wrote her more letters and even dispatched mutual friends, such as Cecil Beaton, to plead his case. It was only with great reluctance, more than a year later, that he agreed to end his pursuit, settling for a place in her life as a friend rather than a lover. Their friendship continued until his death, but he never completely overcame the disappointment of losing her, though he did apologise for his behaviour. 'Some fifteen years later when we met at a social gathering,' Diana writes, 'he generously told me how badly he had behaved to me, a young girl, and how much he regretted it, and I was to answer that there was probably cause for regret on all sides.'[25]

Even before Connolly gave up pursuing Diana, he had become passionately involved with a young woman named, poetically, Lys. Peter Quennell introduced Connolly to Mrs Lys Lubbock, the handsome young wife of a struggling actor and schoolteacher named Ian Lubbock. Quennell had met her just before the war, when she took a job at the advertising firm where he worked as a copywriter. He soon became friendly with Lys and her husband, and when a bomb destroyed his flat in Chelsea early in the blitz he moved in with the 'bohemian young married couple', as he describes them in his memoirs, sharing their large basement flat near Holland Park. (At this time Quennell was finishing his *Byron in Venice*, two parts of which appeared in *Horizon* at the end of the year.) His stay with the Lubbocks, he recalls, 'was brief, but full of emotional dramas and dramatic episodes'.[26] The couple's marriage was on the verge of breaking up. They had been together for only two years, but it had been a troubled marriage from the start, and when Quennell entered their lives Lys was looking for a way to end her relationship with Ian. While Diana was in Oxford, Connolly and Lys had met and fallen in love. She was twenty-two, and he was thirty-seven, but this considerable difference in age formed part of her interest in Connolly. As she recalled later, 'Ian Lubbock was too young to settle down to married life, and it occurred to me, in my innocence, that because Cyril was older and seemingly more mature, he might be easier to live with.'[27]

Lys had grown up in Kent and London, but she was born in the United States. During a visit to Vancouver her English mother had met an American lawyer and had married him in 1916 after a brief courtship. Ernest Dunlap, Lys's father, represented a large mining company in the American West, and shortly after marrying he took his new wife, Ida, to live in the remote and rugged town of Butte, Montana. It was there that the couple's second child, Lys, was born at the end of 1917, but the isolation and severe winters proved too much for Lys's mother. At the end of 1918, pregnant for the third time, she and her children left Montana and made the long trip back to England. Mr Dunlap did not follow and died soon afterwards in a car accident. When Lys was fifteen, her mother died, and three years later, without enough money to support herself, she decided to acquire some secretarial employment skills at a college in London. She found a job in the office of the Dorchester Hotel, and while she was working there she met and married Ian Lubbock.

In some ways Lys was an unlikely person to attract Connolly's romantic interest. She lacked money and family connections and had no strong artistic talents. However, she did possess an almost sultry beauty which he found immensely attractive. At one time a fashion model for British *Vogue*, she had rich dark hair, worn at shoulder length, a pale complexion, large seductive eyes, and full lips. In addition, Lys had a deeply affectionate, unselfish nature which was especially appealing to that 'only-child complex' in Connolly's character. He needed not only a lover but a sister and a mother, and in Lys he found someone who was good at being all three. What Connolly says of his schoolboy infatuations in *Enemies of Promise* can be applied here: 'To say I was in love again will vex the reader beyond endurance, but he must remember that being in love had a peculiar meaning for me . . . Love was an ideal based on the exhibitionism of the only-child. It meant a desire to lay my personality at someone's feet as a puppy deposits a slobbery ball; it meant a non-stop daydream, a planning of surprises, an exchange of confidences, a giving of presents, an agony of expectation, a delirium of impatience.'

It was not easy to resist Connolly's advances. He had learned long before that 'being funny' was a quick way to win approval; with women, he had also learned how to make good use of his soft voice, penetrating eyes, and intense conversational style. 'When he talked to you and looked straight into your eyes,' Lys remembers, 'he could make you feel, for that moment, that you were the only other person in the world, even though you might be in the middle of a large party or sitting in a crowded restaurant.'[28] In his memoirs Anthony Powell observed that Connolly was 'a master of flattery; flattery of the best sort that can seem on the surface almost a form of detraction. There was undoubtedly something hypnotic about him.' He was also a master at manipulating emotions. The painter Francis Bacon, who occasionally saw him entertaining young women at restaurants in the 1950s, described those occasions as 'a lot of oysters and Cyril sobbing into them'.[29] If laughter failed to win over a woman, tears were always in reserve.

By late 1940 Lys was certainly won over to Connolly and ready to leave Ian Lubbock as soon as she could. Early in 1941 her chance came when Connolly found a small studio that was to his liking. It was a pleasant house in Drayton Gardens, a short distance from the Fulham Road. The twins Celia and Mamaine Paget (the latter married Arthur Koestler) owned the house but offered it to Connolly for a year while they went to live in the country. He accepted and asked Lys to live with him. She readily agreed, and at the end of February she left her flat and moved in with him. They were soon joined by Peter Quennell, who was still without a place of his own.

Energetic and by nature domestic, Lys organised the household so that it ran smoothly and efficiently. She looked after Connolly and gave him the pampered existence he had long dreamed of. She enjoyed cooking and showed great ingenuity in preparing delicious meals to suit his gourmet tastes. (Another demanding gourmet, Evelyn Waugh, was so fond of her food that he once asked her to give lessons to his cook.) Lys even tried to put Connolly's financial affairs in order: 'When I discovered that Cyril was not filing income tax returns,' she recalls, 'I found . . . a very good tax accountant, to whom I annually provided all the tax data, including grounds for deducting heavy entertaining expenses.' Throughout the time they were together, she claims proudly, 'Cyril never had to pay a penny in taxes.'[30] Peter Quennell was amazed at how comfortably Connolly, with Lys's help, lived during the remainder of the war. 'Cyril's household, in these wartime surroundings, was a constant source of wonder. He kept the war at bay more effectively than any other man I knew . . . About his own existence he drew a magic circle, with which he pursued his personal affairs and employed his native power of charming.'[31]

Lys also brought new energy to the *Horizon* office, where she went to work about the same time that she moved in with Connolly. She sorted manuscripts, helped with correspondence, read proofs, and generally made herself useful in the daily management of the office. She later became business manager when Bill Makins went off to the army. Except for a two-year period of war work in a government office, she was a constant presence at *Horizon* for the rest of the magazine's life. Indeed, in many ways she was instrumental in keeping *Horizon* going. Artistically, she was not especially imaginative or creative, but she provided the steady, practical assistance the magazine sorely needed.

In their first year Lys and Connolly were content merely to live together. Having just escaped an unhappy marriage, Lys was not ready to think about marrying again, though later she wanted very much to become Connolly's wife. In the meantime, they were hosts to a marriage celebration for another couple. The previous year Spender had met a young pianist named Natasha Litvin, and they married early in April 1941. Lys and Connolly gave a cocktail party for them, the first of many large *Horizon* parties, for which the magazine was famous by the end of the war. They provided real vitality and gaiety when so many writers felt isolated and uninspired, in the dreary period when night life was hampered by rationing and the blackout. One could never be sure who might turn up. At the party for the Spenders the guests included A. J. Ayer, Cecil Beaton, and Louis MacNeice. There was also a charming young man named Guy Burgess, who was then employed as a Talks Assistant for the BBC, and as a spy for the USSR.

With Watson's backing, Lys's help, and the use of a house, Connolly had all the ingredients necessary for successful literary parties, and he made the most of the opportunity. At the end of the war Elizabeth Bowen, a frequent guest at *Horizon* parties, wrote, 'Your parties had something more than even your and Lys's beautiful hospitality can account for, and something without which even intellectual happiness would be desperate: real spirit.'[32]

72

# FOUR

# ART AMONG THE RUINS
## 1941–1942

I

In May 1941 *Horizon* published an admiring article on the painters of
the Euston Road School; it was timed to coincide with a major
exhibition of the group's paintings at the Ashmolean Museum in
Oxford. The magazine included reproductions of works by its leading
members: Graham Bell, William Coldstream, Victor Pasmore, and
Claude Rogers.

The 'School of Painting and Drawing' at 316 Euston Road had
opened in 1938, and for a short time one of its students was Stephen
Spender, who had taken an amateur interest in painting. Knowing
many artists at the school, Spender would have been the most likely
person to write about them, but the article was the work of a novice
writer named Sonia Brownell, who was twenty-two years old. She had
been the subject of several portrait studies by the school's painters, and
had come to be known affectionately among them as the 'Euston Road
Venus'. She was indeed a beautiful young woman, with fair hair, bright
eyes, and a clear round face. (Spender described her as having a 'Renoir
face'.)[1] She had literary ambitions but knew that her talents were
modest, so she sought to associate with those of promise, whose careers
she could help to promote and sustain. William Coldstream, who had
fallen in love with her in 1939, was the first important artist to whom
she gave her devoted attention, and her article in *Horizon* was one way
of serving his talent.

Sonia Brownell had tried a year earlier to be published in *Horizon*.
One night in February 1940 she had been talking casually with Coldstream and Spender at the Café Royal, and had learned that *Horizon*'s
plans for a special issue on young British painters, edited by Kenneth
Clark, had fallen through. She suggested to Spender that she would
like a chance to edit the number, and he told her to give it a try.
Thanks to her association with Coldstream and his friends at the

Euston Road School, she was able to approach various painters and ask them to contribute, but she had no training or experience in art criticism and could not be expected to put together the critical commentaries for the number. Nevertheless, a few days later, while she was waiting to hear from Spender about the magazine's plans, she typed out a neat three-page proposal and sent it to *Horizon*. She suggested that the special issue include statements of purpose and representative samples of work by five artists – Coldstream, Henry Moore, Pasmore, John Piper, and Graham Sutherland. 'After this,' she wrote, 'there ought to be three longer articles by outstanding authorities,' but the names she mentioned under this heading included Desmond MacCarthy and Stephen Spender, neither of whom could conceivably qualify as 'outstanding authorities' on modern art. She also suggested, in perfect innocence, that the issue should end with a reprint of an essay on painting by Winston Churchill. She had been impressed by this essay, she noted, after reading it 'in some anthology of English essays'.[2]

It must be kept in mind that Sonia was only twenty-one when she put these suggestions, but it is extraordinary that someone so young and untried would presume to edit, by herself, an entire issue of *Horizon* on five major British painters. Not surprisingly, Peter Watson turned down her proposal; it would have looked odd, to say the least, if a special issue previously advertised as being edited by Kenneth Clark, director of the National Gallery, had appeared under the editorship of Miss Sonia Brownell, unknown outside the Euston Road group.

Although she failed in her first attempt to publish in *Horizon*, Sonia gained from this experience the acquaintance of another talented man whom she could champion and encourage: Cyril Connolly. Spender had introduced them not long after she had sent in her proposal for the young painters' issue, and Connolly was utterly charmed by her. She could quite easily have become the next major love of his life, but he discovered that loving Sonia was not easy. For her, love was essentially an intellectual affair, or so it appeared in her relationships with men, whose intellects she could worship while placing less importance on their physical attributes.

After Sonia's affair with Coldstream ended in 1941, Connolly did his best to establish a love affair with her, but failed, even though the attraction between them was strong. He liked to claim that it was Sonia's 'Lesbian drives' that kept her from falling in love with him. He never ceased being fascinated by her, and she occupied a place in his life to its end, but their relations were always somewhat uneasy. 'I

always regard Sonia,' he told a friend late in life, 'as my unconscious
enemy – unconscious because unaware of the strength of her Lesbian
drives . . . She has done me more harm than good, she is the enemy of
the male principle, one has to be broken down to win her pity.'[3] In
Connolly's unfinished novel from the late 1940s, 'Happy Deathbeds', a
character who clearly resembles Sonia is described as being, in the
battle between the sexes, 'a commando sergeant fighting behind enemy
lines and disguised as a very pretty girl'.[4]

Still, Sonia never wavered in her conviction that Connolly was a genius
as a literary artist, and she became one of the strongest advocates of
his work. She spent most of the war years working as a clerk in the
Ministry of War Transport, and living in a small flat in Percy Street;
but by the time her first article was published in *Horizon* she had
become a kind of unofficial, occasional assistant to both the magazine
and Connolly. She was an extremely fast typist, reportedly able to
'take down typing at shorthand dictating speed'.[5] She helped out at
the magazine whenever she was needed and whenever her regular job
would allow her time. She was also invited to *Horizon* parties or for
evenings out with Connolly, Lys, and other companions. Only after
the war, when her job with the government had ended, did Sonia
become a regular, paid assistant at *Horizon*, though she spent so much
time with Connolly, and worked so hard to help him, that many people
assumed she was employed by the magazine during the war.

Sonia sometimes carried her devotion to comic extremes. One
summer in the early 1940s she and Connolly went down to a house
party in Sussex given by Connolly's old friend Dick Wyndham, and
during their stay Wyndham, who had drunk too much, got into an
argument with Sonia and began to chase her, half in jest, across the
grounds, pursuing her to the edge of the mill pond which bordered the
terrace of his house. Wyndham began to make advances and when Sonia
found that she could not push him away she jumped into the pond to
escape. Peter Quennell, also an old friend of Wyndham's, came to her
rescue, and pulled her up from the muddy banks of the pond. As she
came out, drenched and shaking, she exclaimed: 'It isn't his trying to
rape me that I mind, but that he doesn't seem to realise what Cyril
stands for.'[6]

She never talked much about her own life, and not many people
knew about her family or her upbringing. She was born in India, in
August 1918, where her father, Charles Brownell, was a shipping
freight broker. Her mother, Beatrice Binning, was a member of an old
Anglo-Indian family, and when Sonia was born Beatrice had only one

75

other child, an older daughter named Bay. Tragically, Charles Brownell died of a heart attack when Sonia was only a few months old, and for the next three years she and her sister lived alone in India with their mother. In 1921 Beatrice married again, but this second marriage also ended unhappily. Sonia's step-father turned out to be an alcoholic who lost his job as a chartered accountant in India and returned, practically penniless, to England in 1926. Beatrice and the rest of the family, which now included a son from the second marriage, also returned; by 1929 she was living apart from her husband, supporting herself and her three children by managing a boarding-house in South Kensington, which she later bought and which she was still operating in the 1940s.

A devout Catholic, Beatrice was determined that her two girls should receive a religious education, and with financial help from relatives she was able to send Sonia and Bay to the Convent of Sacred Heart in Roehampton, south of the Thames in London. From the age of ten until she was eighteen, Sonia's life was dominated by the strict discipline and gloomy environment of the convent. The secular and religious instruction was demanding, and Sonia later confessed that she hated every minute she was there. By her early twenties, she had rejected her religious training. Diana, who became one of her close friends later in the Forties, says that she 'threw over Catholicism completely, and she *really* threw it over. In fact, she always said, "I spit if I see a nun," and when we were walking along the street she'd spit, and I'd say, "what are you doing?" and she said, "I just saw a nun."'[7]

Her experiences at the convent could not have made relationships with men easy. The girls were made to feel that their bodies were things to be ashamed of. When they bathed, they had to keep their bodies covered with long white gowns; and, to prevent them from taking too much interest in their appearances, they were forbidden to own mirrors. The nuns were businesslike and tried to keep the girls from being idle at any moment of the day; at night each girl slept in her own curtained cubicle, preferably on her back with her arms across her breast so that if she died in her sleep she would be prepared to meet God.

It is not surprising that Sonia rebelled against this morbid, repressed upbringing, but she was never fully able to escape its influence. She was not the 'enemy of the male principle', as Connolly charged, but she was certainly the victim of a system which encouraged misunderstanding of sex and mistrust of one's physical nature. Recalling the Sonia she knew in the Forties, Diana says, 'She flirted and went out with men, but underneath it all I think she did have a feeling against them which was deep-seated. She would always be criticising, saying, "Oh, men!" A lot of us used to do that as a sort of joke, but with her I think it was more deep-seated, because she really *did* give the brush-off directly they started getting keen on her, and she was attractive to many men.'[8]

Significantly, one man whom Sonia was drawn to in the Forties was Peter Watson. She had enormous admiration for his taste in art, his refined manners, and his sensitivity. Watson was often touched by her interest in him, though at first he did not really like her. He thought she was too aggressive and ambitious, and was offended by her efforts to work her way into *Horizon*. Eventually he came to care for her deeply and to sympathise with her ambitions. Towards the end of the Forties, he also gave her a great deal of practical help. For all her beauty and intelligence, Sonia had little money, and lived very modestly throughout the Forties. Watson felt sorry for her and would occasionally offer her small gifts of cash. He also gave her money for holiday trips, paying her way to France more than once after the war. He liked to take her out to good restaurants, and from time to time would go with her to a concert or film. Seen out together, they could easily have been mistaken for a young married couple.

Peter Watson had the attraction of being 'safe' – a man whose physical side posed no threat to Sonia. In Connolly's unfinished 'Happy Deathbeds', Elsa (the character based on Sonia) is infatuated with Paul, a rich homosexual who owns the literary magazine for which she works as a secretary. After telephoning Paul at his flat one day and talking briefly to him, Elsa dreamily ponders, in minute detail, her impressions of the call: 'She thought of Paul's thin sad face, his bath running, the faint backwash from an atonal gramophone record, his money, his distinction . . .' Later, we are told that Paul is someone whom Elsa 'could truly love because, being homosexual, he inspired no sexual ambivalence, she could not hate him for desiring her or for desiring another woman. In the sex-war he was a kind of angel of man's who was on her side.'

Sonia's fascination with Watson both intrigued and irritated Connolly. Spender recalls that Connolly would occasionally complain to him, partly in a joking spirit, that Sonia loved no one but Watson. 'Cyril told me that when he went to the office of *Horizon*, if Sonia opened the door, he always knew whether Peter was there: for if he was, Cyril got only 30 per cent of her smile, 70 per cent being reserved for Peter.'[9] Ironically, Watson was always of the opinion that Sonia wanted to be Mrs Cyril Connolly. When she did marry, during the last days of *Horizon*, her choice caught everyone by surprise. The dying George Orwell married her in October 1949.

## II

While Connolly was creating a bright social life at his rented studio in Drayton Gardens, Watson continued to simplify his life, relinquishing many of the outward symbols of wealth once so important to him.

The biggest change came at the end of 1940, when he moved to a new flat in Palace Gate, south of Kensington Gardens. His rooms were in a tall modern building with a flat roof, plain concrete exterior, and wide, rectangular windows. Watson liked the clean, geometric shape of the building and the simplicity of his flat: one bedroom, one bathroom, a small kitchen, and a long living room – almost like a gallery – divided by furniture into a study area, a dining area, and a living room. It was comfortable and the space was adequate; he was content to remain there for the rest of the Forties and beyond. All the same, it was small and spare by the standards of his life in the Thirties. Its modest nature amused Connolly, who could not resist teasing Watson about it. Writing to Diana early in 1941, Connolly reported that he had said 'jokingly' to Watson that if Lansdowne Terrace happened to be destroyed in a raid, *Horizon*'s office would have to be moved to the flat in Palace Gate. 'You will have to move out of this into a single room in Earls Court,' Connolly had quipped. Expecting a laugh, he was stunned to hear his friend agree with him. Indeed, Watson took the plan 'quite seriously', as though it no longer mattered where he lived.[10]

During the war Watson opened his flat to all sorts of people, some of them almost strangers, who needed a temporary place to stay; there was a large day-bed in the living room for them. But there was a limit to his generosity. Brian Howard, a chronic alcoholic, once wanted to stay at Palace Gate while Watson was away in the country, but was bluntly refused. Watson wrote: 'All my friends (and yours) say it is madness to lend you a flat. Are they all wrong? Anyway I would rather even in this socialist age keep my two rooms quiet while I am away.'[11] On another occasion he was saddened to discover that one of his guests, whom he did not know well, had stolen a solid gold cigarette case which had been treasured for many years. After Watson had reported the details of the theft to the police, a friendly Cockney constable warned him: 'If you don't mind my saying so, Mr Watson, in future you should have people staying with you who are more commensurate with your way of life.'[12]

A few people who stayed at his flat might not have been 'commensurate' with his way of life, but most were harmless young artists whom he had befriended. In his first months at Palace Gate, he shared the flat with the painters Robert Colquhoun and Robert MacBryde, both of whom came from Scotland with little money and few prospects for establishing their careers. Watson not only gave them a place to stay but paid for their first studio, at the back of a shop in Kensington High Street. And early in 1941 he wrote to Kenneth Clark, who was then chairman of the War Artists' Advisory Committee, asking whether some work could be found for Colquhoun; the young painter was eventually given a small commission for a textile design. Of course, when Watson came across new artists whose work appealed to him, he was able to promote their careers by including reproductions of their best works in *Horizon*. Colquhoun and MacBryde were helped in this way and so, too, were John Craxton, Lucian Freud, and Lawrence Gowing.

Craxton and Freud were especially close to Watson in the early years of their careers. 'Lucian Freud and I used to haunt [Watson's] flat and read *Verve* and *Cahiers d' Art*,' Craxton remembers. '[Watson] had marvellous taste and was interested in everything new and anything good.'[13] At seventeen, Freud's first drawing – a self-portrait – was published in *Horizon*; Craxton's celebrated 'Poet in Landscape' appeared in the magazine when he was twenty. For two years during the war they both worked in adjoining studios in St John's Wood, and Watson paid the rent. He also introduced Craxton to Graham Sutherland, and arranged for them to spend time drawing together during a summer holiday in Wales. Sutherland, who had sold two major landscape paintings to Watson in 1939–1940, 'Entrance to Lane' and 'Gorse on Sea Wall', became a friend to Craxton and exercised an important influence on his work, teaching him 'how to look at landscape', according to Craxton.[14]

Both Craxton and Freud painted Watson's portrait. Freud's painting, done in 1941, is especially striking, for it depicts Watson as a sad-eyed patient in a hospital ward, so wasted by sickness that he seems to be melting away, dissolving into the dark folds of the blankets covering his sick bed. Lawrence Gowing, whose book on Lucian Freud contains a reproduction of the painting, says that it was based on a dream Watson had shared with his young painter friend. Titled 'Hospital Ward', it captures perfectly the dark, fatalistic side of Watson; the image of doomed isolation it evokes is like something from a novel by Kafka. Indeed, Watson had become an avid reader of Kafka, and in

1941 was recommending the writer to his friends, telling Craxton that Kafka was 'completely satisfactory to read during this War'.[15] No one portrayed the nightmarish, Kafkaesque nature of wartime London better than Henry Moore in his drawings of the shelter dwellers in the underground stations and, as one might expect, Watson was a great admirer of these works. Shortly after Moore began the drawings, two were reproduced in *Horizon* (March 1941) – 'Shelterers in the Underground' and 'Seated Figure in Tube Shelter'.

The list of artists whose work appeared in *Horizon* during the war years reads like a 'Who's Who' of twentieth-century British painters, sculptors, and photographers. In addition to Moore, Sutherland, Craxton, Freud, Colquhoun and MacBryde, and the major painters of the Euston Road School, the magazine published works by Cecil Beaton, Bill Brandt, Cecil Collins, Naum Gabo, Barbara Hepworth, David Jones, Paul Nash, Ben Nicholson, John Piper, Ceri Richards, and Alfred Wallis (and, after the war, Francis Bacon). It was a truly extraordinary offering of the country's best art, consistently done in superior reproductions, at a time when opportunities for viewing such works were very limited. These reproductions were often published with excellent critical commentaries; in effect, Peter Watson was offering readers of *Horizon* continuing, informal education in modern British art. In the process he gave the artists invaluable exposure to a large and influential audience.

It was a major contribution to the cultural life of the nation, and Watson was perhaps the one person in the country who had both the money and the taste to do it. Indeed, the only person who did more to promote British art in the early 1940s was Kenneth Clark, which says a great deal for Watson, who worked without government or institutional support. The musician Priaulx Rainier, who also benefited from his encouragement and support, called him 'perhaps the last true patron of the Arts', using the word 'patron' in its best, traditional sense – the independent, generous person of wealth, intelligence, and understanding.[16] Certainly, when an artist received help from him, it was spontaneous and personal; there were no forms to fill out, no committee meetings to attend, no interviews required – none of the bureaucratic burdens imposed on artists by the more 'advanced' forms of patronage today.

Through *Horizon*'s 'Begging Bowl', which first appeared in January 1941, Watson and Connolly sought to involve readers in the act of patronage. The 'Begging Bowl' announcement took up half a page, and it exhorted loyal readers to help the magazine by finding it new subscribers, and to help contributors by sending them money: 'If you particularly enjoy anything in *Horizon*, send the author a tip. Not more than One Hundred Pounds: that would be bad for his character. Not less than Half-a-Crown: that would be bad for yours ... Do not forget the painters either.' It is not known how much money was raised through this amusing notice, but it was not a great sum. Connolly reported at the end of the year, after the notice had been dropped from the magazine, that the largest donation had been ten pounds. Several gifts of five pounds had also been received, and he acknowledged that he had benefited personally from one such donation. Most responses were a pound or less. Alun Lewis received only one donation after the publication of 'All Day It Has Rained', and that was for 3/6d, which he turned down. All the same, Connolly considered the experiment reasonably successful, and encouraged readers to continue sending money. 'We would repeat that *Horizon* authors are in our judgment underpaid, and that by sending them gratuities the readers of *Horizon* are forming themselves into a new patron class.'

Dylan Thomas was one writer who did receive a substantial sum of money from *Horizon* over a long period, some of it from readers in donations but a large proportion in gifts and loans from Watson and Connolly. It appears that the original idea for 'Begging Bowl' came from a campaign to raise money for Thomas in the spring of 1940. He seemed always to be on the brink of financial ruin, and in May 1940 Spender, Watson, Henry Moore, and Herbert Read combined to appeal to friends for donations which would help Thomas escape from some pressing debts. They raised about one hundred pounds and more went Thomas's way when Watson added a large donation. 'I never thought I'd have so much, and was frightfully pleased,' Thomas wrote to Watson after receiving some of the money. 'I'll be able to settle everything now.'[17] Of course, Thomas ran through the money in no time, and within six months he was writing to a friend, 'After buying a few useless things ... the Watson money disappeared, quick as a sardine.' His creditors were after him again, and once again he turned to Watson, who promised to send more money. In the meantime, Thomas said, 'The debtees will have to wait until my Watson comes in.'[18]

The 'Begging Bowl' was an attempt to keep a trickle of money coming in to help people like Thomas, who were in constant need of funds. But inevitably most of the money *Horizon* gave away came out of Watson's pockets, and Thomas, for one, soon learned to go straight to him. If he was not around, he would plead his case to Spender, Connolly, or anyone else who happened to be in the office. Spender recalls, 'When I was at *Horizon* ... Dylan was always coming in, usually to borrow money.'[19] And Connolly once described buying Thomas's 'poems spot cash from his wallet as if they were packets of cocaine'.[20]

At the end of 1945 Thomas wrote to Connolly, 'Do you remember our conversation ... some nights ago about fifty pounds that I think you said you thought I should have for my poem but for fear that I should spend it? Spend it of course I would ... I'm so much in worry and debt that the money would be wonderful *now*.'[21] Even if the poem in question is the rather long 'A Winter's Tale' (130 lines), as the editor of Thomas's collected letters surmises, fifty pounds would be a large sum to expect for a single poem. What Connolly had in mind was misunderstood; Thomas did indeed receive fifty pounds from the magazine a short time later, but it was not for a single poem. It was the 1945 *Horizon* Prize, awarded to Thomas for the best work contributed to the magazine during that year.

Despite all he was given, it cannot be said that Thomas truly took advantage of his connections at *Horizon*, though at certain times it might have seemed so. Whatever his problems and whatever sums he received, he was the pre-eminent poet of his generation, and he gave the very best work he produced in the Forties to *Horizon*. Ten poems were published in nine separate issues (including one in a special French issue in 1945), and among these were such important works as 'There Was a Saviour' (May 1940); 'Deaths and Entrances' (January 1941); 'The Ballad of the Long-Legged Bait' (July 1941); 'Vision and Prayer' (January 1945); 'Poem in October' (February 1945); 'Fern Hill' (October 1945); 'A Refusal to Mourn the Death, by Fire, of a Child in London' (October 1945); and 'In Country Sleep' (December 1947). *Horizon*'s periodic investments in the spendthrift poet were amply rewarded by the chance to publish these poems.

Through the War Artists' Advisory Committee, many painters and sculptors enjoyed the patronage and protection of the government during the war, but there was no similar scheme for literary artists. While writers were called up for military duty or wasting their talents in bureaucratic jobs at the Ministry of Information, official war artists were paid comfortable salaries to do work which often allowed them a great deal of artistic freedom and opportunity. Henry Moore's shelter drawings, for example, were done while he was an official artist, and even though only thirty artists were paid full-time salaries dozens more received specific commissions.

In October 1941 *Horizon* sought to extend to writers some of the benefits given to artists by calling for 'the formation of an official group of war writers'. The call was made in a manifesto titled 'Why Not War Writers?' and was signed by Connolly, Spender, Orwell, Alun Lewis, and Arthur Koestler, among others. The basic idea was that writers, like the official artists, should be paid to record the human side of the war, and should have the facilities and creative freedom to do the job. At the very least, the manifesto argued, novelists, poets, and dramatists should be counted as workers in reserved occupations, especially since this classification had already been granted to most journalists. To demonstrate the logic of this idea, the manifesto called attention to the parallel case of artists and photographers: 'The Government distinguishes between war artists and war photographers. Both are reserved and the function of each is regarded as distinct. The first has to give a permanent aesthetic significance to the events of the war, the second a news or documentary significance. It would be logical to apply the same principle to writers as to journalists, and give them the same facilities.' The argument had merit, but no one at the Ministry of Information showed interest in supporting it. Nothing came of the ideas advanced in the manifesto, and Connolly later dubbed it '*Horizon*'s most lost of lost causes'.[22]

Alun Lewis and Arthur Koestler were invited to sign the manifesto because they were considered representative of all those writers who were struggling to keep their careers going while doing military service. The circumstances of Koestler's army life were particularly disheartening. In the spring of 1941 he had been dispatched to the Pioneer Corps, and at the time that 'Why Not War Writers?' was published he was at a camp in Gloucestershire spending much of his time digging latrines. It was, of course, disgraceful that a writer so talented should be forced to do such work, and for those aware of his situation his name on the manifesto was a sharp reminder of the government's failure to consider the needs of writers, including those who, like Koestler, had fled to Britain as exiles. Koestler was never given anything better to do in the army, but he managed to get a medical discharge early in 1942.

When Koestler arrived in London, Connolly took it upon himself to provide him with a place to stay, and shortly afterwards helped him to become an established writer in London. In turn, Koestler gave *Horizon* three important articles: 'The Yogi and the Commissar' in 1942, 'The Birth of a Myth' in 1943, and 'The Intelligentsia' in 1944. The second essay, which was about the death of Richard Hillary, was chosen by readers as the most popular work in the magazine for 1943. Moreover, near the end of 1943, Connolly published Koestler's powerful story 'The Mixed Transport', which describes a long train ride by a group of Jewish prisoners headed for Nazi concentration camps.

This was one of the early attempts to demonstrate to the British public how desperate the plight of the Jews had become in the occupied countries. Its last paragraph highlights the relentlessness of the Nazi campaign to exterminate the Jews: 'They [the Mixed Transports] are on no time-table, but every night they run in all directions – ten to twenty cattle trucks locked and bolted, drawn by an old-fashioned locomotive spitting sparks into the night.' Lamentably, *Horizon* received a number of letters from people who doubted whether Koestler's story had any basis in fact. Koestler wrote a reply to one, which was reprinted in the magazine. It concluded boldly, 'As long as you don't feel, against reason and independently of reason, ashamed to be alive while others are put to death and guilty, sick, humiliated, because you were spared, you will remain what you are: an accomplice by omission.'

Koestler remained forever grateful for Connolly's support, saying many years later: 'Cyril took me under his wing. I want to emphasise very warmly my indebtedness to Cyril. Instead of spending my time in loneliness and isolation like so many exiles, or confined to an emigré clique, I was welcomed into the *Horizon* crowd. I wouldn't say that I was exactly an insider – more a strange bird on the periphery: but the important thing was that I felt at home.'[23] For a few months in 1942 Connolly, Lys, Peter Quennell, and Koestler were all living together in the house in Drayton Gardens, but these arrangements sometimes created comic complications. Lys recalls, 'Though the house was not small, there was only one bathroom, and it was amusing to watch Peter and Arthur trying to beat each other to the bath each morning; unlike Cyril, they were both early risers. Peter, as the senior lodger in terms of time spent, not only resented the competition but found the sight of Arthur's hairnet (quite customary on the head of a Central European) revolting.'[24] Quennell relates in his autobiography, 'An absurd squabble presently broke out, followed by an irate correspondence, because I was alleged to have told a girl we both knew that in bed he wore a hairnet; and he protested that I had gravely injured his chances of securing her affections.'[25]

## III

Although as the editor of *Horizon* Connolly enjoyed the relative safety and comfort of a reserved occupation, he could lose that status if

*Horizon* went out of business. The easiest way for that to happen would be if the magazine lost its paper ration – a real and constant threat throughout the early years of the war. As long as Harold Nicolson was at the Ministry of Information, *Horizon* had an influential friend, but in the summer of 1941 Nicolson lost his place as the Ministry's Parliamentary Secretary and was sent off to a new job on the BBC's Board of Governors.

On 21 July Connolly received a short note from Nicolson on Ministry of Information stationery, which read simply, 'I am clearing out of here today and I fear I can do no more to help Horizon. I am very sorry about it.'[26] With paper in extremely short supply, some bureaucrats at the Ministry had been threatening to take away *Horizon*'s ration and pass it on to more 'essential' publications. Once Nicolson was out of the picture, there seemed to be nothing to stop them; at that point, *Horizon* appeared 'threatened with extinction'.[27] Fortunately, Nicolson and Kenneth Clark continued to lobby for *Horizon* among influential people in the government, and by the end of the year Connolly was able to report in 'Comment' that the magazine's 'paper difficulties have so far been surmounted, though only for the time being. Here again the friends of *Horizon* [identified as Clark and Nicolson among others] helped us to a temporary settlement.' Still, Connolly pointed out, 'Like every newspaper with a paper ration we have not nearly enough. To develop a magazine on the trickle which we are allowed is to try to grow figs from a window box.'

To justify the magazine's continued existence, Clark and Nicolson pointed to the favourable publicity *Horizon* had been receiving for the past year in the United States, where the British government was eager to cultivate pro-British sentiments of all kinds. The magazine had a good press in several prominent American publications, including *Time*, and in March 1941 Klaus Mann's new magazine *Decision* – published in New York – contained a seven-page editorial devoted almost exclusively to singing the praises of *Horizon*. Klaus Mann (Thomas Mann's eldest son) recommended the magazine as the best that modern British literary culture had to offer, and he called on the Ministry of Information to increase the number of copies allowed for export. He asked American readers to let the British government know that little magazines like *Horizon* were appreciated abroad: 'We are sure that it would impress the Press Department of the British Embassy in Washington if it should receive a batch of letters stressing the keen interest on the part of young Americans in the doings and ideas of literary and progressive youth in England. The Press Department, for its part, may inform the Ministry of Information.'

85

This was, of course, wonderful ammunition to use against *Horizon*'s foes in the Ministry, and it does seem to have helped the magazine's cause. Shortly after the *Decision* editorial, Mann received a letter from an official at the embassy telling him that the piece had 'been read with great interest here', and he was invited to go to Washington to discuss his ideas in greater detail.[28] *Time* magazine later reported that New York's Mayor LaGuardia was among influential American readers of *Horizon* who, in 1941, helped persuade 'the British government that the magazine should be kept alive'.[29]

Connolly had not asked for Mann's support, and did not know about the editorial in *Decision* until after it had come out. But the two editors knew each other – Erika, Klaus Mann's sister, had married Auden in the Thirties – and Connolly wrote a long, friendly letter of thanks to Mann, even though he had yet to see a copy of the editorial: 'I don't know what you said but I would like to thank you very much for it and to say how much we are all looking forward to seeing it . . . It is a very great pleasure for us to be known in America and the ideals of *Decision* are much closer to us than are a great many activities here.' What is most interesting about this letter is the advice Connolly offers, editor-to-editor, on running a magazine:

> There is so much advice I would like to give you about the horrors of editing – you will find everyone seems to let you down but long after you have given up hope the copy comes in, sometimes a year late. Also everybody abuses your magazine, especially your contributors, but it really doesn't matter as long as they go on contributing. The thing is always to remain perfectly friendly and completely cynical. If you have politics, people will disagree with them – if you have none, they will call you escapist. If you use the same contributors, they will call you a clique, and so on. However, it is very interesting, like sitting all day under a tepid shower, and sometimes one feels one is really helping something or someone. The further people are from the magazine, the nicer they are about it, and readers are always more enthusiastic than writers.[30]

Connolly could speak with some confidence about the support for *Horizon* among its British readers because he had just finished conducting a survey of the subscribers, and the results showed that the readership was indeed enthusiastic. A questionnaire had been enclosed in each copy of the January 1941 issue and by March over a thousand had been filled out and returned. Even before the specific replies had been examined, Connolly was pleased to note that 20% of the readership had cared enough to respond. 'It shows exceptional interest in and affection for the magazine generally.'[31]

The tabulated results revealed much about the backgrounds and tastes of the readers. Most were male and under forty: 75% were male and 85% were under forty. Although, predictably, the readers were primarily from the middle and lower middle class, the survey showed that about 16% made more than a thousand pounds a year, which put them in the 'well-off' category. Another 10% were from the working-class level, which meant they made no more than two hundred pounds a year. To test the loyalty of readers, the survey asked whether they would be willing to continue taking the magazine if the price went up from one shilling to 1/6d; 70% answered yes. Asked to indicate their preferences for material they wanted to see in *Horizon*, readers gave articles on writers and writing the highest approval rate, while politics and current affairs had the lowest.

Perhaps the most revealing thing about the survey was that it demolished the charge often made by the magazine's enemies that the readership was a small band of pampered intellectuals who had little to do with ordinary life. Questioned about their occupations, 17% were serving in the military or full-time Civil Defence; 8% were civil servants; 8% were students, and nearly 20% were teachers. Among the remaining 47%, there were 'clerks and farmers, writers and engineers, parsons and accountants, librarians and businessmen, chemists and secretaries, members of the book trade and nursing profession, house-wives and policemen'. Despite this evidence of diversity, some critics continued to say that *Horizon* had no appeal for the ordinary reader. This misconception could then be used against the magazine within the Ministry of Information.

In the early years of the war the press sometimes stirred up senti-ment against anything which could be labelled 'highbrow', treating the term as a virtual synonym for 'cowardly' or 'escapist'. One expected this from certain papers, but even *The Times* got into the act, running an editorial called 'Eclipse of the Highbrow', in which it argued that the intellectuals of the past two decades had taken art away from the common man and turned it into esoteric 'parlour games'. The demands of the war might lead to a permanent change in taste, the paper implied, in favour of more traditional art; but failing that 'at least it can hardly give rise to arts unintelligible outside a Bloomsbury drawing room, and completely at variance with those stoic virtues which the whole nation is now called upon to practise.'

This prompted a quick response from both Kenneth Clark and

Stephen Spender, whose letters in defence of serious art were published in *The Times* on 27 March 1941, two days after the offending editorial had appeared. The only artist the paper had singled out for specific criticism was Paul Klee, who had recently died, but Spender felt, perhaps rightly, that the attack was directed against his literary generation in particular. Shrewdly, Spender hit back at *The Times* leader writers in a way they could easily understand, telling them that many of the so-called 'highbrow' writers in his generation had been 'the prophets of the present conflict between Democracy and Fascism at a time when ... your leading articles were advocating a policy of appeasement and surrender'.

The philistine sentiments of *The Times* also provoked the anger of T. S. Eliot and brought about, indirectly, his first contribution to *Horizon*. When James Joyce died at the beginning of 1941, *The Times* obituary seemed to Eliot and others to be condescending and unsympathetic to the novelist's artistic experiments. As Eliot later explained in a letter to Spender, he decided that Joyce's achievement had been slighted by the paper, and he fired off a letter to the editor in protest. A fortnight passed without any response from *The Times* and at the beginning of February Eliot decided to withdraw the letter and seek other means of making his disapproval known. (*The Times* later defended itself by saying that space restrictions had kept it from printing the letter.) Eliot turned first to *Horizon*: He told Spender that what he had in mind was to publish his letter in the magazine, giving readers a brief explanation of his original plan to send it to *The Times*, and then adding a second, less polite version in order to say what he really thought of the obituary. He thought this might amuse *Horizon's* highbrow readership, but he also felt strongly that someone like him needed to stand up for Joyce and defend his reputation.[32] In March *Horizon* published Eliot's two letters as well as his added note of explanation, just as he had asked. He had been especially annoyed by the failure of *The Times* to acknowledge the unparalleled achievement of *Ulysses*, but he was also indignant that the paper had failed to say anything about the publication of *Finnegans Wake*. In his second letter he charged that *The Times* had used an obituary prepared years earlier and had not bothered to update it except to insert the date of death. The opinions expressed were those of an earlier time and did not reflect the growth of Joyce's reputation in the last years of his life. By printing outdated facts and opinions *The Times* had revealed the true extent of its philistinism. Obviously it did not regard Joyce as someone worthy of a complete and up-to-date assessment. Such an attitude was unworthy of a great paper, Eliot concluded, and he predicted confidently that time would prove how right he was.

The 'highbrows' were clearly not going to sit idly by while the press used the war as an excuse to push literature back towards the values of some imaginary Edwardian 'golden age'. But, ironically, Connolly was beginning to have doubts about defending writers like Joyce.

In his 'Comment' for May 1941 he confessed that the war had begun to make him question some of the literary reputations sacred among Modernists over the past twenty years. He was in no danger of deserting *Horizon* for a job as a *Times* leader writer, but he was honest enough to confess that the war was having an effect on the way he looked at the recent literary past: 'War shrinks everything. It means less time, less tolerance, less imagination, less curiosity, less play. We cannot read the leisurely wasteful masterpieces of the past without being irritated by the amount they take for granted. I have lately been reading both Joyce and Proust with considerable disappointment ... They both attempted titanic tasks, and both failed for lack of that dull but healthy quality without which no masterpiece can be contrived, a sense of proportion.' Amid the bombed-out ruins of Chelsea and Bloomsbury, Connolly understandably found the playful, linguistic complexity of *Finnegans Wake* tough going. But having taken his swipe at Joyce and Proust, he qualified his criticism by adding: 'Yet we must remember that the life many of us are now leading is inimical to the appreciation of literature; we are living history, which means we are living from hand to mouth and reading innumerable editions of the evening paper. It is as unfair to judge art in these philistine conditions as if we were seasick.' And, he announced, to 'help those of us who are passing through a dark night of the aesthetic emotion', *Horizon* intended to present positive views of Proust and *Finnegans Wake* in separate articles on each (they appeared in July and September 1941).

Connolly infuriated many people by his unpredictable stands in 'Comment', but other readers found this unpredictability and candour refreshing – after all, who has not been of two minds about the reputation of a major author? Of course, it would have been in *Horizon*'s interest if he had withheld his negative remarks about two writers who were easy targets for philistine attacks. No doubt, Eliot found them irritating since he had just gone to so much trouble to defend Joyce, and had settled on *Horizon* as the proper place to make that defence. But by the time Connolly's remarks appeared, Eliot had another, more serious reason to be angry with him.

In April Spender and Connolly had hastily put together a section of

*Horizon* tributes to Virginia Woolf, who had committed suicide the previous month. Among the people whom they had approached for a contribution was Eliot. He agreed to write an essay about her but, because the section was scheduled for the May issue, he had to write it in a hurry. *Horizon* quickly produced galley proofs for him and posted copies to his office at Faber & Faber, but somewhere along the way a misunderstanding arose over the deadline for return of the proofs. Apparently unaware that his copy needed to be returned immediately, Eliot held on to it past the deadline, and Connolly decided to print the initial draft as it stood in proof. When Eliot discovered what had happened, he was furious. Because it was dashed off so quickly, his essay on Woolf is clumsily written in places, and he had been counting on having the chance to revise it. Connolly blamed Eliot's secretary for the misunderstanding, claiming that she had been given clear instructions about the deadline over the telephone. But Eliot was in no mood for listening to excuses. He complained that the proofs had arrived in his office without a cover letter, and that no specific deadline had ever been mentioned to him or to his secretary. He held Connolly entirely responsible for the mix-up and indicated that nothing could persuade him to think otherwise. Because his essay concerned the death of an important friend he could not bear to see it published with so many imperfections, and his letter sharply conveys his disappointment.[33]

*Horizon*'s business manager, Bill Makins, had been responsible for giving Eliot's secretary the information about the deadline and, in a note to Spender written after the misunderstanding, he said: 'Point out to him [Eliot] that . . . light talk of covering letters is all very well in a large publishers' office but damned nonsense here when the telephone arrangement with . . . T. S. E.'s secretary was clear enough for any average moron.'[34] It did not really matter who was to blame; the fact was that *Horizon* could not afford to alienate a contributor and major literary figure like Eliot. It was a mistake which caused much ill-feeling.

By the end of 1941 the list of poets angry with Connolly included far more names than Eliot's. In November he had a new surprise for his readers: 'In this number of *Horizon* there are no poems. This is not accidental, it is rather an act of editorial passive resistance, a negative criticism of the poetry which is submitted.' Connolly recognised that good young poets like Alun Lewis come along only rarely but, with bad submissions inundating the magazine every week, it was becoming harder and harder to spot a good poet among all the bad. Connolly complained that an average of one hundred poems a week were coming in and of these 'seventy should never have been written.' The remaining thirty, he wrote, 'are bad but in a different way. One cannot help feeling that their badness is curable, that they exhibit errors peculiar to the present time, a disease (like night blindness) which we can attribute to a particular cause. If one were to make an anthology of them it would be called The Hampstead Book of Puritan Verse.'

Connolly illustrates his point with an imaginary poet called 'John Weaver', portraying him as the archetypal young poet of the Puritan school – a tame Socialist who writes 'austere' verse in poor imitation of the Thirties poets, singing about 'Love's tracer bullets', and writing poems which begin with lines like 'Heart we have been handed our passport,/ Love's visa has expired.' The portrait of Weaver was detailed enough to offend more than a few poets, critics, and editors of the day. 'He will have been published in *New Verse*, *New Writing*, and *New Directions*,' Connolly said of Weaver, 'and have produced one volume of verse, with an Introduction by Herbert Read, called *The Poet's Thumb*.'

Herbert Read, for one, did not see the humour in this, and wrote complaining that the reference was unfair. Connolly tried to be conciliatory: 'I agree with you that you have never sponsored the John Weaver type of poetry. I put you in hastily after reading your list of New Poets in the Listener. If I get the chance I will retract it.'[35] But Read wrote again with more complaints, and this time Connolly vigorously defended himself:

You seem to have got my editorial completely wrong. I have oppressed nobody except an imaginary poet invented by myself, who represents the Spender-Auden tradition expiring in a Faber New Writing type of youngish poet (25 to 35). To say this kills youthful enthusiasm is just as ridiculous as to accuse an art critic who says he doesn't like the Euston Road group, of hating painting. As for saying it is better to print the timid and the tentative than to print no poetry at all, you seem to be in complete ignorance of the difficulties of running a magazine today if you think that ... Our life has been a constant struggle with Civil Servants to exist at all. If we filled our pages with 'tentative' efforts we would have long since gone out of existence. Nobody seems to realise that the rationing of paper is a direct threat to immature writing because only publications can survive which can put up their price, i.e. appeal to bookstalls, society, and satisfy Ministries that they are part of the war effort.[36]

91

Precisely because the markets for poetry and other types of literature were so limited during the war, Connolly and *Horizon* were expected to be all things to all people. A remarkable thing is that the magazine did represent a wide range of authors while maintaining very high standards. Given the bombings, tight money, paper rationing, political pressures, bruised literary egos, and normal foul-ups, it is a miracle that Connolly managed to keep going at all, much less that he kept *Horizon* going as well as he did.

Late in 1941, writing in a private notebook, he speculated on the reasons for his success:

> Editing a magazine is perhaps the only occupation in which my lack of belief in anything or anyone, and my ambivalence, my passionate belief in the BOTH, can be turned to advantage. In a writer this causes sterility, in an editor it is called 'readiness to give the other side a hearing'. I believe in god the Either, god the Or, and god the Holy Both.[37]

## IV

As Connolly's talk of 'sterility' suggests, he was again beginning to feel guilty about not producing more work of his own. 'The Ant Lion' could have become the first of many imaginative essays to appear under his name in the magazine, but he had chosen instead to make his creative contribution in the form of 'Comment' each month. That contribution was major, but he wanted to be writing something more substantial, which would stand and endure.

Despite this, he rarely had to look far to find an excuse for not writing. The turmoil and hardships of the war provided him with countless excuses, as did his work at *Horizon*, and, in a sense, the magazine was a convenient substitute for a book of his own. It had his name in bold letters on the front cover, and he could show it off with some of the same satisfaction a proud new author might feel. Spender recalls, 'If you invited Cyril around to a party and *Horizon* had just appeared, he would often have copies of it in his coat pockets and would show them to everyone. For Cyril, I think it was almost like having a book of his own appear each month.'[38]

By spring 1942 Connolly had another good reason to put off writing a book. The *Observer* had offered him the job of literary editor and principal reviewer, and he had accepted. It meant a great deal of work, because he planned to combine that work with editing *Horizon*. The new position carried considerable prestige and influence, and came with a generous salary, nine hundred pounds a year. Peter Watson was paying him around four hundred a year, and Jean was sending money occasionally from America, so the financial gain from the new job was substantial. It was also an opportune time to begin working at the newspaper, because David Astor, son of the proprietor, was beginning to take an active editorial part, and was 'trying to liven it up a bit, to make it more in touch with what was going on'.[39] Connolly was expected to recruit top-notch reviewers for the literary page, and to give it a more sophisticated, contemporary flavour. Although he had misgivings about taking on so much editorial work, he could not turn down the chance to take part in the revitalisation of such an important newspaper.

As soon as he had accepted the job, he and Lys decided to look for another place to live. Walking in Bedford Square one day, Lys had found a large, attractive flat to let, and Connolly approved of it right away. Its location in Bloomsbury – within view of the great dome over the Reading Room of the British Museum – was convenient, but it was expensive. With the money from his new job, however, he could afford it. He met the owner, a lawyer who had to leave London for war duties elsewhere, and he agreed to rent the flat for the duration of the war. By May 1942 he and Lys had moved into 49 Bedford Square, a tall Georgian house in which their flat occupied the top two floors. They had perfect arrangements for entertaining – a large dining room, a kitchen, and a very spacious, elegant drawing room with a high ceiling; from the tall windows there was a view of the oval garden in the square, with its magnificent plane trees. On the floor above was a big bedroom and a study. Again, Peter Quennell moved in with them, but this time he had separate quarters above theirs in a large attic flat which they rented to him.

Not long after the move, Lys was called up for national service and assigned a position as a secretary in the Political Intelligence Department of the Foreign Office. *Horizon* had also lost Bill Makins, and in the autumn of 1941 Spender had finally received his call-up papers and was a fireman at a London branch of the National Fire Service. He ceased to serve as the magazine's associate editor, but his old flat continued as *Horizon*'s office, and he contributed material to the magazine throughout the war and gave advice when asked. He had begun to drift away from the magazine by the time of his marriage in 1941. At the beginning of that year John Lehmann had persuaded him to become a regular contributor to his magazine, which had been revived as *Penguin New Writing*, with financial backing from Allen Lane, the founder of Penguin Books. Spender agreed to write a monthly feature called 'Books and the War', and he also contributed other material to Lehmann's hardback anthologies – *Folios of New Writing* and *New Writing and Daylight*.

*Penguin New Writing* was a far more successful publication, in terms of numbers sold, than *Horizon*. Thanks in part to Allen Lane's support, and his large stocks of paper, Lehmann's magazine sold amazingly well, achieving a circulation more than ten times as large as *Horizon*'s. Spender was thus able to reach a very large audience and, furthermore, Lehmann shared his interest in the social purposes of literature. It was this interest that he wanted Spender to develop in the 'Books and the War' feature: he wanted those monthly articles on books to 'provide food for the thoughts that were stirring . . . in the minds of innumerable people who had hardly taken literature seriously before, or felt any need to go to the great poets and novelists for answers to the problems that now obsessed them, and at the same time could be valuable and interesting for the highbrows and professionals; and I believed that Stephen was one of the few writers of our generation who could undertake them successfully.'[40]

Connolly, of course, had little interest in developing such earnest, socially-redeeming plans for *Horizon*, and he did not really regret losing Spender as an active editorial associate. Much later, he wrote that he was grateful to Spender for his help in the magazine's first years: 'It was due largely to him that we printed such good war poetry and such intelligent articles about war aims.' But Connolly also complained that Spender's influence had, at certain points, pushed the magazine too far into politics: '*Horizon* at that time [1939–1941] manifested a tendency to become a Left-wing "school magazine" with a rather naive attitude to other writers.'[41]

He also openly expressed doubts about Spender's artistic talents. In March 1942 he gave a talk on 'Literature in the 1930s' for the BBC's Eastern Service (where Orwell was the producer of the broadcast, beamed directly to India). When he came to the subject of poetry, he told his listeners, 'The Spender of the Thirties is . . . only an indifferent poet . . . in spite of one or two fine poems when he was just beginning. One feels his future lies in prose.'[42] When Spender heard about the broadcast a few days later, Connolly apologised by saying, with perfect innocence, that he had not meant the words to be taken too seriously since they were intended 'only for India'.[43] Spender let the matter pass, but it was clear that he had accomplished as much as he could at

*Horizon*, and that the time was right to move on.

When Lys was called up, Connolly needed someone to work in the office, but the war had made it difficult to find good help. Finally, he decided that the best available person for the job was Diana and she agreed to fill in on a part-time basis. She stayed at *Horizon* for about six months, and at the beginning worked briefly with Lys. They liked each other, and worked well together. Even Connolly seemed happier and easier to get on with, now that he was a prosperous man of letters. 'Cyril has . . . taken an enormous flat in Bedford Sq. and is very much on the up-grade,' Diana wrote to her brother in May. 'He grins a great deal and is hoarding an immense amount of cigars.'[44] But Connolly's good fortune had Peter Watson a little worried. With Spender no longer serving as a back-up for Connolly, Watson did not want his editor enjoying himself too much. 'I have to keep an eye on Cyril,' he wrote to John Craxton in the early spring, adding with typical understatement: 'He is apt to go astray if not watched.'[45]

# FIVE

# THE UNQUIET GRAVE
## 1942–1944

### I

Evelyn Waugh was one of many friends whom Connolly and Lys entertained at 49 Bedford Square. He dined there on several occasions in 1943–1944, while he was on extended leave from military duty, and was served at least one meal which included truffles and lobster according to his report. Despite wartime rationing, Lys managed to put together special meals for her guests week after week, and Waugh seems never to have come away disappointed. 'Cyril Connolly and his delightful mistress give dinner parties which I enjoy very much,' he wrote early in 1944.[1]

Waugh had known Connolly since their undergraduate days at Oxford, and over the years they had developed what Waugh once called an 'always precarious friendship'.[2] Although he had contributed a short piece of fiction to *Horizon* late in 1941 ('My Father's House', a fragment from *Work Suspended*), he did not have a high opinion of the magazine, objecting especially to the frequent presence of contributors from what he termed 'the rump of the Left wing'.[3] He did not care at all for Stephen Spender, whom he once referred to as Connolly's 'semi-literate Socialist colleague', and he contemptuously dismissed Watson as 'a pansy of means'.[4]

Early in 1943 Waugh had some fun at *Horizon*'s expense when he wrote a letter to the magazine ridiculing its recent tribute to the 'primitive' painter Alfred Wallis, who had died in August 1942 at the age of eighty-seven. Despite praise for Wallis's work from Ben Nicholson, Waugh could find nothing artistic about it, and expressed his disapproval in a letter which Connolly published in the March 1943 issue:

Dear Sir,
 Blue, decayed streaks of silliness are healthy in art as in cheese.
 I have the honour to offer a prize of ten pounds annually, as long

as *Horizon* is published, for the silliest contribution, to be called 'The Alfred Wallis Prize', and to be awarded by subscribers. All contributors will be eligible with preference for the old and famous rather than the young and contemporary. The work need not be complete in itself or in anything else.

      Your obedient servant,
      Evelyn Waugh

Waugh's plan was a parody of *Horizon*'s recently announced scheme to give prizes to the authors of the best contributions published in 1943, as indicated by subscribers' votes. But thanks to a sharp response from Graham Greene in the May issue, *Horizon* had the last laugh:

Dear Sir,

    May I record a vote that Mr Evelyn Waugh be awarded the first 'Alfred Wallis Prize' for his little castrated letter, which so admirably fulfils his last condition, that 'the work need not be complete in itself or in anything else'?

    As Alfred Wallis is dead and is unlikely, therefore, to notice Mr Waugh's generous offer, I suggest that the prize might more suitably bear the name of the donor.

      Yours etc.,
      Graham Greene

For as long as they knew each other, Waugh delighted in making fun of Connolly. His published letters and diaries are overflowing with anecdotes about Connolly's various literary, social, and sexual misfortunes, all of which are told in as much detail as possible. (Late in life, Connolly dismissed the diaries as 'all vomit and Debrett'.)[5] Sometimes Waugh would mock Connolly in his presence, and on several occasions he criticised him harshly in print.

Connolly took all this with amazing forbearance, for the most part. He respected Waugh's talent as a novelist, and he wanted his good opinion. There were many times when the two seemed to get on well, taking great delight in each other's witty, fast-paced conversation. 'Evelyn's relations with Cyril were among the most ambivalent of his life,' his biographer Christopher Sykes observed. 'On several occasions Evelyn was rude to him to his face'; at other times, Sykes says, their friendship was marked not only by signs of true 'affection' but 'almost of amorous infatuation'.[6] In the last decade of his life, however, Waugh placed too much strain on his delicately balanced relationship with Connolly. In 1961 he put a thinly-disguised caricature of Connolly into the novel *Unconditional Surrender*, the final volume of his trilogy on the Second World War.

In its second chapter a character named Everard Spruce appears as the celebrated editor of an influential literary magazine called *Survival*. A rumpled dandy in his middle thirties, Spruce lives and works in a large house in fashionable Cheyne Walk, where he is assisted by four devoted young secretaries who not only answer his correspondence and correct page proofs but cook his meals, do his laundry, and clean his house. ('They gave him their full devotion; also their rations of butter, meat and sugar.') Spruce regards himself as one of the true champions of culture in wartime, and the constant concern of his monthly review is the 'Survival of Values'. He publishes writers who represent the latest trends in literature, and two of his secretaries assemble 'art supplements' to give exposure to new painters and sculptors. ('There was one such in the current issue, ten shiny pages of squiggles.') Spruce's magazine has a loyal following and has won the blessing of the Ministry of Information, which recognises propaganda value in promoting a periodical devoted to 'free expression in the arts'. The Ministry sees that the magazine has the paper ration it needs, and arranges for Spruce to be exempted from military service and all other war-related work so that he can concentrate on *Survival*. With four secretaries to help him, his work is scarcely demanding and leaves him plenty of time for enjoying himself, and he spends much of his time entertaining friends and admirers at large parties in his home. Sipping a drink mixed and served by one of his assistants, Spruce idles his time away in literary small talk with the guests who crowd his drawing room during the long nights of the blackout.

This portrait hit too close to home, and Connolly was depressed by the thought that others would recognise the likeness and laugh at both him and *Horizon*. Ann Fleming, wife of Ian Fleming and a friend to both Connolly and Waugh, wrote to Waugh to warn him that Connolly was upset by the book. Disingenuously, Waugh claimed that Spruce was a fictional invention. He accused Connolly of suffering from a 'persecution mania', and told him that it was wrong to 'suppose I would publicly caricature a cherished friend'.[7] Although Waugh's argument was not convincing, Connolly let the matter drop and even gave the novel a good review in the *Sunday Times*. But he was clearly hurt by the whole episode. Later Maurice Bowra, the Oxford don, wrote perceptively to Ann Fleming: 'I am not surprised that Cyril is wounded by Evelyn's presentation of him in *Unconditional Surrender*. It is not very like him, but sufficiently like him to be offensive. It is sad that Evelyn has such an urge to torture him. It must be a form of love.'[8]

Waugh's portrait makes much of the fact that Spruce was 'cared for by secretaries to the number of four', and in one of his letters to Connolly concerning the book Waugh tried to persuade him that two of the young women – described as bohemian and untidy – were not based on Lys and Sonia Brownell. 'As for secretaries,' Waugh wrote, 'Lys was beautifully neat and, as I remember her, Miss Brownell was quite presentable. Some time later you had a barefooted landlady but (surely?) she had no part in *Horizon* and very little part in the delightful parties you gave.'[9]

Waugh is certainly correct about the appearances of Lys and Sonia, and partly correct about the 'landlady' – Janetta Woolley, who was part-owner of a house in which Connolly lived later in the Forties. Connolly had known Janetta since she was a young girl; they first met when she was only fourteen, in 1936. They were close friends throughout the Forties and beyond, and, though she was not 'officially' on the staff of *Horizon*, she helped out occasionally during the war and was often a guest at Connolly's parties. Once, when Waugh visited Connolly on a summer day, he was shocked to see Janetta going barefoot through the house. He took it as a sign that he was in deepest, darkest Bohemia and, according to Janetta, he refused to remove his bowler hat throughout his luncheon, as a show of his disapproval.[10] Diana, Janetta, and Sonia – and to some extent, Lys – were all closely involved with one another as friends in the Forties, drawn together not only by their youth and their enthusiasm for art but by the parts they all played, at one time or another, in the complex drama of Connolly's emotional life. Taken together, these four attractive young women might have provided Waugh with the models for his four secretaries, but at no time were they all working and living together with Connolly.

In developing his caricature of Connolly at *Horizon*, Waugh was probably influenced as much by his reading of another novel as by his memories of life in Bedford Square. In 1951 Nancy Mitford's novel *The Blessing*, dedicated to her friend Evelyn Waugh, was published, and in its final chapters there is a subtle, affectionate portrait of Connolly as a character named Ed Spain, an Old Etonian and Oxford graduate who owns and manages a small theatre in London where 'highbrow' plays are performed. 'He was a charming, lazy character who had had from his schooldays but one idea, to make a great deal of money with little or no effort, so that he could lead the life for which nature had suited him, that of a rich dilettante.' Ed Spain, who is also called the Captain, is assisted in the management of his theatre by 'a band of faithful followers, clever young women all more or less connected with the stage and all more or less in love with the Captain'. Like Everard Spruce, the Captain lives in a large house where his female assistants – most of whom are bohemian-looking – wait on him. One in particular is kept on 'because she was an excellent cook'.

It was clever of Nancy Mitford, who was a frequent guest at Bedford Square during the war, to transform *Horizon* into a theatre where the Captain is as fussy about the plays performed as Connolly was about the contributions that went into his magazine: 'The Captain had too much intellectual honesty to pander to his audiences by putting on plays which might have amused them but which did not come up to his own idea of perfection.' As a clue to the real-life source of her fictional character, Mitford closes her description of the Captain's appearance by remarking that 'his keen blue eyes looked as if they had been concentrated for many years on a vanishing horizon'.

Because of the pains Nancy Mitford took to disguise her portrait of him, and because she stressed some of his more attractive features, Connolly raised no objections when the novel came out. But, as he explained to her in several letters written in 1951–1952, Waugh considered it a mistake to go easy on Connolly. He had only praise for her descriptions of the young women, but he told her that 'the Captain doesn't ring true to me', and suggested that the 'tenderness' she felt toward Connolly had obstructed her artistic vision.[11] On another occasion he complained that her portrait of Connolly was 'so flattering as to be barely recognisable'.[12] When Waugh came to write *Unconditional Surrender* several years later, he clearly wanted to make the model for Spruce identifiable, despite his protestations to the contrary, but the identification arises out of circumstantial information. There is no depth, no complexity to Spruce's character; if we did not know that he edited a literary magazine and lived in a house with his female assistants, there would be little to suggest a connection with Connolly.

Connolly was quite aware that his life at *Horizon* in the Forties had become something of a spectacle, a drama that outraged and amused onlookers. Indeed, he himself found considerable enjoyment in the spectacle. 'He was the spectator of his own life, as though it was lived fiction,' Spender once wrote of him.[13] Since his schooldays he had been playing various parts, all designed to win sympathy or approval from friends and lovers, or simply to attract attention. He might appear as a convincing suicidal lover or as a tormented, tragic artist, while at other times he delighted companions by playing the witty extrovert, the brilliant mimic, the sophisticated man of letters, the smiling hedonist, the innocent buffoon. No one understood the complications involved in acting out these parts better than Connolly, who played them to the hilt while privately berating himself for becoming their prisoner. In an unpublished fragment from 1942–1943, he defined three broad character parts for himself:

> In myself I recognise three beings: one is the lean, romantic anarchist, melancholy connoisseur of sunsets who was once wild-eyed, arrogant and uncompromising . . . who believed in passionate love and once hoped to be a genius; another is a robust eighteenth-century humanist, who enjoys conversation and the classics, motoring, luxury, architecture, convivial evenings with old friends and pretty women, and who relishes the gossiping good-sense of the world; and a third inmate, an efficient, well-informed liberal intellectual who would make a good columnist, editor or publisher. The first of these beings has managed to destroy any chance the other two have had of being happy, but not before they have quietly dragged him down in their common ruin.[14]

Connolly never lacked an audience for any of his parts, and as his importance in the literary world grew his circle of friends expanded, bringing him into new relationships with some wealthy and influential society figures.

At Bedford Square he entertained not only writers and artists, but people such as Edward Hulton, the rich publisher of *Picture Post*, and his glamorous wife Nika, a Russian princess; Christopher (Lord) Glenconner and his wife Elizabeth; and the publisher Hamish Hamilton and his wife, Yvonne. Connolly was also a frequent guest at luncheon and dinner parties given by Emerald (Lady) Cunard in her suite at the Dorchester Hotel, where he mingled with admirals, ambassadors, and government ministers, as well as poets and journalists. Connolly did his best to entertain on a grand scale at Bedford Square, and he haunted shops in search of fine china and silver for his dining room, and antiques and furniture for his drawing room. He usually spent more time looking and dreaming than buying, and his favourite place was Sotheby's, which he began to frequent during the war: 'Week after week I would call in after luncheon, lay out my twopences on a couple of catalogues, and set off round the cases to study.'[15]

Despite his busy social life and his work at the *Observer*, Connolly kept *Horizon*'s contents stimulating and fresh. In the summer of 1942, for example, he helped to launch Denton Welch's literary career. The young writer had sent him an unsolicited article describing an awkward visit to the painter Walter Sickert, shortly before the old artist's death. Although Connolly knew nothing about Welch, he liked the article's mixture of humour and pathos, and accepted it right away. Its appearance in *Horizon* was a great success, and he remained a keen advocate of Welch's work long after the young man's early death in the late 1940s. When Welch had difficulty in 1944 finding a magazine that would accept his story 'When I Was Thirteen', which touches on the theme of homosexual love, Connolly again helped him out, publishing the story in the April 1944 issue. It is Welch's finest short story, but inevitably a few readers protested that it was immoral. One reader wrote an angry letter condemning both the author and the magazine, charging that *Horizon* had abandoned its standards of high literary quality. Connolly responded icily: 'It seems to me it is you who have deteriorated in the last four years, and not Horizon, for I can hardly imagine that the author of your letter can ever once have been the kind of reader whom we hoped to cater for.'[16]

This unhappy reader's complaint was presumably followed by cancellation of his subscription, but losing subscribers was no longer a matter of much concern to anyone at *Horizon*. The magazine was not suffering from a shortage of subscribers, because after 1942 the demand for it was so great that it could probably have doubled its circulation if it had been allowed a larger paper ration. There was a general revival of interest in literature and readers were eager for new material of any kind, but with strictly limited paper supplies there was no chance for the magazine to grow, no matter how good it was. Knowing that each issue was almost certain to be a sell-out, Connolly could risk alienating some of his more conservative readers if he desired; but this freedom had its drawbacks.

In 'Comment' for October 1942 he wrote, 'I wonder how many readers of *Horizon* can understand what it is like to know that however good a magazine one edits were to be, not a single extra copy could be sold, and that, however bad, not a single extra copy would be wasted. Such is the demand of the reading public for anything it can lay its hands on that, were we to print large sections of pre-war Bradshaw upside down, we could still dispose of *Horizon* ... We exist in that station to which it has pleased the paper controller to call us. This fixed circulation produces a numbing effect.' On occasion this 'numbing effect' would lead Connolly to take a dark view of the magazine's future. In his December 'Comment' (at the end of *Horizon*'s third year) he wondered whether the magazine had already seen its best days; he observed that after thirty-six issues it had reached 'a considerable age for a literary magazine', and went on to declare: 'Fifty numbers, that is a maximum; at fifty *Horizon* would be older than the *Yellow Book*, older than *Transition*.' He was already beginning to toy with the idea of ending *Horizon*, although at this stage his threats to close it down were dramatic gestures, not serious proposals.

During this particularly trying period of the war, a new assistant came to work at *Horizon*, and stayed for a little over a year. Her name was Anna Kavan, a strange, deeply troubled woman who had published a critically acclaimed book of short stories in 1940 called *Asylum Piece*. Kavan was born Helen Woods in 1901 and, after she married in the Twenties, she published several conventional novels under the name Helen Ferguson. By the end of the Thirties she had been married and divorced twice, and had spent two extended periods in mental institutions. Before *Asylum Piece* came out, she changed the colour of her hair from brunette to white-blonde, and changed her name by deed poll to Anna Kavan, taking the name from a semi-autobiographical character who appears in two of her earlier novels. In her illness she had become addicted to heroin, and in 1940 she became a registered addict.

*Horizon* accepted her story 'I Am Lazarus' early in 1943 (it was published in May), and when Connolly and Watson discovered that she was desperately in need of a steady job they offered her a position at the magazine, partly out of sympathy but also because they admired her writing. The stark Kafkaesque world of her stories was especially intriguing to Watson, and he became one of Kavan's few close friends. Her closest friend was a bald, frail little man with thick hornrimmed glasses who had written poetry, drama, and criticism in Germany before fleeing to England when Hitler came to power. He was also a doctor, and Kavan was under his care, receiving her allowance of heroin from him. Dr Bluth, as he was called, also became Peter Watson's doctor in the Forties. Kavan either took her injections from Dr Bluth or injected herself. One day in the spring of 1943 Watson arrived at the *Horizon* office and found Kavan sitting in a chair with one arm hanging limply at her side. 'Anna's arm was paralysed yesterday,' he wrote in a matter-of-fact tone to Connolly, 'so I have sent her off to her flat where Bluth is giving her a 'cure' himself. She should be away for about a month.'[17]

Except for the breaks which Watson freely allowed her, Kavan worked at *Horizon* until late in 1944, when Lys returned to work full-time at the magazine. Understandably, Connolly was never comfortable with Kavan, and she did not usually enter into the social life which surrounded *Horizon*, though from time to time Watson entertained her and Dr Bluth. When she was well enough to work, she was by all accounts very good in her editorial job; but she was an odd, rather disturbing presence at *Horizon*. Over the next ten years, she gradually faded from the literary scene, and her reputation as a writer went into decline. In 1968 she died in her London home, where her body was discovered sprawled across her bed. She was still holding a syringe loaded with heroin, and police reported later that they had found enough of the drug in her home 'to kill the whole street'.[18]

## II

In the first few months of his work for the *Observer*, Connolly proved his worth by bringing it a number of first-rate reviewers, including friends such as Nancy Mitford, George Orwell, Logan Pearsall Smith, Peter Quennell, and Stephen Spender. The quality of the literary page improved markedly, and both Lord Astor and his son David seemed pleased with the results of Connolly's efforts.

David Astor was particularly pleased to have Orwell writing for the paper. He had read Orwell's *The Lion and the Unicorn* and was much impressed with its style and argument, finding it a 'masterly' work.[19] It was Connolly who introduced the two men, and, though at that time Orwell was still relatively unknown to the general public, Astor thought he would make a good contributor to both the literary page and the front-page editorial 'Forum'. Orwell and Astor became friends, and their professional relationship proved to be satisfying for both men, though Orwell's independent attitudes sometimes led to difficulties. In September 1942, for example, Connolly asked him to review O. D. Gallagher's *Retreat in the East*, but after the piece was finished and submitted the editor of the paper – Ivor Brown – rejected it on the grounds that its critical comments on the Empire might 'play into the hands of a few ill-disposed Americans', meaning those who were isolationist and anti-British. Angered by the reasons for the rejection, Orwell returned another book Connolly had given him to review, telling him, 'I don't write for papers which do not allow at least a minimum of honesty. There is no point in reviewing a book unless one can say what is in it . . . I had no idea that silly owl Brown had anything to do with the literary page of the Observer.'[20]

Orwell was soon persuaded to write again for the paper, but the problems over his review came when Connolly was beginning to complain that his own work was being hampered by interference from

David Astor and Brown. Apparently they felt that the literary page was becoming too 'highbrow' under his editorship. Unwisely, Connolly began to voice his complaints about David Astor behind his back, entertaining friends with elaborate parodies of conversations with him, and condemning what he considered to be the philistine character of the paper. Eventually some of his remarks reached Astor, and their relationship quickly soured. Arguments broke out, and by the summer of 1943 it was clear that Connolly's days at the paper were numbered. Late in August he received a letter from Astor sharply rebuking him for his behaviour:

> You have frequently tried to convince me that I am cynical, unscrupulous, power-seeking, uncouth and barbarous; that I am an enemy of 'intellectuals' and a disparager of art.
>
> But you have done more. These views of me are given at dinner parties by your friends whom I don't even know, such as Quennell and Harold Nicolson. Incidentally I have also heard how you yourself describe the 'atmosphere' at the *Observer* in a disparaging way to entertain your friends, while continuing to accept whatever the *Observer* has to offer you.
>
> The last time we met you exceeded your previous degree of abuse, ending with a denunciation of my family.
>
> I agree that we are bad for each other.[21]

One of the immediate causes of this letter was an argument between Connolly and Astor over the reviewing done for the paper by Quennell. As Astor explained later in another letter, he believed that Quennell dealt too often with books which were too obscure and academic for the readership of a mass-circulation paper. He maintained that 'a paper like the Ob with a circulation of a quarter of a million required a less specialised type of book reviewing,' and he thought that in selecting books and reviewers Connolly gave more consideration to 'their effect on his fellow littérateurs than on the Observer readers'.[22]

Connolly strongly defended himself and Quennell against these charges, but the argument soon got out of control. In a draft of a letter which might not have been sent, Connolly told Astor, 'If we are literary haberdashers you are the customer whom we all dread. You have chosen to be a Philistine because your interests are political and practical . . . Since you are interested in the world of action and not the world of art, admit the fact, and be tolerant.' Connolly concluded the letter with a warning: 'I like your one-sidedness, but don't get your teeth into me, I won't play!'[23] Each man was too quick to judge the other, but a dispute of this nature could not continue for long. David Astor's father soon put an end to it. Early in September Connolly was sacked, in the interest – Lord Astor politely informed him – 'of having harmony and mutual confidence among those working for the paper'.[24]

Although not unexpected, the dismissal was a blow. Later, Connolly was able to joke about it, teasing Quennell that he had lost his job defending him. But at the time he was bitter, and complained to some of his friends that the paper had hired him solely because the Astors wanted him to bring important writers into the *Observer* fold, and that after he had helped to do this he was unfairly let go. Even if this were true, he did not help his case much by picking fights with the owner's son, but it should be remembered that, apart from his brief tenure as a reviewer at the *New Statesman* in the Twenties, Connolly had never held a regular job in a real business until, at thirty-eight, he went to work at the *Observer*. Editing *Horizon* for a benevolent and indulgent Watson had spoiled him, and he was not prepared to take orders or to conform to the normal rules and practices of a large business. As far as his work was concerned, he gave the Astors exactly what he thought they wanted – a literary page of high quality and sophistication. He preferred to think that his only mistake was that he had done his job too well, so when disagreements arose he was in no mood for compromise.

Fortunately, he had *Horizon* to fall back on, and he was even able to persuade Watson to give him more financial help when his income from the newspaper stopped. Hamish Hamilton also put him on the payroll of his firm as a literary adviser. Still, for some time he remained defensive about his 'failure' at the *Observer*, especially when he looked back on it as a defeat in the 'world of action', where one part of him wanted so much to find success. Despite his angry words with David Astor, Connolly had found a great deal to admire about him, and in the first few months of his time at the paper the two men had been on very friendly terms. Although he later criticised Astor for being more interested in action than in ideas and art, he was first drawn to him precisely because the young man was such a handsome character of great energy and enthusiasm. Connolly once observed of Ian Fleming that 'he had the attraction the man of action always exerts over the intellectual', and to some extent this comment can be applied to Connolly's early relations with Astor.[25]

Connolly's problems in adjusting to life at the *Observer* were exacerbated by his general feelings of restlessness and frustration after four years of wartime life in England. He loved to travel, but the war had cut him off from the places he liked to visit most – Paris, the South of France, Spain, Italy, Switzerland. Admittedly, it was a small price to pay in a world where thousands were dying every day as a result of the fighting, but that did not prevent Connolly from missing the South of France. To recapture some of the excitement of going abroad, he made special trips to Scotland (which he liked to pretend was a foreign country, just for the sake of adding adventure to the visits) and to Ireland. For an escape to a warm spot within England, he would sometimes go down to Devon and Cornwall for short visits. It was not exactly thrilling, but it was the best he could manage. During a visit to Lord Glenconner's Scottish castle in 1943, he wrote to Lys, who was having to work at her government job in London: 'Our chief topic of conversation is still the South of France. That [a future visit to France] will be my treat for you!'[26]

His growing restlessness was reflected in *Horizon* by a series of travel articles called 'Where Shall John Go?' The first of these – 'New Zealand: Answer to an Inquiry' – came out in September 1943, and was the work of Anna Kavan, who had once lived 'down under'. (This series ran to nineteen instalments, including one on Jamaica written by Ian Fleming.) In addition, the magazine began to feature the glories of France and its culture. There were numerous essays on French writers, ranging from Molière to Rimbaud, and at the end of 1942, *Horizon* also sponsored the English publication of Louis Aragon's wartime poems, *Le Crève-Coeur*. During a stay in Edinburgh, Connolly gave a talk at the Franco-Scottish House on 'French and English Cultural Relations', and in June 1943 this was published in *Horizon*. His celebration of the natural beauty and cultural greatness of France reveals how deeply he longed to travel there again:

The great blessing France confers on the artist is anonymity. When an English writer goes there, one by one the layers of his social personality peel off, he finds there are more and more things he can do without, and more and more he comes to be preoccupied with his central situation, his creative possibilities. For in France he is not an ordinary nobody. This nobody, who leaves behind his old social or academic skin, is offered all that is most rare and delightful in life: masterpieces of painting and architecture, natural beauty, congenial climate, cheap food, good wine, a room to write in, a café to talk in . . . For the painter, there is outdoor light at all seasons and the world's centre for pictures. For the writer, health and constant exhilaration. He has the Mediterranean for a sun-lamp, and Paris as his oxygen-tent.

His speech at Edinburgh reached its climax in a detailed description of the exact itinerary he had worked out for his first trip back to France, whenever that might be. He fondly describes the roads he will take, and the sights he will see, declaring, 'I know in my own case how much the thought sustains me of my first visit to France after the war.' As he explains it, the highlight of this triumphant return will be his arrival in Saint-Tropez:

> There for several months I shall lie on the beach without moving, like a lump of driftwood, until I have regained what Rousseau called the 'sensation of existence stripped of every other feeling, which is in itself a precious sense of contentment and peace', and without which we cannot develop the best that is in us, and then, when the cicadas are silent and the nights turn cold, it will be time to think of Paris.

Despite its rather bland title, 'French and English Cultural Relations' is an extraordinary performance, and shows Connolly at his best as he manages to move smoothly through his subject, taking on, by turns, the parts of literary critic, cultural commentator, autobiographer, travel writer, humorist, and lyric prose-poet. Such were the possibilities when the subject and the occasion were right, and the necessary motivation and inspiration were with him.

It was impossible for Connolly to spend so much time thinking about France without also thinking about Jean and the many experiences he had shared with her there, beginning with the events of that cold winter of 1929 when they first met in Paris. In all the time since her return to America, he had never really stopped thinking about her, and his dreams of France intensified her image in his mind, reviving one vivid memory after another. But until the war was closer to its end, there was no more chance of seeing her than there was of seeing France; nevertheless, he still sent off periodic pleas for her to return, without ever making it clear what kind of relationship he had in mind if she came back to him. The distance separating them and the difficulty of sending letters across the dangerous waters of the Atlantic combined to heighten the emotional drama of it all, but he never seemed to grasp the absurdity of asking her to brave a crossing for an uncertain future with him.

The comic elements of this drama emerged in June 1942, when Connolly arranged for Brian Howard to help him send a 'desperate' letter to Jean in New York. The idea was that Howard would deliver the letter into the care of a sailor friend, who was leaving for America in a matter of hours aboard a ship in a large convoy. The plan back-fired. Howard got drunk and not only failed to get the letter to the sailor in time but opened the letter, read it, and began telling his friends about its contents. Drunk again, he spotted Connolly at the White Tower restaurant one day and, as he passed his table, could not resist stopping for a moment and whispering, 'I am so tired of not being respectable'. Connolly immediately recognised this as a quotation from his letter to Jean, taken from a passage in which he had complained to her about the social guilt brought on by their marital separation.

Connolly left the restaurant in a rage. Howard later tried to make amends, returning the opened letter and pleading his innocence by blaming the sailor friend for opening it first. According to Howard, his friend had become drunk and decided to take a look at the letter. It was then left behind and found its way back to Howard with some of the sailor's other belongings. Connolly did not believe this story, but his anger over the incident soon cooled, especially after he read Howard's sadly funny, hopelessly confused letter of explanation: 'I did not, for instance, either open your letter or arrange for it to be brought to me. If I had done either, I can assure you (a) that the letter would not have given the appearance of having been opened. I am not an idiot. And (b) you would not have heard about it.'[27]

Connolly's agitation and grief over losing Jean eventually led to something productive. In the autumn of 1942 he began keeping a jour-nal in which he randomly recorded his impressions not only of his past with Jean but of his position as a civilian living and working in wartime London. Many writers of the period kept wartime diaries, but Connolly did not intend anything so regular and methodical. He did not really have any plan or purpose. He just wanted to have a convenient means of recording ideas, observations, and memorable quotations as they came his way, though most were connected to one of the three subjects that interested him most – his relationship with Jean, his life in London, and his love of France.

After a year this journal had taken up three small notebooks, and somewhere along the way Connolly saw the pattern of a book emerge. By the end of 1943, following his dismissal from the *Observer*, he was busy putting together the manuscript that would become *The Unquiet Grave*. In the spring of 1944, Lys and Sonia prepared a typed copy of his first draft, and over the next few months he made so many revisions that the entire work had to be typed again. Finally, the Curwen Press printed the book on handmade paper in a limited edition of one thousand copies, with *Horizon* identified as the publisher. It went on sale in December 1944.

## III

Connolly wrote that literature 'offers the only complete participation in another human personality. We can never know Mozart as we know Montaigne.'[28] In *The Unquiet Grave* he opens wide the doors to his own personality and takes the reader on an intimate tour of the interior. It has its dark, clammy recesses, where fear, guilt, and remorse predominate – as well as its bright, sunny spaces, where wit, innocence, and love hold sway.

Connolly shows us all the views, and is forthright in his commentaries on them. He is unsparing in his criticism of himself: 'A fat, slothful, querulous, greedy, impotent carcass'. He expresses sharp insights into problems of a more general kind: 'There are many who dare not kill themselves for fear of what the neighbours will say'; 'Somewhere in the mind are crossed the wires of fear and lust and all day long nature's burglar alarm shrills out in confusion'; and his most famous remark, 'Imprisoned in every fat man a thin one is wildly signalling to be let out'. Most confessional writing is unremitting in its seriousness and increasingly painful to read, but Connolly's confessions are lightened by his keen wit and unfailing sense of comic irony. His prose style is redeeming; its richness and elegance cast a glow over his darkest moments of self-reproach. It is no wonder that he once remarked, 'Secretly I am convinced that there is no happiness outside my prose.'[29]

Strictly speaking, the author of *The Unquiet Grave* is 'Palinurus', the pseudonym Connolly adopted and the character through whom he projects his thoughts and feelings. No attempt was made in the first edition to identify the author as anyone other than 'Palinurus', though most readers were aware of his identity, which 'was never regarded as top secret', according to Connolly. So why did he go to the trouble of obscuring his identity in the first place? One reason was that he wanted 'a coat of varnish to protect what might otherwise seem too personal a confession'.[30] But he also regarded the Palinurus myth as a powerful representation of his position in life, and he hoped to draw attention to its significance. (It had fascinated him for years: a brief reference to Palinurus appears in his first signed review for the *New Statesman*.)

The story, told in Virgil's *Aeneid*, seems simple enough. Palinurus is Aeneas's master pilot, and is renowned for his navigational skills, calmly steering his ship past Scylla and Charybdis and other ocean perils. But, mysteriously, sleep overtakes him one night and he falls overboard. After three days in the ocean, he is swept ashore, where savages unceremoniously murder him for his clothes. His naked corpse is left unburied on the sands. Later, when Aeneas travels to the underworld, the ghost of Palinurus begs him to see that his bones are properly laid to rest so that he can be delivered from his unquiet grave.

Connolly liked to think that Palinurus did not fall overboard by chance, but that he abandoned Aeneas and his proud place in the hero's grand adventure. As he argues at the end of *The Unquiet Grave*, 'Palinurus clearly stands for a certain will-to-failure or repugnance-to-success, a desire to give up at the last moment, an urge towards loneliness, isolation and obscurity. Palinurus, in spite of his great ability and his conspicuous public position, deserted his post in the moment of victory and opted for the unknown shore.' Whether this interpretation is correct is debatable, but what matters is that Connolly believed in it and that he applied its meaning to himself. As a Palinurus figure, he sees his 'will-to-failure' as the cause of much of his distress in life, but he is also proud of himself for not accepting success and happiness. He is caught up in a recurrent pattern of behaviour which makes him want to sabotage chances of achievement and contentment that come his way.

As a lover, he relentlessly pursues women, then turns his back on them once they have surrendered; the only thing that will revive his passion is to feel their rejection. As a critic, he is respected and influential, yet he takes particular pleasure in discounting the importance of criticism. In *The Unquiet Grave*, for example, he declares, 'We are becoming a nation of commentators, of critics and hack-explainers, most of whom are ex-artists. Everything for the milk-bar, nothing for the cow!' As an artist, he knows that he has the talent and ambition to be successful, but he is unable to push them far enough to gain what he desires. The closer he comes to reaching his goal, the less he cares to have it, and he will not make the necessary sacrifices. Palinurus/Connolly 'would like to have written *Les Fleurs du Mal* or the *Saison en Enfer* without being Rimbaud or Baudelaire, that is without undergoing their mental suffering and without being diseased and poor'.

Even in less exalted literary ambitions, he will not make the extra effort to succeed. His comments on the Palinurus myth were written around the time when he was dismissed from the *Observer*, and it seems that his explanation of the myth's significance was influenced by his recent 'failure' at the paper, where he turned his back on David Astor, the 'man of action', and deliberately provoked a confrontation he could not win. What Connolly says in this quotation is meant to refer to Palinurus, but it seems to fit Connolly better:

> And as with so many of those who resign from the struggle, who quit because they do not want to succeed, because they find something vulgar and even unlucky in success itself – immediately he feels remorse and misery at his abdication and wishes he had stuck to his job. Doing is overrated and success undesirable, but even more so the bitterness of failure.

Although he had placed himself in an impossible situation, his book abounds with plans to improve his life, ranging from losing weight ('a good writer must be in training') to avoiding *angst* ('*Angst* is an awareness of the waste of our time and ability, such as may be witnessed among people kept waiting by a hairdresser'). Of course, none of these remedies will cure the patient until he rids himself of his 'Palinurus complex', but the patient does not want to be cured. No matter what the cost, he wants to be the romantic, doomed Palinurus. The secret, exotic, subversive self brings endless intrigue and dramatic complications to an otherwise uneventful life. 'As I waddle along in thick black overcoat and dark suit with a leather briefcase under my arm, I smile to think how this costume officially disguises the wild and storm-tossed figure of Palinurus; who knows that a poet is masquerading here as a whey-faced bureaucrat? And who should ever know?' For all his complaints about unhappy love, frustrated desire, and artistic failure, Palinurus/Connolly would not have his life any other way. He is tortured by the needless confusion and chaos he brings into his life, but he would be profoundly bored without it.

*The Unquiet Grave* is a lament for the many precious things he has lost in life – 'sensation of what is lost: lost love, lost youth, lost Paris' – but it is this very sensation which seems to give him most pleasure. Once things are lost or, better yet, on the verge of being lost, they acquire a beauty and magic which nothing won can give him. 'Pining' for such things is a favourite pastime. He speaks of the 'torture of two faces', which is a reference to his love for both Jean and Diana at the end of the Thirties, but his writing takes on a note of vitality and excitement which he cannot disguise when he writes about this 'torture', indulging his passion for what he calls elsewhere 'erotic nostalgia':

> The two faces. Everything connected with them is excruciating: people, places, sounds, smells, habits. An old letter coils up and

explodes like a land-mine, an inscription in a book pronounces a life-sentence, gramophone records screech from the grave; even the harmless sunbeam and the green surge of summer out of doors are decoys which ambush the heart at a sultry corner. *Da dextram misero!* O, never to have met or never to have parted! [31]

When told by a friend that his 'vice' is 'inconstancy', he defends his Palinurus complex with a strange, eccentric logic: 'But is it not rather constancy? Fidelity to the experience of abandoning all the world for a new face with an invitation to ecstasy?' This suspect but amusing appeal to reason is disarming and an example of the way he redeems the indulgences of self-pity with humour and irony. Just when he seems to be falling into an abyss of despair, a flash of wit pulls him back: 'MESSAGE FROM THE ID: If you would collect women instead of books, I think I could help you.'

*The Unquiet Grave* is divided into three major sections, and the last is the best. It includes a long and moving account of his early days in France with Jean, the days in 1929–1930 when they lived first in Paris and then in the South of France. Like the rest of the book, it is made up of fragments – observations, quotations or spots of time captured for a moment's reflection. He recalls vividly long, lazy Paris afternoons spent in 'the quiet of hotel bedroom and of empty lounge; the bed covered with clothes and magazines, the *Chicago Tribune*, the *Crapouillot*, *the Semaine à Paris*'. He remembers touring with Jean in a hired car, 'peeling off the kilometres to the tune of "Blue Skies", sizzling down the long black liquid reaches of Nationale Sept, the plane trees going sha-sha-sha through the open windows, the windscreen yellowing with crushed midges, she with the *Michelin* beside me, a handkerchief binding her hair'. The entire section is alive with what Connolly terms 'the memory of physical pleasure':

Early morning on the Mediterranean: bright air resinous with Aleppo pine, water spraying over the gleaming tarmac of the Route Nationale and darkly reflecting the spring-summer green of the planes; swifts wheeling around the oleander, waiters unpiling the wicker chairs and scrubbing the café tables; armfuls of carnations on the flower-stall, pyramids of lemon and aubergine, *rascasses* on the fishmonger's slab goggling among the wine-dark urchins; smell of brioches from the bakers, sound of reed curtains jingling in the barber's shop, clang of the tin kiosk opening for *Le Petit Var*. Our rope-soles warm up on the cobbles by the harbour where the *Jean d'Agrève* prepares for a trip to the Islands and the Annamese boy scrubs her brass. Now cooks from many yachts step ashore with their market-baskets, one-eyed cats scrounge among the fish-heads, while the hot sun refracts the dancing sea-glitter on the café awning.

In his precise poetic descriptions Connolly tries to recapture some of what the past has taken from him, carefully cataloguing impressions of lost moments like a collector arranging priceless objects for public display.

His approach works well in his poignant tribute to the exotic pets he and Jean kept during their marriage, substitutes of a sort for the children they could not have. The lemurs and ferrets and other small animals were a delight to Connolly because they led an existence 'without thought, guilt or ugliness wherein all was grace, appetite and immediate sensation'. He names and describes his favourites – the ferret English Rose, the lemurs Whoope and Polyp – each defined in his memory as vibrant, individual personalities. He recalls the 'pale golden eyes' of English Rose, and Polyp's brash responses to strangers: 'He judged human beings by their voices; biting some, purring over others, while for one or two well-seasoned old ladies he would brandish a black prickle-studded penis, shaped like a eucalyptus seed.' He tells us that Polyp 'died of pneumonia while we scolded him for coughing'. These descriptions are among the finest and most touching passages in Connolly's work. They even won praise from Evelyn Waugh, who wrote that they were 'as beautiful as any passages of English prose that I know'.[32]

Ironically, *The Unquiet Grave* did not languish in obscurity after publication, contrary to its author's expectations. Readers and critics loved it, and the limited edition sold out quickly. It was followed by a general trade edition, which was also a success. By planning to issue the book only through *Horizon* and in only a limited quantity, without any reference to his own name, Connolly had done his part to keep the book from becoming successful. The plan went awry because it added to the appeal of the book, giving it the attraction of a rare and slightly mysterious private confession. It deserved its success, though Connolly was at first mystified by the enthusiastic reaction to it, and he eventually came to feel that the confessional aspects could have been handled in a less indirect fashion. Not long after its publication, a friend – the painter Ethel Sands – wrote to ask why he seemed to show such an 'intense mistrust of life'. He was quite candid about the deeper reasons for his discontent:

'Why this intense mistrust of life?' Well I think probably from a sense of insecurity – perhaps because I am an only child and was sent home by my parents who were abroad – for 2 years when I was five, which made me feel that I didn't really exist unless perpetually reassured of the fact by affectionate contacts – or perhaps because, belonging to what was called after the last war, the 'new poor' I was too conscious of the difficulties of life as compared with the comfortable expectations which I had been led to expect of it – or perhaps I had too much early success ... As for *content* – you are wise and right about it – it has never existed for me, except as a momentary physical sensation – my natural states are either *pleasure* or anxiety-boredom-guilt. How does one learn content if one is always dissatisfied, always feeling that one has disappointed everyone and let them down? [33]

Perhaps the best comment on *The Unquiet Grave* came from Jean, who read it in America and wrote: 'I think you are one of the few people whom self-pity or unhappiness develops rather than shuts in. Only you mustn't stop there, let the next grave be a pyramid.' [34]

## IV

To some extent, the self-pity in *The Unquiet Grave* was occasioned by Connolly's fortieth birthday in September 1943. This event depressed him enormously; he claimed later that the gloomiest parts of his book were written during a period of several months which ended in August, just before the arrival of middle age.

He confessed in *The Unquiet Grave* that forty is a 'sombre anniversary to the hedonist'. With each passing month, he had imagined that the few remaining traces of his youth were being stripped away: 'Sometime in that long year Middle-age angrily flung youth's last belongings out of the room ... Locks of hair, teeth, kisses, memories and hopes; all perished during those slow months.' [35] The dismal prospect of advancing years and the image of the decline that would come with age was made more painful by the slowness with which the war dragged on; each month seemed interminable. With its end nowhere in sight, pleasures remained on indefinite hold, and that was a grim thought indeed for an ageing hedonist. The invasion of Normandy was not far off, but civilians like Connolly did not know that. All he could see was that life was increasingly drab and austere. In *Horizon* he complained openly of London's 'shabbiness and expense, its dirt and vulgarity'. [36]

After five years under siege the urban landscape was indeed depressing; Connolly noted for his readers some of its dismal sights: 'The contraceptives in the squares, the puddles of urine in the telephone boxes, the sulphurous wines and goat-stew in the restaurants, the bored, pale, ferrety people milling round the streets.'[37]

One escape hole, where the cares of war could be put aside temporarily, and the attacks of middle-age *angst* alleviated was Tickerage, the Sussex millhouse owned by Connolly's friend Dick Wyndham. (It is celebrated in *The Unquiet Grave* as a 'cure for *angst*'.) Wyndham, who was away much of the time, often allowed friends the use of the house for weekends or longer stays, and Connolly loved to go there. It was within easy reach of London, and the setting was nothing less than idyllic. He describes it in *The Unquiet Grave*:

> The red lane through the Spanish chestnut wood, the apple trees on the lawn, the bees in the roof, the geese on the pond, the black sunlit marsh marigolds, the wood-fire crackling in the low bedroom, the creak of the cellar-door and the recurrent monotonies of the silver-whispering weir – what could be more womb-like or reassuring?

Another delight at the millhouse was located beneath that 'creaking' door, where Wyndham kept his well-stocked wine cellar. Early in 1944 Connolly was delighted when Peter Watson decided to rent Tickerage for a year. The general drabness of wartime London had begun to depress Watson too, and he wanted to use Wyndham's house as a regular retreat.

Watson was not one to complain openly about his troubles, but the middle years of the war were almost as painful for him as they were for Connolly. He was lonely much of the time, living quietly and keeping to himself. The slow passage of the war had taken its toll on his spirit. In 1943 he wrote to Brian Howard: 'The whole thing [the war] has been going on much too long I feel, and . . . it is very depressing for me to have lost all sense of contact with Denham . . . After four years the sense of tension is unbearable.' Moreover, he did not see much reason to be optimistic about the future, his own or anyone else's: 'It seems to me no one believes in the future, which is tragic and unbearable as time is passing so relentlessly: in fact 30 years are going to be sandwiched into the 5 or 6 (?) of this present war.'[38] In Denham Fouts's absence, Watson was sometimes desperate for a confidant. Although Brian Howard's drinking and irresponsibility angered him, Watson regarded him as an old friend, and the two were frequently together. They shared gossip and confidences, maintaining their relationship despite occasional bitter arguments. Watson was brutally frank with Howard when the drinking got out of hand, telling him in the summer of 1943, 'You have got to stop all this nonsense and drinking soon or you will complete your own self-destruction, which is what you are aiming at. You are a bloody nuisance to everyone and the whole thing is just inflated egotism which you have the impudence to call love.'[39]

Howard squandered his literary talents, which had seemed so promising in the days of the *Eton Candle*. Although he was constantly talking about works that he wanted to write, he produced little in his lifetime and his decline as a writer was viewed with both disdain and sympathy by Watson. At one point Watson made an unusually candid confession to him: 'Without some money I would have acted worse than you. I can't do anything and I hate *doing* things.'[40]

Renting Tickerage brought some much-needed brightness into Watson's life. After living so long in the small flat in Palace Gate, he enjoyed having the extra room of 'Tick Tock', as he came to call the millhouse. Before moving in, he went to great lengths to achieve the simplified, clean modern interior he preferred. The furniture was old-fashioned, and the rooms full of clutter. He did not want to cause Dick Wyndham any inconvenience, so before he moved anything he asked John Craxton to come down and make precise drawings of the placement of furniture in every room. Then the furniture and other items belonging to Wyndham were put in store, and new furniture and modern paintings brought in to give the room the look Watson wanted. When his lease was up, he planned to remove the new pieces and put the old furnishings back in their exact positions.

When he was settled at Tickerage, Watson began leading an active social life again, inviting friends to come down for small but stylish parties. Priaulx Rainier recalls that 'weekends there were an oasis in the drabness of war', and she has written a vivid description of finding him on one visit in 'a spotless white suit, sitting at the head of the dining table, having spent considerable time gathering food from nearby farmers – duck eggs and other wartime luxuries – to entertain his guests'. 'The only item missing was good wine,' she writes, and goes on to explain why that was:

> On my first visit he beckoned to me secretly before dinner. Descending a staircase to the cellar below, he switched on a light. There, securely encaged within a fine steel grill could be seen dozens of bottles of vintage wine!

'Which shall we choose for dinner?' [he asked] smiling at me. 'Let us enjoy in imagination at least our choice!' [41]

Unfortunately, the serenity of even this retreat was disrupted in the summer of 1944, when the Germans began their desperate V-1 flying bomb attacks. Launched from bases in the Pas de Calais, these 'doodle bugs', as they were called, were generally aimed at London, but many fell short over 'Bomb Alley' in Kent and Sussex. At Tickerage, Watson found himself besieged. The sky was filled with the buzzing roar of the doodle bugs as they raced towards London. If the engine of one cut out, the next sound would be a loud explosion as the bomb crashed to earth. Writing to Craxton from Tickerage in the middle of the summer, Watson let it be known that these terrors were almost more than he could stand: 'The doodles are so bad for the stomach. I bit the carpet for hours last night.' [42]

There was no point in returning to London. Things were far worse there. For a time in June more than fifty of the bombs were managing to reach Greater London every day, causing widespread, indiscriminate damage. One of the bombs hit the gardens outside Connolly's flat in Bedford Square. Terrified, Connolly decided it was time to begin going to the public shelter when the air-raid siren was sounded. 'Cyril decided that he wanted to go well-prepared,' Lys remembers, 'so one night we headed for the shelter with Cyril trudging along carrying blankets, a flask, cigars, and a hot water bottle. But almost as soon as we got there, he wanted to . . . come home. All the noise, crowding, and smells were too much. That was our one and only experience with the shelters.' [43] Towards the end of the doodle-bug attacks, Connolly wrote in *Horizon*, 'I know one is not supposed to say so, but I don't care for flying bombs: to all guilty people (and by now all civilians are guilty), they are the final appointment in the dentist's chair.' [44]

One reason he dreaded these bombs was that one had fallen on his father's hotel in South Kensington. Major Connolly, who was now seventy-two and rather frail, was not injured in the explosion, but his room – with its precious collection of shells – was covered in dust and rubble. Lys and Connolly helped to move his belongings to a similar hotel around the corner, where Lys had managed to find the major a room. For years he had refused to move because he had grown so accustomed to his arrangements at the old hotel, and because it was close to his beloved Natural History Museum. He was lame from arthritis and gout, but had faithfully made his way to the museum almost every weekday, crossing the Cromwell Road waving his cane to fend off the traffic.

Overnight the routine of his life had been shattered, and all of his accumulated treasures had to be gathered up and deposited in a strange place. For the major's son, as well as for the major, this move was a difficult and painful experience. Ironically, Connolly had written to his father just a few weeks before the bombing to ask him to move to safer quarters, perhaps in the countryside around Bath. But his father had resisted, writing, 'It is good of you to take an interest in my welfare, but there is nowhere for me to go . . . and to tell the truth, I have not fagged down all the way to the shelter in the cold and dark, but stayed put with my head beneath the clothes for fear of blast. If I were to go anywhere, it would mean giving up my work at the Museum.'[45]

Connolly had begun to grow closer to his father at about the time the hotel was bombed. He had not seen his mother since the late 1930s – the war had kept her from travelling to London from her home in South Africa – and he had gradually become more involved in his father's life. There had been periods in the past when he could barely tolerate his father, who could sometimes be a great embarrassment in public; he once joined his son at a posh restaurant wearing a nice dinner jacket but no socks (they were difficult to put on because of his arthritis). He was stubborn and overbearing at times, and his son found it difficult to be assertive with him. On one occasion in the Thirties Connolly had mentioned to W. H. Auden that he was having problems dealing with his father, and Auden had sternly advised him to make some show of defiance that would put the major in his place. 'Stand up to him, make him see you don't need him any more,' Auden had declared. Years later Connolly recalled his awkward, unsuccessful attempt to follow his friend's advice: 'My father lunched with me in Soho, a treat he always enjoyed, and on the way back I stopped the taxi outside my door . . . He clearly expected to be invited in for a talk and a brandy but I bade him an abrupt farewell and gave the driver his address. Clutching his two thick cherrywood sticks with the rubber ferrules, his legs crossed, his feet in pumps, for owing to arthritis he could not stoop to do up the laces, he fingered his grey moustache while a tear trickled down his cheek. I don't know which of us felt more unhappy.'[46]

When his father's health grew worse towards the end of the war, Connolly became more tolerant and sympathetic. Moreover, his endearing qualities became more apparent as he aged, as did the similarities between father and son. After all, his passion for collecting shells and filing them away in boxes was not that far removed from collecting literary contributions and arranging them neatly in magazines. Indeed, in the early Forties he had applied his skills to the task of compiling the semi-annual index for *Horizon*, with his usual efficiency. In the letter which accompanied his finished work, he wrote: 'Herewith Index to Vol. III, which I suppose will come in useful to you. I suggest that Horizon give me for it an Honorarium of 5/-. The British Museum values my time at 4/- an hour, and as this has taken me exactly 6 hours to make out, (4 × 6 = 24/-) I imagine it is cheap at 5/-.'[47] It is not easy to feel affectionate towards someone with a mind like that, but as the war brought him closer to his father, Connolly did his best to be a good son.

Just before the doodle bugs began to rain down on London, Connolly became friends with a writer whom even the major could admire – Ernest Hemingway. Of all the writers Connolly knew, Hemingway might seem the least likely to find anything of value in Connolly's work or his life. When they first met in the late Twenties at Sylvia Beach's bookshop in Paris, they did not get on at all. But when Hemingway arrived in London in May 1944 as a war correspondent, Connolly quickly sought him out and volunteered to introduce him to literary friends at a party in Bedford Square. The party was a success, and the two men found themselves enjoying each other's company. It was an exciting time, just before the D-Day invasion, and perhaps the excitement of the moment made it easier for them to strike up a friendship; they drank together, and talked long into the night. Connolly invited Hemingway to write a 'Cuban Letter' for *Horizon*'s 'Where Shall John Go?' but nothing came of the idea, even though Hemingway vaguely said that he would try. On another occasion Connolly took him to visit Emerald Cunard at the Dorchester. The burly, bearded Hemingway and the heavy-set, round-faced Connolly must have been a sight to behold as they entered the rarefied atmosphere of Lady Cunard's suite. According to one account, Hemingway did not try to ingratiate himself. When Lady Cunard asked him what he thought of Russia, he replied gruffly, 'There is the pro as well as the con about Russia. As with all these fucking countries.'[48]

Oddly enough, he became a great admirer of *The Unquiet Grave*. He read it when it first came out, and found its comments on *angst* fascinating. He also seems to have appreciated the difference between his personality and Connolly's. All the time that he was in London in May and June, he could not wait to jump into the thick of battle; yet he found Connolly's intellectual and emotional distance from the war intriguing and even admirable. In the late Forties he wrote what can only be called a fan letter, full of praise for *The Unquiet Grave*. It is touching in its way, and Connolly treasured it, coming as it did from a 'man of action':

> I always get involved in wars but I admired the way that you did not. It would be wrong for me not to fight but it was many times righter for you to do exactly as you did. I am no good at saying this sort of thing but I wanted you to know how strongly I felt it and to tell you how much the Palinurus book meant to me.[49]

# SIX

# THE SPOILS OF VICTORY
## 1945

### I

A few weeks after the publication of *The Unquiet Grave*, Cyril Connolly finally had a chance to see Paris again. The long German occupation had ended late in August 1944, and Connolly began asking for official permission to travel there as a 'journalist' reporting for *Horizon*. It was difficult for anyone not connected with the government or the military to go to Paris then, but by the end of the year he had managed to win the necessary approval, and in mid-January 1945 he flew across the Channel, over French countryside which, in his words, 'looked very wild and empty, all snow and forests'.

Paris was very cold and covered in ice and snow. Although the city had suffered little damage from bombs, it was plagued not only by a harsh winter but by severe shortages of food and fuel. Milk, butter, coffee, and meat were in short supply (even horse meat was hard to come by); many homes were without heat, and electricity was cut off for most of the daylight hours; except for the Métro there was almost no public transport. Connolly quickly found that walking was the best way to get around, though it meant cold, wet feet. The empty streets and freezing weather reminded him of Petrograd rather than the Paris he remembered, and in his first letter to Lys, he wrote: 'Tell Peter I don't think he really misses much – it is not the Paris we knew but an unreal city.' [1]

Although this was not the glorious return he had dreamed of, he was happy to be there: an 'unreal' Paris was better than no Paris at all. And thanks to the hospitality of Duff and Diana Cooper, he was spared the ordeal of having to stay in a dark, unheated hotel with bad food and little service. Shortly after the liberation of Paris, Duff Cooper had been sent to serve as British Ambassador, and when Connolly arrived the Coopers offered him a room in the Embassy, an elegant eighteenth-century building which was an island of luxury in the French capital. His room was warm, the food was good, the telephones and electric lights worked and the Embassy was 'almost the only place in Paris with hot water'.[2] Best of all, Diana Cooper gave grand parties which brought together fascinating people from all over Paris, and Connolly was delighted to be a guest at these gatherings. He was even allowed to arrange one Embassy party on his own, inviting André Gide and several other French writers to join him for lunch with Duff Cooper.

He visited the publisher Gallimard, where he exchanged literary news with the critic and former editor of *La Nouvelle Revue Française*, Jean Paulhan. He saw Valéry, who entertained him with stories of London literary life in the days of the *Yellow Book*. Connolly's happiest moments, however, were spent in the smoky interiors of Left Bank cafés, where he met many of the promising literary figures of the day. Among these establishments the Café de Flore, near Saint-Germain-des-Prés, was the most popular; it teemed with writers and editors discussing plans for new books and magazines. Even though the Flore could offer only weak imitations of beer and coffee, there was a good stove and gas lights for illumination when the electricity was off. 'This pleasant haunt has now become a kind of literary *bourse*,' Connolly reported in *Horizon*. 'The brokers are the editors who sit round with their *sommaires* or contents page of the magazine they are going to bring out (when they can get the paper!), and these *sommaires*, which are handed round and discussed like a V-Day menu, are the kerb-prices of literary reputations.'[3] Although Connolly was self-conscious about his rusty French (complaining to Lys that he spent his days and nights 'gibbering my bad French like a marmoset'), he entered enthusiastically into the literary wheeling and dealing, sifting the most interesting material to use in *Horizon*. He found just what he was looking for when he talked to Simone de Beauvoir.

The Flore had been a favourite haunt of Jean-Paul Sartre and Simone de Beauvoir throughout the Occupation. They would sometimes sit there throughout the day, surrounded by books, pens, and paper, reading, writing, or discussing literature, philosophy, and politics with their friends. By the end of 1945, Sartre's fame as the leader of a new 'existentialist' movement meant that he could no longer work peacefully at the Flore; but at the beginning of that year, his work – particularly the play *Huis Clos*, first staged in May 1944 – was only beginning to gain international recognition. It was still possible to meet him at his usual spot in the café, 'between the telephone and the toilets, among drafts and questionable odours', according to one account.[4]

Connolly was unlucky; he arrived in Paris a few days after Sartre had left on a long visit to America. But Simone de Beauvoir stayed in Paris, and was sitting at her usual place in the Flore when he walked in one day. He was thrilled when she gave him a copy of Sartre's manifesto for *Les Temps Modernes*, the now-famous magazine which was then only in the planning stage. The manifesto was an attempt to explain his theory of 'committed literature', a theory which would soon exert extraordinary influence in French literary circles. Realising its importance, Connolly obtained permission to publish part of it in *Horizon*. This was a coup, for its appearance in May 1945 was the first publication anywhere – it did not appear in *Les Temps Modernes* until nearly six months later, when Sartre finally launched the magazine. *Horizon* was one of the first English journals to describe the exciting new work being done not only by Sartre but by the young Albert Camus, whose *L'Etranger* and *Le Mythe de Sisyphe* had been published by Gallimard during the Occupation. In 1945 and 1946 *Horizon* published a major series of articles on Sartre and Camus by A. J. Ayer, and in October 1945 the magazine brought out, as a separate book, the first copies of *Huis Clos* printed outside France.

At the time of Connolly's visit the main battlefront was only 150 miles away, in the Ardennes, and memories of the Nazi occupation of Paris were still painfully fresh. 'The presence of the Germans could still be felt,' Connolly later wrote in *Horizon*; 'in the café chair where one sat they had sat not so long before.' Taken to see one of the Gestapo's execution chambers, he found the sight of it 'horrible beyond description'. It was housed in what had once been a shooting gallery, and at the end of the building visitors could still find several 'bullet-torn posts' with 'blood-stained rags attached to them'. Along the asbestos walls 'the innumerable impressions of hands' were still clearly visible. This was a side of the war which British civilians like Connolly could only have guessed at; the air attacks on Britain had been bad enough, but no bomb or rocket could convey 'the sensation of utter evil and misery which emanates from these human abattoirs'.[5]

This graphic reminder of Nazi repression heightened his strong appreciation for the writers of the French Resistance. He was amazed not only by their political courage but by their interest in art for its own sake. He observed in *Horizon*: 'It is to be wondered that once they had learnt to watch their friends die in agony and to carry their own death with them in a capsule as their most precious possession, any of them could even contemplate literature, as an end in itself and not merely a means for bringing people back to the truth.'[6] During the period of the occupation, Connolly had not neglected these writers; he did as much as anyone in Britain to promote Resistance literature. *Horizon* published important works by Louis Aragon and Paul Eluard, and Connolly prepared the first English translation of Vercors's *Le silence de la mer*, one of the most famous pieces of Resistance writing.

*Le silence de la mer* tells of a French family's effort to avoid being seduced into collaboration with the Germans. Jean Bruller, using the pseudonym 'Vercors', had written the short book with the support and encouragement of a British secret agent in Paris, who was helping to organise underground publications. But just as the book was about to be printed, the premises were raided by the Germans. They arrested the printer and took away his equipment, but the manuscript remained safely in Bruller's hands. It was published in 1942 by Bruller's underground press, Editions de Minuit. When Connolly received a smuggled copy, he was struck by what he later called its 'exquisite moderation', its calm, steady approach to a subject surrounded by passion and controversy. He was impressed enough to attempt a translation of it, and Macmillan published his English version in both London and New York at the beginning of 1944.

After less than a fortnight in Paris, Connolly returned to London at the end of January 1945, filled with 'exhilaration'.[7] The French literary scene excited him because it seemed so new and dynamic after the isolation of the war years; by contrast, the atmosphere in London seemed to him to have grown stale and dull. There was nothing to compare with the interest and enthusiasm that the recent works of Sartre and Camus had generated in Paris. Connolly was so fascinated by the French cultural revival that he maintained a stream of *Horizon* articles about it throughout 1945: Nancy Cunard and Philip Toynbee contributed reports on the Paris scene; André Malraux gave an interview; Stephen Spender wrote 'Impressions of French Poetry in Wartime'; Paulhan submitted a piece on the painter Braque (Peter Watson translated it); the French art dealer Daniel Henry Kahnweiler wrote 'The State of Painting in Paris'; and Cecil Beaton contributed several photographs of Picasso's studio in Paris. The May 1945 issue was devoted entirely to French culture, and a special issue in French had the title *La Littérature anglaise pendant la guerre*. By the end of the year it must have seemed to many English readers that *Horizon*'s subtitle could more accurately be 'A Review of French Literature and Art'. Connolly's last 'Comment' of 1945 announced that his number one resolution for the new year was 'to have fewer French articles'.

Even without all the French contributions, there was still a strong international flavour to *Horizon* during this period. Connolly had long been critical of the English for being too insular – 'You're full of hate against other countries,' he wrote; 'you talk of Frogs and Yanks and Wogs, and write to *The Times* against Picasso' – so he was only too happy when the end of the war brought so much foreign culture within his reach again.[8] Between early 1945 and early 1946, *Horizon* published poems by Boris Pasternak (translated from the Russian by Maurice Bowra); a short story by Alberto Moravia; an essay by the Italian philosopher Benedetto Croce; several articles on post-war Germany; an appreciation of Paul Klee's paintings by Robin Ironside; an entire number (February 1946) devoted to Swiss culture; and an essay on modern Greek poetry. America was represented by an article on Thornton Wilder's plays and contributions from Randall Jarrell ('The Death of the Ball Turret Gunner'), Edouard Roditi, and Edmund Wilson. The international character of *Horizon* is neatly reflected by Wilson's article, which offers an American perspective on the works of two European writers, André Malraux and Ignazio Silone.

Several foreign writers who visited London were entertained by Connolly in Bedford Square, but none was more warmly received than Edmund Wilson, whose work he had long admired. Although the two men had not previously met, they occupied roughly similar positions in the literary establishments of their respective countries, and each had come to regard the other as a natural ally in the battle to win greater popular acceptance and support for modern literature. Although Wilson was a far more disciplined and rigorous critic than Connolly, they both had a gift for writing literary journalism which was polished, sophisticated, and inspired. Wilson had been a regular reader of *Horizon* throughout the war, and admired it not only for the quality of its contributors but for its overall editorial character. Writing in the *New Yorker* in 1945, he observed, 'Though *Horizon*, to the occasional reader, may have appeared rather relaxed and casual, you came to feel, if you followed it month by month, that the magazine must have behind it a personality of some courage and distinction.'[9]

Wilson arrived in London only a few weeks after Connolly's return from Paris. After meeting Connolly and discussing some of the details of *Horizon*'s struggles during the war, Wilson had even greater admiration for the magazine's achievements. As a former editor at both *New Republic* and *Vanity Fair*, he was impressed by the degree of editorial independence and authority Connolly had managed to carve out for himself. Not long after his trip to London, he remarked of Connolly,

It seemed to me a proof of his merit ... that, in the literary and Left political worlds, almost everybody complained about him and [*Horizon*], but that everybody, at the same time, seemed in some degree dependent on them ... Mr Connolly appears to have published only things that he himself has found interesting, and to have been constrained as little as possible by preconceptions – the worst handicaps for a magazine – of what *Horizon*'s clientèle would like to read.

Wilson also admired his determination to keep the magazine 'quietly anti-nationalistic', and praised him for helping 'to re-establish the wrecked communications between different parts of the world'.[10]

During their time together in London, Wilson and Connolly became close friends. Both men enjoyed matching wits in good-natured literary arguments, and they spent pleasurable afternoons and evenings testing each other's opinions about books and authors. As conversationalists, both were intense and full of conviction in their literary judgments, but each had respect for the other's good taste, intelligence, and integrity. As fellow critics and as friends, each seems to have possessed a keen understanding of the other's strengths and weaknesses. Writing in 1950, Wilson answered some of Connolly's critics by pointing out that 'it is no use being angry with Connolly. Whatever his faults may be – he has himself described them more brilliantly than anyone else is likely to do – he is one of those fortunate Irishmen, like Goldsmith and Sterne and Wilde, who are born with a gift of style, a natural grace and wit, so that their jobs have the freshness of *jeux d'esprit*, and sometimes their *jeux d'esprit* turn out to stick as classics.'[11] After Wilson's death in 1972, Connolly fondly described his friend as 'a passionate, sensual Johnsonian polymath', a description which could just as well be applied to Connolly.[12]

Connolly considered Wilson's 1945 visit a success, but many other literary people in London took a less favourable view. At a Bedford Square party in April 1945, Connolly tried to help Wilson become better acquainted with Evelyn Waugh, but the results were not happy. Under the influence of a bottle of champagne, Waugh agreed to take the visiting critic around London, and an appointment was arranged for the next day; the plan went sour when Waugh 'chucked' his appointment with Wilson. He had come to the conclusion that this 'insignificant Yank' was not worth the bother.[13] Hamish Hamilton gave a party for Wilson, where almost no one seemed comfortable with the American, who appeared bored and irritated. John Lehmann

remembered that all the 'literary "top brass" were on their best behaviour, but the little man in the drab clothes who was the guest of
honour lurked rather silently in corners, was difficult to draw out, and
gave a distinct impression of displeasure.' [14]

Writing later in *Europe Without Baedeker* (the book based on his
1945 visit), Wilson provided a clue to his uneasiness at the Hamilton
party. He seems to have been sensitive to any hint of élitism or snob-
bishness among the English, half expecting to be the target of some
repressed anti-American feeling. Waugh might have been the first to
touch that nerve, but it was exposed and raw when Wilson entered the
Hamilton party to face the literary figures who had gathered to meet
him. Listening to two of the guests – Stephen Spender and Peter
Quennell – discussing their work in the fire brigades, Wilson was put
off by their comparisons of life at their public schools with life in the
'classless' fire service. Wilson assumed the comparison was drawn to
reveal the limitations of the brigades: 'I gathered that what was lacking
was the spirit of the school team: the Cockneys who were sometimes in
command merely counted on people to do the right thing in a more
matter-of-fact-way.'

Quennell later objected to Wilson's account of this conversation,
explaining that he and Spender were making a quite different point:
'One of the most engaging features of the Service, we agreed, was
its complete lack of the bourgeois *esprit de corps*.' [15] Whether he
misunderstood them or not, Wilson concluded that this episode was an
illustration of the class consciousness he so much resented in the
English; presumably he registered his disapproval by keeping his
distance at the party. He would not take the incident lightly, insisting
that the exchange between the two writers spoke volumes about the
difference between his America and their England: 'Such a conversation could hardly have taken place between graduates of American
prep schools, in their late thirties as these men were, because even an
expensive education does not usually unfit Americans to work with
other kinds of Americans and also because at that age Americans would
not still be looking back to their school days.' [16]

*Europe Without Baedeker* came out in 1947 and it contained enough
unpleasant remarks about England to make most English readers
unhappy with Wilson. In his determination not to reveal any sense of
inferiority, he used a broad brush to depict London as a city of faded
glory, its best years behind it. He portrayed it as a seedy, decrepit ruin
peopled by dull, weary citizens who looked as though they would be at
home trudging the streets of another shabby capital – Moscow.

Understandably, the book did not make Wilson welcome in England again, but Connolly did not take offence. He later argued that *Europe Without Baedeker* was 'not so much anti-British as anti-Establishment'.[17]

Connolly had been protesting against the ugliness and gloom of London ever since the middle of the war, and many of Wilson's comments are similar to some of his remarks in 'Comment'. Indeed, when Wilson's book came out, Connolly was complaining in *Horizon* about how dismal English life appeared when measured against the vitality of America: 'Here, the ego is at half-pressure; most of us are not men or women but members of a vast seedy, over-worked, over-legislated, neuter class, with our drab clothes, our ration books and murder stories, our envious, stricken, old-world apathies and resentments – a careworn people.'[18]

Because Wilson found so much that disappointed him in the London cultural scene, he was especially generous in his praise of those things which pleased him, including not only *Horizon* but *The Unquiet Grave*. A few weeks after he returned home, he wrote an enthusiastic review of the recently published American edition of *The Unquiet Grave*. In the *New Yorker* he said that the book represented an important triumph on the cultural front of wartime Britain: 'One used to hear it said in London that Cyril Connolly was out of key with the wartime state of mind, but I think we ought to be grateful that . . . one good writer has persisted in producing, not what patriotism demanded, but a true natural history of his wartime morale.' Wilson particularly liked the book's fond tribute to pre-war France, calling the descriptions of Paris and the South of France 'delicious and crisp, like good food to the taste, fresh and bright'. That such vivid passages were composed against the grey background of London during the last half of the war made them all the more remarkable. In Wilson's view the book offered the reader a fascinating case study of the indomitable powers of the artistic imagination. Concluding his review, he declared: 'The truth is, perhaps, that the unquiet grave has been but a kind of bomb-shelter which is giving up a still-living man.'[19]

Thanks in part to Wilson's praise, Connolly's reputation as a writer and an editor rose rapidly in America. *The Unquiet Grave* sold well and attracted considerable attention in the New York literary world. In addition, demand was strong for the limited number of *Horizon* copies available for export to America. The magazine acquired something of the mystique which attaches itself to a treasured collector's item. There was great curiosity about it and about the enigmatic

'Palinurus' who served as its editor – so much so, that even *Time* magazine considered the subject worthy of a substantial article.

A few months after Wilson's *New Yorker* review, the *Time* article ('Highbrows' *Horizon*') noted that the influence of Connolly's magazine was 'out of all proportion' to its modest circulation, and declared that it had 'come closer than anything in sight to filling the void left by the US's famed *Dial* . . . and T. S. Eliot's London *Criterion*'. *Time*'s account of *Horizon*'s wartime existence, told in the typically effusive house style of the period, extolled Connolly as a plucky and resourceful defender of the 'cultural ramparts': 'Of all times to start a literary magazine in Britain, Cyril Connolly picked December 1939. Europe's lights were blinking out and England was in for it, when he lit his brave little cultural candle.' It was clear that *Time* thought this was the stuff cultural legends are made of, but Connolly was wary of the growing interest in him and his magazine. 'He has a horror of becoming too fashionable,' *Time* observed, reporting that Connolly had remarked, 'We don't want to be known as the *Vogue* of literature.' Connolly tried to warn *Time* that their story about him might not appeal to very many of their readers. 'According to your standards,' he bluntly informed them, 'I'm just a sissy writer.'[20]

## II

In 1945 one of the few major contributions to *Horizon* from a British author was the long story 'Ivy Gripped the Steps', by Elizabeth Bowen. Set at a resort town on the South Coast of England, it is concerned with the life of a middle-aged man who yearns to recapture a lost love from his past. It is the kind of story that appealed to Connolly's romantic sensibilities, but he had a general fondness for the richly evocative world of Elizabeth Bowen's fiction, and always counted her as one of his favourite contemporary writers. She was also an especially cherished friend. During the war they saw a great deal of each other, and Elizabeth Bowen regarded Connolly's *Horizon* parties as highlights of her wartime life. She frequently invited him to dinner parties at her spacious house in Clarence Terrace, one of the magnificent Nash terraces bordering Regent's Park. This part of London strongly influenced her imagination, and features in two of her best-known novels – *The Death of the Heart* (1938) and *The Heat of the Day* (1949). By 1944 Connolly had also developed a special affection for the area, and had begun to think it might prove the ultimate urban haven for him, if only an affordable house could be found.

Such a house came on to the market in the spring of 1945. It was in stately Sussex Place, a long, curving terrace of houses near Elizabeth Bowen's home. Designed by John Nash in the 1820s, Sussex Place is impressively adorned with pointed cupolas and grand porticoes supported by Corinthian columns. It is set back a comfortable distance from the road, and its high windows offer stunning views of the lake in Regent's Park. The house at 25 Sussex Place had four large floors, but it was reasonably priced because it had a short lease of eighteen years. Connolly and Lys planned to share the cost of buying the house with their friend Janetta Woolley, who was then breaking off a wartime affair which had resulted in the birth of a daughter two years earlier. There was more than enough room for Janetta and her daughter to live comfortably in their own separate quarters, leaving Connolly and Lys the use of a large bedroom, study, formal dining room, drawing room, and kitchen. (Several months later Janetta invited Robert Kee to live with her; they married in 1948 and Sussex Place was their home until they separated in 1950.)

Connolly was eager for the move; he felt he needed a change of scenery after spending so much time in Bloomsbury during the war, and he hoped that living so near the Park would provide him with a fresh charge of inspiration. Anticipating the possibility of writing fiction again, he teased Elizabeth Bowen that they would have to divide the Park into separate zones for use as settings in their novels. His friends were impressed by the new house, and he had ambitious plans for beginning a new series of *Horizon* parties there. The only friend to question his plans was Evelyn Waugh, who could not resist telling him, apparently with a straight face, that the inhabitants of the house would all be evicted by the Crown authorities 'for living in sin'. Waugh noted with satisfaction that this malicious attempt at prophecy 'scared' Connolly.[21]

When Major Connolly learned of the proposal to establish joint ownership with Janetta, he objected for practical reasons. Always ready to subject any idea to cold calculation, he advised in a letter, 'I am sure that divided ownership *cannot* possibly be a success or work smoothly – you will grow to hate each other every time you meet on the stairs or that the other gives a noisy party, let alone babies!! And supposing they clear out or sublet to undesirable people?? Eighteen years is a terribly long time.' Connolly's father argued that it was too long to be under any obligation, regardless of the other party's intentions. Solemnly, he warned his son to remember the 'most important [point] of all – you are a Connolly, and I imagine fairly typical of the race – we are all ever wanting to be on the move, never staying long in the same place.' Since his son was indeed 'fond of travel and foreign life', the major told him that the most sensible thing would be to take a modest *pied-à-terre* in London, which would allow him freedom to come and go as he pleased, but he was under no illusion that this recommendation would be welcome. At the close of his letter he remarked in exasperation, 'I expect you will have come to a definite decision before this reaches you, so my well meant advice, even if you would have considered it, is all wasted!'[22]

His father was right; Connolly was determined to have his dream house in Sussex Place, and nothing was going to keep him from acquiring it as soon as possible. By the end of June – a month after the end of the war in Europe – the purchase was complete, and Connolly, Lys, and Janetta were preparing to move into their grand new home. But, as the major might also have predicted, these preparations were barely under way when Connolly decided to leave London for a long trip abroad.

Peter Watson was anxious to see Paris again, and had won permission to travel after he and Connolly had convinced the authorities that both of them were needed in France on *Horizon* business. Officially, the purpose of the trip was to collect some more French articles for the magazine, and to solicit work for a proposed issue on Switzerland; but privately both men were glad to have an excuse for visiting some of their old haunts on the Continent at the height of the first post-war summer. In addition, Watson needed to determine what had happened to the money and personal property he had left behind in 1939. His fear was that some of the best pieces in his art collection had been lost, because he had heard reports that certain of his paintings had ended up in the hands of European dealers or in the collections of prominent Nazis. He had written several times to Sherban Sidery, the caretaker of his Paris apartment, asking for explanations, but had not had any satisfactory answer.

With *Horizon* left in the care of Lys, Watson and Connolly flew to Paris on a sultry day in mid-July. They went straight from the airport to the apartment in the Rue du Bac. What they found confirmed Watson's worst fears. The rooms were dirty, curtains were torn, nearly all the furniture was broken or missing. 'My flat's a shambles – really heartbreaking and so filthy,' Watson lamented to John Craxton.[23] Worst of all, the art collection was gone. Over the years practically everything of value – from large paintings to small silver and gold items hidden away in cupboards and closets – had been removed.

Sidery claimed they had all been stolen, but Watson found pawn tickets for some of the items, which left little doubt in his mind about the real culprit. 'I think Sidery is really responsible for the disappearance of most of the things,' he declared to Cecil Beaton.[24] Watson had placed his trust in the Rumanian, despite the fact that he had known him only a short time. He did not imagine that Paris would be out of reach for so long or that Sidery would be in the apartment for years. He assumed that some of his things would be missing, but not that the place would be stripped bare. He was furious, but decided not to go through the ordeal of taking legal action against Sidery. He did manage to reclaim a few things by tracking them down through dealers and museums; most pieces, however, were never recovered. The material loss was bad enough, but he was even more distressed by the realisation that his trust and friendship had been betrayed. He remarked bitterly, 'I think Sidery a revolting sort of person, preserve me from aesthetic Roman Catholic homosexual snobs.'[25]

Despite the shabby condition of the apartment, Watson and Connolly stayed there during their visit. They did their best to tidy it up, but Connolly found the place 'terribly depressing, empty of everything, no hot water, no clean sheets . . . My bed is a sofa in the dining room – nowhere to unpack anything, and I have to go through Peter's room whenever I want to go to the bathroom.' He also found that the apartment held too many sad memories of his life before the war. He was haunted by two particularly painful reminders of that past. One was a faded portrait of Jean, photographed by Man Ray, which was pinned to the bathroom wall, exactly where Denham Fouts had left it in the summer of 1939. Elsewhere, suspended from the ceiling, was a ragged bunch of dried mistletoe which Connolly had watched Jean put up during the Christmas season of 1938. No one had bothered to take it down. These ghostly images intensified his unease, leaving him with the sensation that he was living in a 'mausoleum'. In a letter to Lys, he remarked, 'It is so strange that Peter, who once had a genius for "gracious living" now comes to symbolise morbid discomfort to me.'[26]

Connolly did not have to worry about the weather on this trip. The city seemed almost like a Mediterranean port in the mid-summer heat. 'Paris is absolutely beautiful,' he wrote, 'intensely hot, but a much drier heat than London, walking is not unpleasant and the trees and the river are the most wonderful green with the houses bleached with heat like Rome or Marseille. It is extraordinarily Southern and rather overpowering.' Although he was in Paris for only a week, he packed it with non-stop activity. While Watson was busy sorting out his personal affairs in the Rue du Bac, Connolly explored the city, sometimes on his own but primarily with English friends engaged in government and military missions in France.

The writer Christopher Sykes had the use of a military jeep and, to Connolly's great delight, chauffeured him around the city several times. Diana Cooper invited him on a 'canoeing party' in the countryside, and on one memorable evening he went out on the town with A. J. Ayer and the distinguished government scientist Solly Zuckerman ('We all got absolutely plastered and went to two night clubs, where we behaved rather badly'). He had lunch with Gide ('very gay and full of life at 76') and dinner with the painter Balthus ('a depressing and anal gentleman'). He went through a few antique shops, looking for pieces to decorate the rooms of Sussex Place, but was shocked at the 'colossal prices'. Indeed, he was disappointed to find that almost everything had become much more expensive since his visit in January. 'In fact,' he told Lys, 'the expense of everything slowly paralyses one's enjoyment.' His only real indulgence was a meal at Maxim's with Watson. Several nights later the two friends gave a large cocktail party in the empty rooms of the Rue du Bac, entertaining literary celebrities and old friends from Watson's earlier years in Paris ('The French call Peter and me Laurel and Hardy, at least his smartyboots do').[27]

On Bastille Day Connolly stayed out late at night on his own, watching fireworks as he strolled along the quays by the Seine. While 'the opaque green river slid by the immense poplars', he grew pensive, reflecting on how much the city had changed since the Twenties, when he had first come to know it well. As he later described his thoughts, it was not difficult for him 'to decide what was missing':

> For one thing about ten thousand American girls, with their satchels and sketch-books, their exotic looks and wholesome voices to animate all the small hotels on the Left Bank, now miserably functionless and sombre; then a quantity of genuine artists and writers from other countries, lovers of Paris and serious ease, to argue in cafés and crouch in the bookshops, and sit too long over lunch. Then a horde of rich tourists and Latin Americans to pour money into every tattered courtyard and shabby street, and last a French government which would welcome all this money and food and appreciation with dignity while continuing to experiment in the new possibilities of living and thinking and painting that have made this most beautiful of all northern cities pre-eminent.

But as the night wore on, he began to reproach himself for dwelling on past images of Paris. He told himself that he was merely indulging in 'a kind of middle-aged mumbling over the grave of youth', and in a philosophical mood he asked sadly: 'Even were this young man's Paris to be resurrected, who can give back the eyes and heart which first explored it?'[28]

By the end of the week, his feelings about Paris were painfully confused. 'It is all the same and all so changed,' he wrote, 'very upsetting, like a beautiful woman who has had a stroke.'[29] Both Connolly and Watson were now anxious to set off for Switzerland, where they anticipated finding a part of Europe which still offered the pleasures of pre-war life. Late one night they boarded a hot, crowded train for Bern and, after a fifteen-hour journey mainly standing or sitting in the corridors, they reached the Swiss border. There was very little to eat or drink on the train or in the few stations where they stopped; but the discomfort and inconvenience ended as soon as they crossed the frontier.

'The entry into Switzerland was dazzling,' Connolly wrote. 'On the one side gloomy hungry France – dirty, corrupt, inefficient – and on the other, at Les Verrières, slot-machines full of cigarettes and sweets, a trout-stream singing by the station hotel, a meal of trout, cheese, and apricots with two kinds of Swiss wine (out of twenty) for about 12/- for both of us. Then a clean gay electric train through the Jura and, suddenly, the lake of Neuchâtel shimmering in the sun, its blue water lapping green hills covered with vineyards and its beaches full of bathers and small racing yachts. Oranges and lemons for sale in the stations, windows full of cigars, window-boxes in every house.'[30] While the sleek train sped through the mountains, he could hardly contain his excitement. As he later recalled in his 'Comment' for the special Swiss number of *Horizon*, 'Such was our intoxication, Alp-starved since 1939, that every sleeper on the track, every cable and pylon, every newly born aroma of mountain sunlight and fir-forest and the name of every station appeared the last unbearable saturation-point in the rebirth of feeling.'

Connolly felt like a prisoner who had thrown off the last of his chains. Arriving at the Bellevue Palace hotel in Bern, he gleefully surveyed the view from the balcony of his room ('I had almost forgotten that hotels had balconies'): in the distance were mountain peaks and a wide expanse of forest, and directly below him – some two hundred feet down – was a long fast-moving stretch of the River Aar. He was so taken with the view that he had his breakfast served on the balcony the next morning, and during the rest of his stay he repeated the experience as often as possible. In the evenings he sat under an awning on the balcony and lazily scanned the pages of 'some immensely provincial Swiss newspaper', occasionally looking up to observe the lights coming on in the hillside suburbs. Watson thought the Bellevue Palace was 'like a dream of a hotel in a novel', and Connolly remarked that the clean, orderly city of Bern was, 'after five years of England, sheer hallucination'.[31] It was almost possible to imagine that the war had never happened.

The two war-weary Englishmen were supposed to be spending their time in Switzerland interviewing intellectuals about the nation's cultural life and collecting articles for the special Swiss number, but they found the tourist pleasures far more interesting than artistic or intellectual concerns. They went on shopping and sightseeing expeditions to Zurich and Geneva, visiting museums and buying small gifts to send home. And, like a couple of young students on holiday, they travelled several times into the countryside to go swimming in the clear mountain lakes and streams. 'The swimming is beyond belief,' Connolly reported. 'The first day we tried the town baths – artificial waves, sun-bathing, etc. – just where the country begins. Yesterday we took the train to Interlaken, then a cab, and lunched in a chalet-hotel by the lake of Thunersee. Then 2 hours of swimming in the warm blue water, surrounded by woods and snow mountains . . . Today we swam in the Aar – you undress and change and then walk up the riverside path for as long as you like, then plunge in and are carried down by the current to where you undressed – a wonderful feeling.'[32] It is hard to believe that these youthful, exuberant sentences were written by a man who a year earlier had spoken in the *angst*-ridden tones of the middle-aged Palinurus. Beautiful Switzerland was no place for *angst* attacks. It was a land where the daily practice of the 'Craft of Living' had come close to perfection. It was, in short, 'a bower of bourgeois bliss' where even the 'waiters are never rude'.[33]

When Connolly finally turned his attention to filling the proposed issue on Swiss culture, he discovered that good material was difficult to locate. Accustomed to working with writers in the lively literary circles of London and Paris, he was disappointed to find that the literary life was not lively, or – for a visiting Englishman in midsummer – accessible. The idea of going to Switzerland, with its landscape and economy unravaged by war, had been so appealing that he had not considered whether he could justify his business excuse for the trip. At the end of July he conceded that his plan was not working: 'It's impossible to get stuff for a Swiss number here, there are hardly any Swiss writers and they are all on holiday in unapproachable valleys.'[34] Life in Switzerland might be perfect for businessmen and tourists, but Connolly soon decided that its 'bourgeois bliss' had not done much to stimulate literary culture. 'One can't be an intellectual in this atmosphere,' he concluded, 'where watches are discussed like old masters and where to swim is the most important daily question.'[35] He began to doubt the general worth of living in a nation so comfortably neat and prosperous. There was no denying the impressiveness of the material wealth on display in every part of the country; but, as a cosmopolitan writer and editor, he was uncomfortable with the thought that this wealth had been acquired at the expense of a national tendency towards complacency and conformity. 'One wants, as in so many Swiss towns, to let loose some Senegalese, some French sailors or workmen, some drunken American women, some props of moral worthlessness, someone to walk on the grass or spit in the funicular.'[36]

The material Connolly and Watson eventually assembled for the Swiss number was not first-rate, except perhaps for a short piece of poetic prose by the novelist Charles-Ferdinand Ramuz, the most important French-Swiss writer of his time (he died in 1947 at the age of sixty-eight). Generally speaking, the contributions were pedestrian, with dull titles such as 'Switzerland in Europe'; 'Swiss Composers of Today'; and 'The Cultural Position of German Switzerland' (which was a reprinted academic address by Dr Karl Georg Schmid, Professor of German Literature and Philology at the Zurich Polytechnic). All in all, the issue did not do much to spark enthusiasm for Swiss culture. One contributor, reviewing the condition of the arts in his nation, complained that serious writers and artists in Switzerland suffered because they lived in a land where 'there is a really excessive respect for money. Too many banks!'

In 'Comment' Connolly did not try to give any explanation to those readers who might have wondered why he had suddenly taken a keen interest in the Swiss. One reason was that he had a strong curiosity about foreign cultures in general, but in this case that was not the most important reason. His unusually long 'Comment' (around 5000 words) says little about the nation's literature or art, except to note that its writers and artists were compelled to struggle 'against the essential uncreative smallness of Switzerland'. No one can read his remarks, however, without recognising the primary sources of his interest – the beauty of the landscape and the material wonders of the nation's 'pre-war' standard of living. His 'Comment' was essentially a long travel essay which could stand on its own. It is a splendid piece of writing, and does much to redeem the mediocrity of the rest of the issue. As usual, he excels at conveying the precise physical atmosphere that surrounds a particular experience, as in this description of one of his day trips:

> Let's be tourists again. First a practice run; the early train to Interlaken, an open carriage to the lake; a swim in the cobalt water of the Thunersee. Lying on one's back in the water, until forced to submerge against a dive-bombing attack from horseflies, one looks up at the icy pinnacles of the Jungfrau. The glaciers tower above us, the water temperature is seventy degrees. After lunch and some hours of sunbathing we return on the lake steamer, sometimes hugging the cliffs and woodlands of the shore, sometimes dashing across to a lake village with its vineyards and bulbous yellow church, its ruined castle and its café under the chestnut trees, while we exchange one group of sunburnt summer visitors for another, and the swans glide round the landing-stage.

At the beginning of August, Connolly travelled alone to the resort town of Gstaad, where he stayed for a few days while Watson visited friends elsewhere in Switzerland. The two men had arranged to travel back to England together on 10 August, but Watson came down with an attack of jaundice. He decided to delay his return until his health was better, and went to Vulpera, in eastern Switzerland, where the local 'waters' were supposed to be good for liver complaints.

Connolly returned to Bern, paid 'a last farewell' visit to the grand Bellevue Palace hotel, and began the long journey home. After nearly a month away from Lys (the longest they had been apart since their relationship began), he was missing her deeply, and was quite ready to put his Swiss adventure behind him. 'I really can't bear being away from you for so long,' he had written towards the end of his trip, 'and I hope it will never happen again – a fortnight is the limit, after that one finds out the emptiness of everything in life except being with the loved one! I dare say it is neurotic to depend so on someone else, but if love is neurosis give it me every time. It seems quite natural to me that two people who live together grow into one and I really feel as if I was going about cut in half, with only half of myself there, and that the ugly one.'[37]

## III

On his return, Connolly took up residence in his new home at 25 Sussex Place, which Lys and Janetta had been decorating during his absence. He was immensely pleased with the look of things; the large, beautifully designed rooms provided an ideal setting for his growing collection of fine furniture, silver, and china. He was looking forward to a long, productive future in the house, and was beginning to feel cautiously optimistic about his prospects as both a writer and an editor. While he had been away, the Labour Party had come to power with a stunning victory over the Conservatives in the general election, and Connolly hoped this change would mean more government support for art and literature.

In his September 'Comment' he celebrated the results of the election as a triumph of intellectualism over philistinism, praising the new political leaders as 'reasonable people, people like ourselves who are "we", not "they"'. Although he felt that in the past Labour had not done enough to assist the arts, he believed that in power they would prove far more accommodating on cultural issues than the Conservatives (some of whom he brashly called in *Horizon* 'the millionaire hoodlums whom we have just put out'). In his private correspondence, he was equally quick to put his faith in the goodwill of Labour and to condemn, with harsh words, the record of the Conservatives. Writing from Switzerland, shortly after news of the election victory had reached him, he had declared, 'It will be so nice to be governed by intelligent and *quiet* people – not those horrible money-loving roistering anti-intellectual exhibitionists – I think Horizon will be able to play a far more influential role.'[38]

Connolly had in mind specific ways in which the new government might help the literary profession. He thought, for example, that book royalties should be officially considered capital, not regular income – a distinction which would exempt the money from taxation. This arrangement, he reasoned, would not only put more pounds in writers' pockets but would provide them an incentive for working more on books and less on hack journalism. In addition, he wanted tax advantages for all private citizens who gave writers financial assistance. He was wary of the state taking upon itself the provision of direct payments to writers, unless the money could be given with no strings attached. (During the war he had learned enough from fellow writers about their jobs at the BBC and the Ministry of Information to conclude that the state should have as little control as possible over how writers employed their talents.) At the very least, he wanted the new Labour government to encourage greater public appreciation of literature, and to promote the sale of British books and magazines overseas. He was expecting some sign that the state now recognised literature's importance in society, and that it respected writers as a professional class.

In *Horizon* he had often addressed the question of the writer's place in society and, at the beginning of 1945, he had decided that he wanted his best editorials on the subject to be a separate unit in his first collection of essays, *The Condemned Playground*, planned for publication later that year. When the book came out in October, less than three months after Labour's victory, his editorials were grouped under the heading 'Writers and Society, 1940–1943', as the final section of the collection. Given his ambition to influence the cultural policy of the new government, he could not have managed better the timing of his book's publication. The argument of 'Writers and Society' received prominent attention in many of the reviews of the book. Elizabeth Bowen was so impressed that she suggested it 'would, for the purpose of wide circulation, merit publication in pamphlet form'.[39]

'Writers and Society' provides a fascinating anatomy of the social attitudes and forces which keep most serious writers underpaid, overworked, and generally unappreciated. Connolly takes aim at publishers afraid to take risks on unconventional books; popular press barons whose papers cultivate an air of 'jaunty philistinism'; government leaders who are content to 'do nothing for literature, except to grant occasionally a miserable pittance for some half-starved veteran'; government and corporate bureaucrats who sponsor, not the creation of culture, but the 'diffusion' of it (that is, spreading culture through lectures, readings, discussion groups, pamphlets, films, and radio talks); and the 'increasingly illiterate rich' who have no interest in supporting literature or who give their patronage to bad authors willing to supply them with shallow entertainment.

Connolly saves his greatest scorn for 'Pinhead' critics who attack writers for narrow ideological reasons, and who are quick to discourage any show of independence or innovation in the work of young writers. Such critics are happiest 'when they have persuaded a painter to abandon colour for abstraction, or a poet to write a political pamphlet, or to suppress a novel "for personal reasons". Fortunate is the artist today who is able to follow his invention without one of these poor bald old homo-puritan Pinheads blowing down his neck.'

Connolly's response to this survey of literature's enemies is to suggest that writers will never find the going easier until society's view of art undergoes a transformation. 'We must radically change our attitude to art here: we must give art a place in our conception of the meaning of life and the artist a place in our conception of the meaning of the state which before they have never known. Never again must our artists be warped by opposition, stunted by neglect, or etiolated by official conformity.' He knew well enough that this was unlikely to occur soon, but he wanted to set the change in motion. Winning the support of the Labour government would make a good start.

Working on his own, he could not have directly affected government cultural policy, but he could use his position at *Horizon* to raise public awareness of the problems facing writers and artists, and thus create more pressure for government action. Such pressure was already achieving results in 1945. In June the Arts Council was founded and was granted an annual government subsidy of nearly a quarter of a million pounds, leading its chairman (Lord Keynes) to declare in the *Listener*, 'I do not believe it is yet realised what an important thing has happened. State patronage of the arts has crept in.'[40] Indeed, within the first four years of the Council's operation, the state's contribution to its budget more than doubled. Ironically, none of this money went to writers or literary magazines; it was reserved primarily for opera, ballet, music, drama, and the visual arts. As state support for the Arts Council grew in the late 1940s, Connolly continued to call for some provision for writers, but nothing was done. The Arts Council did not begin helping literature in a significant way until the 1960s, and even then the help was not without the bureaucratic entanglements Connolly had foreseen.

Public support for the arts is only one of many themes taken up in *The Condemned Playground*, which brought together the best of Connolly's literary journalism from the beginning of his career to the last years of the war. It was published by Routledge in the same month that Hamish Hamilton issued the first trade edition of *The Unquiet Grave* (a revised version of the earlier *Horizon* limited edition). With two important books out at once, the 'failed' author of *Enemies of Promise* finally seemed to be coming into his own. The emergence of this new 'successful' Connolly was appropriately commemorated by a large, impressive frontispiece to the essay collection, showing the author in a meditative, youthful-looking pose, captured by Augustus John at a sitting early in 1945.

Regular readers of *Horizon* knew from 'Comment' that his talents as an informal essayist were considerable, but many of his most interesting pieces in this genre were from the Twenties and Thirties and had been largely forgotten, gathering dust in old volumes of *Life and Letters* and the *New Statesman*. *The Condemned Playground* resurrected them and demonstrated to the reading public the range and intensity of Connolly's prose art. Among the book's highlights are critical pieces on Gide, Horace, Joyce, Mann, Rimbaud, and Swift; a delightful parody of Aldous Huxley ('Told in Gath'); an amusing satire on genteel literary folk ('Felicity'), and a masterful send-up of the literary Left of the Thirties ('Where Engels Fears to Tread'); a travel sketch of Athens during an aborted coup ('Spring Revolution'); a series of candid autobiographical musings selected from Connolly's Twenties journals ('England Not My England'); his best essay from *Horizon* ('The Ant-Lion'); and his mordant assessment of life as a book critic ('Ninety Years of Novel-Reviewing'): 'The reviewing of novels is the white man's grave of journalism; it corresponds, in letters, to building bridges in some impossible tropical climate. The work is gruelling, unhealthy, and ill-paid, and for each scant clearing made wearily among the springing vegetation the jungle overnight encroaches twice as far.'

In his brief introduction to *The Condemned Playground* Connolly explains that the title has three separate meanings. It is a reference to the literary atmosphere of the Thirties, which had been so full of hopes and ambitions until the war dashed them. Secondly, it is a phrase to describe the artists' haven of pre-war Chelsea, the urban landscape he had enjoyed in the Thirties but which wartime bombing had badly damaged. Finally, it is a reference 'to Art itself . . . man's noblest [but ultimately doomed] attempt to preserve Imagination from Time, to make unbreakable toys of the mind'. This definition is the most revealing. By collecting his literary journalism into a book, Connolly had managed to save some of the bright creations of his youth from sinking any further into the obscurity which awaits so many periodical pieces. Seeing these essays in the brittle pages of old journals made him more aware of how fragile and vulnerable his art was; despite his success in the Forties, the prospect of failure and loss haunted him still, and his title reflects that fact. He knew how close he had come to failing during the first half of the Forties, and recognised that had he failed there would have been no chance to reprint his earlier work. All those wonderful essays would have been forgotten, and probably lost forever – everything in *The Condemned Playground* would have been 'condemned' indeed.

Nevertheless, Connolly assumes an apologetic tone in his introduction, insisting on portraying himself as a writer of modest talent who wrote a few promising things in his youth but who has since gone 'off the boil'. He apologises for not developing into a more accomplished critic, suggesting that his critical ability has been corrupted by the pressures of writing so much journalism: 'I wish I had been a better critic and that I had not written brightly, because I was asked to, about so many bad books.' Before the reader has a chance to read the essays, Connolly seems to be saying, 'Don't get your hopes up. Most of it is not that good anyway.' As in the case of the limited edition of *The Unquiet Grave*, he courts failure and obscurity while making it clear that what he really wants is success and fame. Like *The Unquiet Grave*, *The Condemned Playground* met with success after all, gathering good reviews and adding lustre to Connolly's reputation. At this stage, good fortune pursued him doggedly in spite of his eccentric attempts to evade it.

## IV

A serious misfortune had befallen Peter Watson: the jaundice which had prevented his leaving Switzerland had worsened. When he wrote to Connolly at the beginning of September to tell him the bad news, he was still in Vulpera: 'I have just had one of the most depressing fortnights of my life. Ever since I came up here I [have] felt worse . . . sick all day and could only lie on my bed with hardly enough energy to climb the stairs.' He had considered going home for treatment, but the local doctor attending him had advised against the idea. 'The doctor says it is madness to go through France in my present state. I would get dysentery and have more jaundice which is fairly chronic with me now.'[41] By the middle of September, his condition was no better, and he was moved to a clinic in Lugano, in southern Switzerland. Even this short trip was almost too much for him, for he reported that the day spent in the train 'has affected me most adversely, as I am much greener and my skin is now peeling and I feel worse'.[42]

The clinic was, in Watson's words, 'a marvel of . . . modern spaciousness and Swiss cleanliness', but his health continued its alarming decline.[43] He became dangerously ill, and the doctors told him that he might have to stay at the clinic for up to four months. He was put on a strict diet which consisted of nothing but spaghetti and rice with mashed turnips or carrots and three glasses of grape juice a day. He was given mud packs, purges, blood transfusions, and other unpleasant 'cures', one of which he described in painful detail: 'Oh dear I am now being submitted to the most undignified treatments. I have to swallow a tube which I can only do with the greatest amount of horror and retching, wait 4–5 hours until I digest the nozzle and the bile pours out. Then they give me a lavage of magnesium which leaves one completely washed out for 3 days.'[44]

After three weeks of such gruelling treatment Watson could see no improvement. 'I am afraid I can't report any progress at all, just a slow deterioration. I have just got to go through all the hoops and stick it until the liver decides to absorb again which must happen in a fit of boredom one day soon. The nausea and the depressive neurasthenia are the worst sides of the disease, but the cheery professional optimism of the nursing home can get on one's nerves. Pee the colour of black coffee and boils on the legs are the latest delights – all quite biblical only they haven't got me to my knees yet.'[45]

His vivid descriptions of his illness and treatment caused considerable alarm among his English friends and some began to fear that he might be dying. Cecil Beaton was particularly worried, and offered to go out and help his friend in whatever way he could. Connolly made a similar offer, but Watson dissuaded both men, saying that it would be 'such a waste of time, money and valuable exit permits. It isn't as if I were dying and wished to communicate the secret of life.'[46] Always ready to help others in need, he was reluctant to make himself a burden to anyone else, though there was no question that he was seriously ill. Moreover, in his weakened state, he simply did not feel up to dealing with friends, no matter how good their intentions.

The reasons for Watson's reluctance to see Connolly went beyond the immediate circumstances of the illness. In a letter written from the clinic in mid-October, he told Beaton that he had experienced a very difficult time with Connolly earlier in the summer. Their personalities, so completely different, had conflicted under the strain of travel, and Connolly had almost exhausted his friend's patience. Watson bluntly expressed his frustration:

> He is so vain, so touchy, so anxious all at the same time. I am quite the wrong person to deal with such a mixture over a long period. He used to lose his temper with me in front of other people which I find quite inexcusable. Of course I know he is everything I am not, impulsive, enthusiastic, quickly deceived and satiated, easily distracted from one thing to another. He can never get over the fact that I *won't* behave like a conventional rich man, always go to the best restaurant, hotel, travel first class etc. I suppose the rich reassure him . . . This must sound very jaundiced but it really isn't. He just makes me feel deeply unhappy after a time, all that welter of unsatisfied desires, jealousies.[47]

Watson preferred to avoid confronting problems, and he never let Connolly know how he felt about their time together on the Continent. Certainly the many letters Watson wrote to him from the clinic show no hint of lingering anger. He saw nothing to be gained by complaining, and the underlying goodwill between them would not allow either to hold a grudge or engage in a serious quarrel. But Watson did not want to invite any trouble between them by having Connolly come out during his illness. Explaining why it would be unwise to make the trip to Lugano, Watson wrote, 'You would die of boredom and I of anxiety neurosis!'[48]

By the end of October there was some improvement in his condition. His appetite returned and he was able to go off his spartan diet. 'The pleasures of life return one each day which is really a delicious sensation,' he wrote. 'The first café au lait is a rediscovery like the first fresh pear.'[49] But his recovery was slow, and he was not able to leave Switzerland until the end of November. Throughout the period of his illness, he tried to keep up with *Horizon* business, writing detailed instructions to Connolly about office matters and the content and arrangement of the magazine's art pages.

One important question concerned the magazine's paper ration. Government action that autumn relaxed controls on paper supplies, and *Horizon* found its allowance increased by 33%. Watson agreed with Connolly that the increase should go not to expanding the size of the magazine but to raising its circulation, though they disagreed on how many copies should be reserved for export. Connolly wanted to begin sending more copies to their distributors in America and France immediately, and wrote enthusiastically about printing 10,000 copies for sale at home and abroad. Watson pointed out politely that the current circulation of 5000 could not be doubled if their paper supplies increased by only a third; and regarding exports he observed, 'It's surely much better to take up our full circulation in England first and then export, less trouble, more profit and more important for us.'[50] Watson always took the practical, cautious view, and in his discussions of business matters one can almost detect his self-made millionaire father's influence.

If he could not win Connolly over by gentle persuasion, Watson usually avoided pressing his point further. (On the question of increasing exports, he soon acceded to Connolly's wishes.) On editorial matters unrelated to visual art, he would rarely bother to make his views known. He wanted Connolly to have as much editorial freedom as possible, and by 1945 he knew that without Connolly in the editor's chair *Horizon* would lose its distinctive appeal. He no longer gave serious thought to finding a replacement in the event of Connolly's departure. *Horizon* and Connolly had become so closely identified that it had become impossible to think of anyone else's name emblazoned on the cover as the editor.

From time to time Connolly suffered periods when he doubted his usefulness to the magazine; then Watson would hasten to assure him that he was indispensable. While he was recovering at the clinic, the special Swiss number was in preparation, and because good material for it had been so hard to come by Watson had himself solicited some literary contributions for it. Confusion arose over which pieces would be included in the issue, and Connolly questioned whether he had to publish the contributions Watson had commissioned. He was already depressed over the generally poor quality of the contributions, and indicated that his friend could probably do the job just as well without him. Watson assured him that no one could replace him. 'On the contrary Horizon needs *you*, Cyril. You are the editor and I really don't want to have anything to do with the belles lettres side. It's not my thing at all, and I only guess at things whereas your judgment is sure with experience.'[51] Whenever his editorial involvement threatened Connolly's territory, Watson retreated as fast as possible. (During his stay at the clinic, he even told Connolly, after seeing the latest issue of the magazine, 'I think Horizon is much better when I am away.')[52]

When Watson was well enough to leave Switzerland, he travelled to Paris and rested there for several days before beginning the last leg of his journey home. His digestion was still not back to normal, and he complained of 'frightful pains after meals at even the most wholesome restaurants'.[53] By the time he arrived in England, he had been away almost six months, and many of his friends were shocked to see how pale, thin, and weak he had become. But he was determined to complete his recovery quickly and get on with his life. Soon the last of his symptoms disappeared, and he began to feel that his health was returning to normal. Psychologically, however, his sickness took a lasting toll. Some of the brightness and good humour of his personality was lost, and the fatalistic, gloomy side of his character became more dominant. 'A certain spark seemed to go out of him,' Lys recalls. 'After that long illness, he was never quite the same man again.'[54]

CYRIL CONNOLLY and STEPHEN SPENDER at a party, in the 1930s, with Dick Wyndham (far left) and Tom Driberg.

PETER WATSON, mid-1930s

WEDDING PARTY for Stephen and
Natasha Spender at Drayton
Gardens, 1941

LYS LUBBOCK, 1941

CYRIL CONNOLLY: THE EDITOR AT EASE, 1942

LAURENCE VAIL and JEAN CONNOLLY, 1945

WALDEMAR HANSEN (right) with Lucian Freud, 1947.

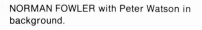

NORMAN FOWLER with Peter Watson in
background.

PETER WATSON, mid-1940s

CONNOLLY at 53 Bedford Square, London WC1,
HORIZON'S LAST ADDRESS, 1948

SONIA BROWNELL and LYS CONNOLLY at
53 Bedford Square, 1948.

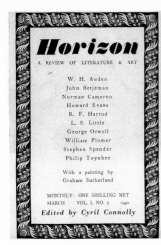

ROY HARROD
THE SURRENDER OF FREE CHOICE

IGNAZIO SILONE
ON THE PLACE OF THE INTELLECT AND THE
PRETENSIONS OF THE INTELLECTUAL

ALAN PRYCE-JONES
DOING GOOD

JOHN RUSSELL
THE OLD AGE OF ANDRÉ GIDE

IAN FLEMING
WHERE SHALL JOHN GO? XIII—JAMAICA

C. M. BOWRA
AN ITALIAN POET: SALVATORE QUASIMODO

BOOKS OF 1947—A QUESTIONNAIRE
POEM BY DYLAN THOMAS
REPRODUCTIONS OF RECENT LITHOGRAPHS BY PICASSO

*Edited by Cyril Connolly*

VOL. XVI
DECEMBER 1947     96     MONTHLY
2s. 6d.

TWO VIEWS OF HORIZON, 1940 and 1947

CONNOLLY mugshots, 1950

PETER WATSON, 1947

TWILIGHT: CONNOLLY in his late sixties

# SEVEN

# LITERARY LIVES
## 1945–1946

### I

During the war Lys had obtained a divorce from Ian Lubbock, and in the summer of 1945 she and Connolly decided that they should marry. He had to summon up courage to break his ties to Jean once and for all. Connolly had expected her to return to England after the war, and had promised Lys that he would begin divorce proceedings as soon as Jean was back in London.

In the early autumn of 1945 he was surprised to discover not only that Jean had ruled out returning to England but that she had filed for divorce in America. From Reno, Nevada, she sent him a packet of legal documents and asked him to sign them so that the divorce could go through without delay. He had known for years that divorce was inevitable, but facing up to it was too much for him, so he put off giving her a reply. He even began having second thoughts about marrying Lys, and was angry with Jean for trying to push him into a quick decision. As the days slipped by without any response from him, Jean began dispatching urgent cables and letters from Reno, pleading for him to sign the papers. In one letter, which was signed 'your hopeful ex-wife', she told him that if he did not send back the documents, the divorce would take three months instead of six weeks.[1] This brought a response: 'Did not ask you to divorce me but to come back. Think you are making greatest mistake of your life and can't conceive what is 3 months, anyway I waited here 5 years.'[2]

Jean had learned long ago not to take such talk seriously. She knew how he enjoyed creating romantic complications in his life, and she was not about to let herself be swayed by his appeals. Moreover, she now had someone else in her life. In 1943, shortly after the end of her affair with Clement Greenberg, she had fallen in love with Laurence Vail, a Surrealist poet and short-story writer who had been prominent in the social life of literary Paris during the Twenties. (He had been known variously as the 'King of Montparnasse' or the 'King of Bohemia'.) Married and divorced twice, he had five children from the two marriages. His first wife was Peggy Guggenheim, and his second the writer Kay Boyle. He was nearly twenty years older than Jean but, after living happily together in New York and Connecticut during the last two years of the war, they had decided to get married. After visiting California in the summer of 1945, they travelled to Reno, and Jean had set about winning her freedom.

Her job was not made easier when Connolly learned that she wanted to marry Vail, whom he regarded as a decidedly inferior match. In one of her letters from Reno, Jean defended her choice, saying of Vail, 'He is not very young, but he is not the burnt-out end of dreary candlesticks you seem to imagine, and I am not so young myself. A dim railway station light is still my most becoming.' [3] Despite what Jean thought of her looks at the age of thirty-five, Connolly longed to see her again. Perhaps he thought that by vigorously opposing her plans to marry, he might convince her to come back to England and discuss her plans with him. It is doubtful that he wanted their marriage to continue; what is more likely is that he wanted an excuse to see her once more before going ahead with his plans to marry Lys. Like many things in his life, Jean would not have been an object of fascination and desire had she ceased to be inaccessible. But for Connolly's sake, as well as her own, Jean wanted him to forget her and go on with his life. Her determination was unmistakable, and Connolly realised that it was pointless to oppose her. He gave in, the divorce was finalised, and in January 1946 Jean married Laurence Vail.

Connolly prepared to go ahead with his marriage to Lys, but he soon learned that the marriage could not take place until a divorce from Jean was granted in an English court. To his dismay, he discovered that Jean was free of him in her country, but that he was not free of her in his. More unsettling was the realisation that an English divorce would take months, and would involve more transatlantic paperwork. Neither Connolly nor Lys wanted to plunge into this legal thicket, so for the time being they settled on the next best thing. Before January was out, Lys Lubbock had legally become Lys Connolly, by using the legal convenience of a deed poll to change her name. In due time, they assured each other, they would have a proper wedding ceremony.

Domestic life in Sussex Place settled into a smooth routine. During the week Lys went off to work at *Horizon* in the mornings, while Connolly stayed at home and tried to write. He had signed a contract with Hamish Hamilton to do a short (60,000 words) 'biographical and critical study of Flaubert', and each morning he would work on it a little; but he would mostly spend his time reading books on other subjects, or thinking of ideas for new literary projects, or simply daydreaming; and from time to time he would jot down interesting ideas or sentences that came to him. Sometimes he would remain in bed all morning, not dressing until it was time for lunch. On other days he drew a hot bath and soaked in it for hours while he meditated on art and life with the aid of a big cigar. Some mornings might find him strolling through Regent's Park, lost in thought. The afternoons were spent at *Horizon*, and then he and Lys would occasionally dine out. More often they would entertain at home, having a few friends over for dinner, with perhaps more guests for drinks later in the evening. Connolly was happy playing host at such gatherings, unless someone asked him how his writing was coming along. It was a taboo subject with him when his work was not going well, and innocent questions were often met with a scowl and a painful silence until conversation was steered around to another subject.

A few weeks after surrendering his hold on Jean, he learned that he had lost another person from his pre-war 'condemned playground' days. On 2 March 1946, his old friend and first patron, Logan Pearsall Smith, died at the age of eighty. In his last years Pearsall Smith had suffered from severe manic depression, and had alienated some of his friends by the irrational conduct typical of the illness. Connolly had seen a great deal of him during the early years of the war, and had kept in touch to the end, but had found the older man's erratic behaviour increasingly difficult to tolerate. By the end of the war, they were still friends but were no longer as close as they had been in the Twenties and Thirties. All the same, he never forgot how much Pearsall Smith's early support and encouragement had meant to him when he was a young writer. He had a lingering affection for this 'father-figure' of his apprentice years, and he was saddened when news of the death reached him.

Asked by the *New Statesman* to write an obituary, he turned out a long, glowing tribute, recalling the admirable qualities of character and art which had made themselves felt in a literary career of more than fifty years. He had high praise for Pearsall Smith's 'radiant prose', but most of all he remembered the older writer's generous concern for so many younger writers, including such recent protégés as the art critic John Russell and the historian Hugh Trevor-Roper. For these men, and for himself, he asked plaintively, 'Who will care now how we turn out, or warn us when we decline, or advise us how to surpass ourselves?'⁴

This tribute was sincere, but it did not give a complete picture of his relationship with Pearsall Smith, which was always characterised by a mixture of feelings on Connolly's part, from fondness and admiration to resentment and envy. Shortly after his piece appeared in the *New Statesman*, he confided some of his misgivings about his old patron to Robert Gathorne-Hardy, who had taken the post that Connolly once occupied – private secretary to Pearsall Smith. Gathorne-Hardy had remained in the job until the last year of his employer's life, when a series of bitter quarrels led to his dismissal. In a long letter, Connolly acknowledged that Pearsall Smith 'always had a vein of cruelty' in him, and recalled the way in which promises of money and property had been used to practise a subtle form of emotional blackmail: 'He was wicked to brandish wills the way he did. I remember him taking me round Chelsea and showing me all the houses in all the streets which he had left me, and it is awful how these things get into one's subconscious.'⁵

Connolly had been powerfully drawn to the kind of literary life Pearsall Smith had enjoyed. During the early years of the century such a life took place in a world Connolly described fondly as one 'in which people of independent means devoted their lives to art, living near together in creamy Georgian houses and going abroad at the same time to the same places. Chelsea was its centre – leafy, well-to-do, fig-ripening Chelsea, from Carlyle Mansions to Ebury Street, where luncheon would last till five o'clock.'⁶ Although this world was passing when Connolly went to work for Pearsall Smith in the late Twenties, he retained an idealised vision of it and had been pursuing that vision ever since. On the other hand, Connolly knew the dangers of living in such a fantasy world. He could see how, under its influence, Pearsall Smith's talent had decayed, and he recognised that his determination to make a similar life for himself – first in Chelsea, then in Bedford Square and Sussex Place – posed a threat to his creative energies. Whenever he felt guilty about this, he became resentful of Pearsall Smith for making the dream tantalising in the first place.

When Gathorne-Hardy announced that he was writing a book about his years with Pearsall Smith, Connolly asked to see part of it for possible publication in *Horizon*. But the candid portrait of Pearsall Smith proved too painful for Connolly. When he read a long excerpt in 1948, he was reminded of all the things he had disliked in his old friend and was depressed to see the glamour stripped away from a literary life which once had seemed ideal. After deciding not to publish an excerpt in *Horizon*, he wrote to Gathorne-Hardy to explain the reasons for his decision, which he admitted were personal rather than literary:

Dear Bob,

I have read your portrait of Logan with great interest and fascination, but I have decided not to publish it in Horizon. At first I thought this was because I found it too unflattering and because I was so fond of him, but we know each other too well not to be absolutely honest, and I am not sure that your article did not bring out in me the other ambivalent feeling I had for him which can only be expressed as sullen rage. He said so many unjust and silly things, and repeated himself so interminably and, when manic, would exhibit himself like a cockatoo whose harsh screams undo all the good created by its quieter moments of charm. I mean I felt I really couldn't bear to be reminded of all this again. Whatever I feel it is very strong and not at all simple, and I don't want to have anything more to do with it. I realise now that I don't think I could write about him myself . . . Please don't quote me on this very much, because of course I am devoted to him as well, but I had repressed the other side unwittingly . . . As for Logan as a literary mentor, I think one feels about him as the goose feels about the farmer who is stuffing its liver – worth it doubtless in the long run, but eating should somehow be more enjoyable!

Yours ever,

[Cyril Connolly] [7]

On the day before Pearsall Smith died, he had telephoned Connolly asking about George Orwell, whose recently published *Animal Farm* he had just read. 'Who is he? What is he like?' he had asked, explaining that the book had delighted him and that he could not wait to learn more about its author. Connolly could have humoured the old man by telling him stories about the school friend Blair who had become so famous as Orwell; but he was in a rush and put him off. 'I'll tell you all about him at tea tomorrow,' he had said. 'No. Tell me now,' Pearsall Smith had insisted. Connolly again refused, but before he had hung up Pearsall Smith declared sharply that Orwell 'beat the lot of you!'

Connolly told Gathorne-Hardy that he deeply regretted that this abrupt conversation had been his last with Pearsall Smith, admitting that he had not been 'nice enough' on the telephone. It was unfortunate, he wrote, that after such a long friendship he had not had one last proper talk with him, a chance 'to say goodbye'. Instead their talk had ended with a gruff reprimand of Connolly and those whose careers had been watched closely by Pearsall Smith: they all stood accused of failing to match the achievement of this fellow Orwell, who had come out of nowhere and 'beat the lot of you'.[8] Connolly never begrudged Orwell his success, but he must have found it ironic that Pearsall Smith, at the end of a long life of privilege and ease, should finish his days singing the praises of an author who despised privilege and whose literary labours were anything but easy.

Connolly knew better than most how difficult Orwell's life as a writer had been, but he was in no danger of concluding that a literary life had to be hard to be good. He had been tempted in the past to give up 'worldly pleasures' so that he could devote himself to his art, but the temptation passed as quickly as it had arisen. A hair shirt would not have become him. Although his desire to live well interfered with his work, it is unlikely that he would have become a better writer by suppressing his love of the good life. His occasional efforts to practise self-denial produced only frustration and anxiety. What sets him apart from a writer like Pearsall Smith, however, is the eloquence with which he expresses flashes of self-knowledge. The eloquence may come in short bursts, but it has a sharp ring of truth. He knows his faults and is not afraid to name them. His best writing is not merely a pretty 'chime of words' – the phrase Pearsall Smith used to describe his own highly polished sentences – but a fresh, unforced tone which captures the writer's true voice.

Because living well and writing well were both so important to him, Connolly was always curious to know how other writers regarded the difficulties of earning a living from literature. In the spring of 1946, a short time after Pearsall Smith's death, he decided to gather some facts on the subject for a special feature in *Horizon*: 'The Cost of Letters'. He made out a brief questionnaire and sent it to a few dozen writers; some were well known and others were beginning their careers. Predictably, some did not respond; according to Connolly, this group included 'about half a dozen of the most successful novelists'. Still, many prominent writers took the time to reply, including John Betjeman, Elizabeth Bowen, C. Day Lewis, Robert Graves, George Orwell, V. S. Pritchett, Herbert Read, Stephen Spender, and Dylan Thomas.

Most of the responses were long and detailed. 'The Cost of Letters' appeared in *Horizon* in September 1946; with a few exceptions, Connolly published each writer's answers in full. The questionnaire contained six items. Connolly wanted to know what a comfortable income for a writer was, and whether this money could be earned solely from writing. If a second job was necessary, what sort of work was most 'suitable'? In the long run was a writer helped or hindered by having a second occupation? And what more could the government or other institutions do, if anything, to help writers earn a decent living? Finally, Connolly asked, 'Are you satisfied with your solution of the problem and have you any specific advice to give young people who wish to earn their living by writing?'

Many writers were quite specific when it came to identifying a comfortable level of income. J. Maclaren-Ross wrote that he required 'a minimum of £20 a week to live on, given the present cost of living; and that's *not* including rent'. The art critic and painter Robin Ironside specified that he needed 'a net income of £15 a week', adding that this was 'an amount I have never possessed and am never likely to possess'. William Sansom was willing to accept 'a minimum of £400 to £500 a year'. The lowest figure was given by C. Day Lewis, who wrote that '£150 to £300 a year' would be 'small enough not to encourage laziness or dilettantism', but 'large enough to relieve the worries, obsessions and grosser expedients of poverty'. At the opposite end of the scale was Elizabeth Bowen's figure – a substantial '£3500 a year net'. Most were in favour of a steady £1000–2000 a year. In his own completed questionnaire, published with all the others, Connolly offered a sound middle figure, and gave equally sound reasons for it: 'If he is to enjoy leisure and privacy, marry, buy books, travel and entertain his friends, a writer needs upwards of five pounds a day net. If he is prepared to die young of syphilis for the sake of an adjective he can make do on under.'

The results of the survey left no doubt about the difficulty of earning a decent living from writing. Herbert Read (who could speak with authority both as a publisher and a writer) observed that if an author required two to three years to finish a book and wanted also to have a regular income of one thousand a year, he 'would have to sell between thirty and fifty thousand copies of each book: in all probability he will sell only three to five thousand copies'. Maclaren-Ross pointed out that most advances were so inadequate (averaging only £100 for fiction) that a writer could not support himself for more than a few months, which would hardly allow time to write a good novel. There were numerous suggestions for second jobs, but none of the respondents seemed confident that there was anything 'suitable' for a writer to do apart from his own work. The most imaginative response came from John Betjeman, who answered, 'I can speak only for myself. I would like to be a station-master on a small country branch line (single track).'

The great majority of authors were opposed to the government's giving direct assistance. 'Those who pay the piper call the tune,' Robert Graves remarked. 'The state (or any state-sponsored institution) is a dangerous patron of literature.' V. S. Pritchett put it even more succinctly: 'State writers are bought and censored writers.' However, many shared Connolly's belief that some form of indirect subsidy was necessary. Day Lewis wrote that in the event the government decided to help a promising poet, 'state support should involve him in no obligations except to his poetry; therefore it would best come from some non-political organisation such as the Arts Council.' Only William Sansom was bold enough to express unqualified faith in state patronage: 'Patronage from any source is invaluable. It is wrong to assume that strings are attached to every generosity, right to marvel that a fairly disinterested good does exist at all in the human arena.' Nearly all the authors had advice for the young, though most of it was not encouraging. Perhaps the most sobering words came from Orwell, who warned that a serious writer could never hope to find much acceptance from society. 'If one simply wants to make a living by putting words on paper, then the BBC, the film companies and the like are reasonably helpful. But if one wants to be primarily a *writer*, then, in our society, one is an animal that is tolerated but not encouraged – something rather like a house sparrow – and one gets on better if one realises one's position from the start.'

Several respondents mentioned university teaching as supplying a regular income, but no one thought much of the idea. 'The snag,' Robert Graves wrote, 'is the difficulty of getting a salaried post that does not involve so much routine teaching that [the writer] cannot get on with his real work.' That is still the 'snag' today, but the extraordinary growth of the academic world since 1946 has made universities – for better or for worse – the most important patrons of writers in our society. In *Horizon*'s day no one could have anticipated such a change, and discussions tended to focus on government grants, tax exemptions, and the like. Nevertheless, 'The Cost of Letters' reveals how great the needs of writers were, and Connolly hoped that its findings would bolster his campaign for some form of government assistance to the profession. Yet, though the issue meant a great deal to him, he did not take it too seriously. To the question, 'What do you think is the most suitable second occupation for [a writer]?' he responded: 'A rich wife'.

## II

The typing and posting of the questionnaire, and the preparation of the responses for publication, were done by Sonia Brownell, who was now a full-time, salaried assistant at *Horizon*. Her job at the Ministry of War Transport had ended in the summer of 1945, and early in the autumn Connolly had put her on the payroll at *Horizon*. She wrote two long book reviews for the magazine in her first few months, but ordinarily she handled basic editorial and secretarial chores.

Sonia performed this routine work with enthusiasm and efficiency, and soon made herself indispensable to the daily operation of the magazine, dominating the office as no other assistant had done before, including Lys, who worked with her. Firm and purposeful, she knew how to get things done, and was quick to assert herself when the need arose. Her self-confidence was clear; when she disapproved of something, she spoke her mind freely, using words like 'rubbish' or 'nonsense' to emphasise her disapproval. Her opinions of literature were particularly strong, although not always well informed or precise. She worked tirelessly as an editorial reader at *Horizon*, often providing Connolly with detailed reports on submissions to the magazine, but she was sometimes hasty in condemning what she did not like, and her confident pronouncements sometimes seemed pretentious. It was her zeal and exuberance, not her critical judgment, which impressed Connolly.

One of her responsibilities was to write letters of acceptance or rejection to authors. Connolly signed some of them, but in other cases they were signed 'Sonia Brownell, Secretary'. A surviving example is a letter written in July 1946 to Theodore Roethke (then thirty-eight and still a relatively unknown poet), informing him that *Horizon* had decided not to publish his submission, 'The Lost Son', a long poem which many critics now regard as one of his finest works. On two previous occasions Roethke had tried to place poems in *Horizon*; in each of these instances his work had been returned with a handwritten note from Connolly encouraging him to send in more poems. When he submitted 'The Lost Son', in April 1946, he was hopeful that he had at last written a poem Connolly would take, calling it in his covering letter 'the best thing I have done so far'.[9]

When he heard that the poem had been turned down, he was furious. It hurt to know that he had failed a third time, but what upset him was the wording of the rejection letter. The decision to send back the poem had been Connolly's, but he had left to Sonia the job of explaining why it was being returned. In her zeal to serve him and the magazine, she was inclined to take her work too seriously, and this was evident in her remarks to Roethke. She took a condescending tone with the poet, using generalisations to lecture him about the shortcomings of American poetry. Instead of a brief, polite rejection, she seemed to feel that he deserved a reprimand. His poem, she says, suffers from flaws typical of

> a great deal of American poetry which seems to us to have become a heartless and rhetorical activity just as most English poetry seems sloppy and thoughtless. We don't necessarily like all the poetry we print though we liked immensely Dylan Thomas's recent poems which, we thought, combined American perfection of form with European passion. But really we are looking for the poems which have something immensely moving about them without caring much how or why it gets there. It seemed to us that your poetry was in a way very American in that it just lacked that inspiration, inevitability or quintessence of writing and feeling that distinguishes good poetry from verse.[10]

How much Sonia knew about American poetry in the Forties is anyone's guess, but she was content to use 'very American' as a definition of verse not good enough to be real poetry. No wonder Roethke was angry. Indeed, as his biographer noted, this letter of rejection so incensed him that for weeks afterwards he continued 'fulminating against "the god-damned limeys"'.[11]

Relatively few poets, British or American, received much encouragement from *Horizon* in 1946. Most issues that year contained one or two poems or none at all – of these, the best was C. Day Lewis's 'Emily Bronte', a good but not a great poem. There was just not enough good poetry around, Connolly felt. He was so unimpressed that he decided not to follow the magazine's usual practice of publishing an annual review of poetry, announcing in 'Comment' that 'we do not consider the volumes produced in 1946 to justify one'.[12] One might object that he was not paying enough attention to new American poets like Roethke; but he was concerned primarily with the state of British poetry and he was right about its lack of distinction in the second half of the Forties. The best of the war poets – Keith Douglas, Sidney Keyes, and Alun Lewis – were dead; T. S. Eliot's major work was behind him; and the best poet of the next generation, Philip Larkin, had not yet discovered his voice. For Connolly, there were only two British poets still doing important work: Dylan Thomas was one, Edith Sitwell the other.

Neither Thomas nor Edith Sitwell appeared in *Horizon* in 1946. Thomas's work was well represented in earlier issues, and from 1944 Edith Sitwell's work received prominent attention. In December he published her poem 'A Song at Morning', and four more of her poems over the next four years. In 1947 he dedicated an entire issue to Edith Sitwell and her two brothers, complete with a long essay by Kenneth Clark, 'On the Development of Miss Sitwell's Later Style'. Her poetry of the war years touched Connolly deeply, and his re-discovery of her work aroused a nostalgia for the years in the 1920s when the Sitwells stood out in England as 'the natural allies of Cocteau and the École de Paris, dandies, irreproachably dressed and fed, who indicated to young men just down from Oxford and even Cambridge that it was possible to reconcile art and fashion'.[13] Carried away by his new enthusiasm for her poetry, Connolly wrote her letters full of praise, and surprised her by asking whether she would be his literary executor.

The shining examples of Edith Sitwell and Dylan Thomas were not enough to brighten Connolly's dismal view of British poetry. There were simply no new poets whose work excited him, and *Horizon* increased its dependence on critical articles. This brought readers an abundance of rich and engaging essays in the first years after the war. In November 1946, for example, Connolly began an entertaining series of articles called 'The Best and the Worst', in which writers made an effort to discuss objectively the works of one of their favourite authors. Philip Toynbee contributed a piece on Virginia Woolf; this was followed by Rose Macaulay on Evelyn Waugh (December 1946); John Russell on Lytton Strachey (February 1947); V. S. Pritchett on Arthur Koestler (May 1947); and Evelyn Waugh on Ronald Knox (May 1948). Connolly encouraged this sort of essay, and several noteworthy variations of it appeared in *Horizon*. Among them, which one could subtitle 'the famous-on-the famous', are Auden's essay on Henry James's *The American Scene* (February 1947); Robert Penn Warren's article on Hemingway (April 1947); and Bertrand Russell's review of A. J. Ayer's *Language, Truth and Logic* (January 1947).

In April 1946, *Horizon* published one of the best and most influential essays of the decade – Orwell's 'Politics and the English Language', which quickly became famous for its criticism of the way in which the corruption of language feeds the growth of political tyranny (a connection no less demonstrable today). Orwell's phrase 'the defence of the indefensible' is still an apt description of the writing and speech-making of the world's politicians and government bureaucrats.

What is interesting about this article from the standpoint of *Horizon* is its similarity to an earlier piece in the magazine, a 'Comment' in October 1941 where Connolly jokingly demanded that an official 'Word Controller' needed 'dictatorial powers to clean up our language . . . War journalism and war oratory have produced an unchecked inflation in our overdriven and exhausted vocabulary.' Connolly had suggested that the Word Controller would need to begin by requiring anyone who wished to address the public, in speeches or in print, to obtain a special 'licence (like driving licences)', which could be revoked or 'endorsed' if the holder were guilty of using words such as 'vital', 'vitally', 'virtual', and 'virtually', or 'democracy', 'justice', 'freedom', 'jackboot', 'serious consideration', and 'island fortress'.

Orwell criticises the over-use of some of these words in his essay, and although Connolly's proposal was made in a spirit of fun the logic behind it was the same as that in Orwell's serious argument. Orwell's principal point is that 'the slovenliness of our language makes it easier for us to have foolish thoughts', and this is also the point of Connolly's satire: 'As [the Word Controller] became more autocratic and more like other controllers he would find out that there is a connection between the rubbish written, the nonsense talked, and the thoughts of the people, and he would endeavour to use his censorship of words . . . to affect the ideas behind them, or, rather, he would give priority to statements of fact over abstractions, and to facts which were accurate rather than incorrect.' The examples of jargon-ridden prose Orwell criticises have their parallel in Connolly's piece, which takes a passage of rhetoric from the *Daily Express* and gives a simplified translation of it to demonstrate what the writer was trying to say.

Unlike Connolly, Orwell develops these points into a sustained and compelling argument. His essay is five times the length of Connolly's 'Comment', and he is able to flesh out ideas merely hinted at in his friend's piece. Too often Connolly wasted ideas in works too short and undeveloped to bring recognition, and, because he could never write at length without humour, readers often did not take his arguments seriously. His 'Comment' on the Word Controller is easy to dismiss as a sketchy outline for Orwell's longer, more accomplished piece, but its compact prose reaches a level of refinement and inspiration beyond anything to be found in the sober sentences of 'Politics and the English Language'. The last paragraph of the 'Comment' – written when the survival of England, not merely the English language, was in doubt – brings to vivid life the question of language usage:

We are all prisoners in solitary confinement: when at last we give up trying to escape through mass emotion or sexual union there remains for us only the wall alphabet in which we tap our hopes and thoughts. Nobody should learn this alphabet who can abuse it, who jerry-builds the English language as if it were the English countryside, who wastes the time of his fellow prisoners by tapping out stale rhetoric, false news, or untranslatable messages, and so brings a perfect achievement of civilisation into confusion.

Brief as it was, Connolly's piece must have been read by Orwell (one of whose essays, 'The Art of Donald McGill', had been published in *Horizon* the previous month). He might also have looked at it again in October 1945, when it was reprinted in the 'Writers and Society' section of *The Condemned Playground*. The time of his reading is not as important as the fact that he and Connolly saw each other often during the first half of the Forties, and one may assume that they had discussed the ideas behind 'Politics and the English Language' long before it was written.

Ironically, this piece was not only Orwell's best essay in *Horizon* but his last. Following its publication, he went to the Scottish island of Jura, and began work on his last book – *Nineteen Eighty-Four*. The success of *Animal Farm* had given him the freedom to concentrate on writing fiction, and he limited his work for newspapers and periodicals. Three years later he finished his novel, and seven months after its publication his long struggle against tuberculosis ended in his early death.

It was during the war that Orwell first made Sonia's acquaintance. They met at a dinner party given by Connolly in Bedford Square. Sonia had just finished reading *Burmese Days*, which she had enjoyed; when she heard that its author would be dining at Connolly's place, she arranged to be there. Recalling the meeting many years later, she confessed that her initial impression of Orwell had not been good. 'His first few sentences were quite off-putting. He said that one should never write anything the working classes don't understand. He then said one shouldn't use adjectives and Cecil Day Lewis [who was also dining at Connolly's that evening] said, "What about Shakespeare?"' When dinner was served, 'He was very quiet and said something about you've put foreign stuff in the food but sat down and enjoyed it.'[14]

Orwell's first wife, Eileen, died in March 1945; in addition to this loss, he had the responsibility of caring for the infant son he and Eileen had adopted nine months earlier. Sonia befriended him in this difficult time. She still had doubts about him, but his problems aroused her sympathy. She visited his London flat several times and eventually took a few turns at babysitting his young son, though this was not work which came easily to her. ('Oh the smell of cabbage and unwashed nappies', she once remarked, summing up her impressions of caring for the baby.)[15] Orwell fell in love with her, and asked her to marry him. He was attracted by her beauty and lively spirit, but he was also rather desperate for a companion who could help him with his work and his child. His proposal was flatly rejected; Sonia considered marriage to be out of the question. She had grown fond of Orwell, but she was not in love, and she was certainly not ready for instant motherhood. At twenty-eight she had no interest in settling down. The war had kept her from enjoying her youth fully, and there were too many things she wanted to see and do.

Orwell did not give up hope that Sonia would change her mind. Even when he went to Jura, he kept in touch with her, encouraging her to visit him at the large farmhouse he occupied there. In one letter he told her she could have a nice room which 'looks out on to the sea', and he described some of the island's attractive features, telling her of its 'uninhabited bays . . . where there is beautiful white sand and clear water'. A journey from London to the island involved a train journey to Glasgow and another eight hours of travel by train, boat, and bus. There was little chance that she would attempt it, but he made sure she had exact directions. 'I do so want to have you here,' he wrote.[16] She did not take up his invitation, but he could not get her out of his mind. Her image inspired one of his most memorable characters in *Nineteen Eighty-Four*: the assured, plainspoken, energetic Julia, Winston Smith's lover, who oversees the operation of 'the novel-writing machines in the Fiction Department'.

## III

While Orwell was spending the summer in Jura writing his novel, Sonia was busy managing the *Horizon* office, working on her own for a good part of the time. Connolly and Lys were away from London in August and in the first two weeks of September during that summer of 1946, enjoying a 'honeymoon' tour of France, which included a long stay on the island of Corsica. It was now easier to go abroad, and Connolly was able to fulfil his promise to show Lys some of his favourite places in France. Sonia wrote him long letters about developments at the office, but with the exception of major editorial decisions she was free to manage things as she saw fit. When he had been away in the spring for a few weeks, she had written, 'All is fine so have NO ANGST but a lovely time.'[17] Her enthusiasm sounded positively school-girlish at times.

In August she was preparing final copy for the September issue, which featured 'The Cost of Letters'. Although this piece had needed a great deal of work from her, she could not contain her excitement about it, telling Connolly: 'The Questionnaire I find absolutely fascinat-ing. I've read it entirely now 3 times in page proof and everyone to whom I have mentioned the idea is wildly enthusiastic ... I think the No. is very very good as it stands.'[18] She enjoyed her position so much that she seemed not to mind having to look after *Horizon* while Connolly and Lys enjoyed the Mediterranean sun. One day Connolly was feeling moody and wrote to her that he and Lys might come home early from Corsica; Sonia made it clear that she was doing fine on her own, and had no desire to see their trip cut short: 'I was rather sad to hear that you're coming back so soon – not because I'm not longing to see you both – I am, but because I hope it doesn't mean that everything isn't delicious or that you've run out of money or something horrid. Please don't worry about Horizon because everything is magnifi-cent.'[19]

Peter Watson was also away from London for much of the summer. His health was still not as good as he might have wished, but by the spring he was well enough to want to travel again. He had visited Ireland early in April and, not long after returning, had made up his mind to go back to Paris. He still had his apartment in the Rue du Bac, and decided to spend the summer there refurbishing it. Like Connolly, he was still attracted to France, despite its post-war problems. He hoped to be able to spend part of each year there and, with Sonia in command of the routine business at *Horizon*, he was less concerned about being away for extended periods.

He did not look for any new material in Paris to use in the magazine. 'I imagine there is more than enough French stuff to hand,' he wrote from the Rue du Bac, 'I shan't ask for anything unless you specially write for it.'[20] Although his sympathies were more and more with Continental writers and artists, he realised that *Horizon* needed to give attention to post-war British culture. By and large Watson was dis-appointed with the state of British art after the war and, as art editor, gave very little coverage to it. He published more reproductions of works by Lucian Freud and John Craxton, but the only other important artists to receive attention were the Scottish-born sculptor Eduardo Paolozzi, and Francis Bacon. Paolozzi was only twenty-three when some of his work was featured in *Horizon* in 1947; and Francis Bacon was just emerging as a major figure when Watson published the painter's powerful triptych 'Three Studies for Figures at the Base of a Crucifixion' in 1949. Most of his and *Horizon*'s attention was focused on the Continent and when he made an effort to include a young artist who was not Continental he appeared to do so without a strong sense of conviction. During his trip to Ireland in the spring of 1946 Watson had discovered Louis Le Brocquy's paintings, and an article about this Irish painter and several reproductions of his work appeared in the summer of 1946. The work is respectable, but the decision to publish it was not based entirely on the artist's merits. In his letter of 17 July to Connolly, Watson wrote: 'Will you put in Louis Le Brocquy for August please. It's time for another Horizon British (Eire) art discovery. This is the only way to reconcile undue interest in Continental artists.'

During that summer at the Rue du Bac, Watson was reunited with Denham Fouts. They had been apart for nearly six years. At the end of the war Fouts had left California and had moved to New York, where he had sold the last of the paintings Watson had sent with him in 1940. He put together his remaining funds and made his way back to Europe. Shortly after Watson arrived in Paris, Fouts appeared at the apartment and made himself at home again. The reunion was not a happy one. Watson could accept the matter of the lost paintings, but Fouts had resumed his old drug habit with a vengeance, and was now displaying it openly. He would stay out all night at clubs, then return with complete strangers who would spend the day sleeping in the apartment. Fouts did not begin his day until it was dark, and most of it would be spent in a cocaine and heroin haze.

Watson tried to help him, urging him to enter a clinic for some of the detoxification treatments he had resorted to in the past. Fouts refused, and his presence made it impossible for Watson to lead an ordinary existence. But he did not have the heart to evict Fouts, so Watson had to go elsewhere. In August he went south to Cannes and stayed on the Riviera for the rest of the month, leaving the Paris apartment to Fouts and an odd assortment of Fouts's 'friends' who drifted in and out.

Before Watson had left London for the summer, Connolly had raised with him the possibility of putting together a special American number of *Horizon*. During the war Connolly had tried to drum up interest in an American issue, but had not been able to find enough good contributors. He had settled instead for a special section in the February 1944 number featuring works by eleven contemporary American poets (among them were Randall Jarrell, Delmore Schwartz, and Wallace Stevens). He now wanted to go to the States and collect material for a special number which would be larger and more ambitious than the French and Swiss issues. He proposed to Watson that they make the trip together in the autumn and spend four weeks in New York and two in California. Among other things they could visit Auden in New York, and Isherwood and Aldous Huxley in Los Angeles.

Despite unpleasant memories of their trip to Switzerland, Watson agreed to the plan. They decided to sail to New York in November, relying on Sonia and Lys to look after *Horizon* while they were away. Before returning to England to prepare for the trip, Watson went back to the Rue du Bac to check on Fouts. Nothing had changed; nothing he could say or do would bring Fouts out of his self-destructive binge. The landlord of the building was complaining angrily that he did not want Fouts in the flat any longer: late-night noise, strange guests, and drugs were too much for the neighbours to tolerate. Yet Fouts could not be persuaded to leave, and Watson was incapable of forcing him out. Frustrated and bitter, Watson took the boat train back to England. After years of longing to be reunited with Fouts, he now wanted to be free of him for good. He hoped that while he was away in America Fouts would leave the Rue du Bac or be forced out by the landlord.

Connolly's enthusiasm for the trip to America was increasing; he expected a warm reception in New York, where his literary reputation was high. In addition to the praise he had received in *Time* and the *New Yorker*, the *Saturday Review* had published a portrait of him on its cover in July 1946, and had included a review of *The Condemned Playground* which lauded 'the brilliance, the wit, and the frequent insight' it offered. A few months earlier, in April, the influential *Atlantic Monthly* had published a lengthy critical analysis of his work. Written by Jacques Barzun, critic and 'Professor of Cultural History' at Columbia University, the piece was titled 'Meet the Modern Ego', and is chiefly remarkable in that it presents Connolly to American readers 'as a representative modern mind: a mind so full of our own high and low spirits, our own anxiety – and at the same time so competent in self-analysis – that to read him is to explore many neglected corners of oneself'. Barzun's talk of 'anxiety' and 'self-analysis' was part of the fashionable literary jargon of the time, and was a sure sign that Connolly's work was being taken 'seriously' in American intellectual circles.

Even critics who did not care for him were inclined to inflate the 'cultural significance' of his work. Writing in the *New Republic* in July

1946, a critic from Harvard – Harry Levin – complained of Connolly's determination 'to wear his *angst* upon his sleeve', and said that this decadent display had ominous implications. At the end of his article, Levin reached a rather extraordinary conclusion: '[Connolly's] work serves more or less authoritative notice that England, long declining into a second-class power, has begun her decline into a second-class culture.' It is difficult to believe that many readers of the *New Republic* would have taken this statement seriously, but they must have been left thinking that this Englishman was a literary figure to be reckoned with. Any writer whose work could be said to signal the cultural decline of the land of Shakespeare and Milton was worth looking into.

Cass Canfield, Connolly's publisher at Harper's in New York, had no trouble recognising that all this critical attention, good and bad, could boost the American sales of his author's books. Harper's had published the American edition of *The Unquiet Grave*, and had joined with Hamish Hamilton to advance Connolly three hundred pounds for the rights to his proposed book on Flaubert. There was every reason to believe that his literary future in America could be bright, and Cass Canfield wanted to have as much of the author's work as possible. However, Macmillan had stepped in and secured the American rights to *The Condemned Playground*, and according to Hamish Hamilton other American publishers, including Doubleday, were 'wooing' Connolly. When Canfield learned of Connolly's intention to visit New York, he arranged to do some 'wooing' of his own, planning a large cocktail party in the writer's honour, as well as a dinner party and a few informal lunches. 'I think the more attention we can pay him, the better,' he told his staff.[21] In a letter from London, Hamish Hamilton suggested one way to secure Connolly's goodwill: 'His greatest material ambition seems to be to purchase an American car and have it shipped to this country. I don't know whether it is still possible to get one for $1500 or thereabouts but, if so, it might be worth your while to consider advancing him enough money for this purpose against royalties to be earned on his next books ... The success of *The Unquiet Grave* and *The Condemned Playground* is encouraging him to take more time for the production of books, and I believe that even if he never tackles the Flaubert, he will do other books within the next few years.'[22]

On 19 November Connolly and Watson boarded the *Franconia* and began a ten-day voyage across the Atlantic to New York. More than sixteen years had passed since Connolly had last been on such a voyage. He had been a hopeful young writer going to America to marry a rich girl from Baltimore. The rich girl had long since left him, but he had found success on his own. He was now the author of four books, the editor of a great magazine, and – according to the Professor of Cultural History at Columbia University – nothing less than 'a representative modern mind'.

# EIGHT

# AMERICAN HORIZON
## 1946–1947

### I

The autumn voyage brought Connolly and Watson to New York the day after the Thanksgiving holiday. Rough weather, overcrowding, and bad food had made the passage difficult, but Connolly had tolerated it all with surprising equanimity. Reading *Les Fleurs du Mal* had so absorbed his attention that he had blocked out some of the unpleasantness of the trip. Writing in his diary, he commented on how much this reading of Baudelaire had affected him: 'Read and re-read and annotated my edition until B's presence became real at every moment.' Inspired by this, he drew up a list of resolutions for the New Year, vowing in one to spend even more time away from the *Horizon* office 'and live for literature on my return'. In another he told himself 'never to forget for one moment that Flaubert and Baudelaire are *for me* The ideal – Re touchstone. They are L'ART et L'AMOUR.'[1]

Throughout the voyage the two friends were on good terms; one night, according to Connolly's diary, they enjoyed a 'long and delicious conversation' on Baudelaire, 'genius', and other less serious topics. The diary even goes so far as to praise 'the charm of my sweet Peter'. For their stay in New York, however, they had made separate hotel arrangements. It was best not to become too caught up in each other's lives, as they had discovered on their Swiss visit. Connolly's reservation was at the Grosvenor Hotel in Greenwich Village, while Watson was uptown at the St Regis, where he had frequently stayed in his 'playboy' days before the war.

On the morning of arrival Connolly got up at six to see the Statue of Liberty and the New York skyline at dawn. It was cold and foggy, and the hour was much too early for him, but the view heightened his excitement and impressed upon him that he had, for the time being, put the Old World behind him. 'Europe seems infinitely remote; England like a week-end cottage which one has abandoned with all the washing-up undone.'² Connolly went straight to his hotel, where Auden was waiting in the lobby. ('Wystan charming though very battered looking. More American than ever and much less self-conscious than in London'.)³ They went off to lunch together at a restaurant on Third Avenue, and during the meal Auden took pains to warn Connolly about 'the perils of the big city', advising him to watch out for thieves and the heavy traffic. When Auden had left, Connolly made his way cautiously back to the hotel, 'hugging' his wallet and eyeing intersections and traffic lights apprehensively as he dashed across busy streets. Later that evening Watson treated him to dinner at a fashionable French restaurant on Park Avenue, but the first day in New York had been too long and hectic, and Connolly did not enjoy the meal, pronouncing it 'disappointing except for avocado pears'.⁴

Watson and Connolly saw each other infrequently during their New York visit. Watson spent much of his time with three old friends from the Thirties: Pavel Tchelitchew, Charles Henri Ford, and Parker Tyler. He had known Tchelitchew the longest, having met him on the Continent in the early Thirties. A Russian exile, Tchelitchew painted in the neo-romantic style, creating strange illusions out of realistic details. He was also a celebrated ballet designer, and his friends included George Balanchine and Lincoln Kirstein. Foremost among his admirers in England was Edith Sitwell, who nurtured a deep but unrequited love for him over a period of thirty years. Most of Tchelitchew's love was reserved for Charles Henri Ford, whom he had met in Paris in 1931, when the young poet from Mississippi was living with Djuna Barnes. Parker Tyler was one of Ford's best friends, and many years later he would write Tchelitchew's biography. These three friends had divided their time between Europe and America in the second half of the Thirties, and Watson had visited them in New York almost every year.

In 1938 Watson had paid the publication costs of Charles Henri Ford's first full-length book of poems – *The Garden of Disorder* – and early in 1939 the poet had asked his wealthy friend to help him and Parker Tyler start a magazine in New York. According to Ford, 'I said to Peter let's start a magazine, and he was so inclined.'⁵ If war had not broken out in Europe that year, Watson might very well have done so; in which case, *Horizon* might never have come into being. He would have become the publisher and patron of *View*, the name his two American friends gave the magazine they started on their own in 1940. Eventually, they received financial backing from a number of distinguished people (some of whom were very rich, such as Mrs Vincent Astor and Helena Rubinstein) and the two editors were able to keep

*View* going in New York throughout the war. It never came close to matching the literary quality of *Horizon*, but its contributors from the art world were impressive: Alexander Calder, Marcel Duchamp, and Fernand Léger were among those who provided cover art for the magazine.

While Watson was renewing his friendships with Tchelitchew and the editors of *View*, Connolly was trying to keep up with a stream of social and professional invitations all over Manhattan. Macmillan and Harper's were paying him a great deal of attention. After giving a large party on 3 December, Cass Canfield wrote a summary of what his author had discussed with him during the evening. One of his concerns was that Macmillan was making an all-out effort to acquire the rights to Connolly's future work. According to Canfield's notes, it was 'obvious that Macmillan [was] making [a] great fuss over him'. A consolation for Harper's was that Macmillan's efforts were not working very well. 'Their publicity head sees him constantly and has worried him by making a lot of useless engagements,' Canfield observed. Although Harper's was not inclined to make extravagant offers -- no fancy American automobiles were mentioned -- Canfield did impress upon Connolly the advantages of publishing with Harper's and went away feeling his arguments had been persuasive. 'The talk with him was very satisfactory,' he recorded in his notes, 'and I think that if we play the cards right we should get most if not all of his books.' [6]

Connolly was amused by the wheeling and dealing in the New York book world. He liked the attention, but he could see that a major reason for it was his standing as a hot, 'new' author in America. In that consumer-driven society he was the latest commodity with 'highbrow' appeal and, given the right marketing approach, a wise publisher could make that appeal yield a profit. Connolly was now a 'name' which was in demand in the publishing world; the American market, Connolly observed, had an insatiable appetite for 'new' names. As he wrote not long after his visit, 'The hunt for young authors who, while maintaining a prestige value (with a role for Ingrid Bergman), may yet somehow win the coveted jack-pot, is feverish and incessant. Last year's authors (most of the names that have just reached England) are pushed aside and this year's -- the novelist Jean Stafford, her poet husband Robert Lowell or the dark horse, Truman Capote -- are invariably mentioned. They may be quite unread, but their names, like a new issue on the market, are constantly on the lips of those in the know. "Get Capote" -- at this minute the words are resounding on many a sixtieth floor.' [7]

On 12 December Connolly's name was heard in thousands of New York homes when he was the featured guest on the radio programme 'Author Meets the Critics'. For half an hour listeners could hear a literary discussion between Connolly and a panel of three critics, one of whom was Orville Prescott, the well-respected editor and reviewer at the *New York Times*. Two days later, readers of the *New Yorker* could learn more of him in an interview with, as the magazine put it, 'the round, bouncing man of forty-three'. His market value seemed to be rising every day, although his public comments could not have gladdened the hearts of the publicity people at Macmillan. The picture he painted of himself in the *New Yorker* interview was honest, but not an image many Americans would have found inspiring:

'I have a tendency to brood,' he said, lighting a Turkish cigarette. 'I try to escape this horrible business of writing by daydreaming and dozing in the bathtub for hours at a time. Sometimes, I get one adjective from an afternoon in the tub. I go through cycles of distraction. I have a vast store of general knowledge, acquired through such escapist enthusiasms as bridge, chess, old furniture, china, rare books, antiques, and travelling . . . Right now, I am on fish. Last summer, in Corsica, I concluded that fish are most misunderstood. People only think about eating them. I spent the summer staring at them through goggles, in the Mediterranean. They do everything just right – play and eat and roam about in pairs and show a great capacity for happiness. This autumn I spent reading about all the fish I'd met in the summer.' [8]

It was all true, but it was hardly promising material for a publisher's blurb.

Connolly enjoyed teasing interviewers, but one of his jokes took an unexpected twist when a radio producer asked him a few questions before a broadcast. The producer – a very earnest woman – enquired: 'What is your religion?' With a straight face, he replied, 'Cummingism'. Perplexed, she asked him to repeat his answer. 'Cummingism', he said again, but seeing that his joke was going nowhere, he explained, 'I'm a devotee of your American poet E. E. Cummings.' Suddenly, it was clear to her. 'You mean you *were*,' she responded confidently. A little confused himself, Connolly insisted, 'No, I *am*.' 'How can you say that,' she said, 'after the terrible things he did!' 'What things?' he asked. 'Living in Italy and broadcasting for fascism: don't you know he's a traitor?' Connolly did not know what to say, then he recognised her mistake. 'You're confusing him with Ezra Pound, aren't you?' The woman thought a second, shrugged her shoulders, and said, 'Oh well, it was one of those three – Eliot or Pound or Cummings.'[9]

Connolly was serious when he declared himself an admirer of Cummings. (He later wrote that what first attracted him to the poet's work was a 'vein of erotic realism'.)[10] One of the reasons that he had come to New York was to talk to Cummings. At the end of 1945 he had read a copy of $1 \times 1$, which had been published in America during the war; he had enjoyed it so much that he had written to the poet to enquire whether *Horizon* could bring out a limited edition of it in England. 'I was tremendously impressed by "One × One",' he wrote to Cummings in February 1946, 'which I think is far and away the best book of poems produced recently in America.'[11] *Horizon* had published a total of four books, including *The Unquiet Grave*, but Connolly had hopes of doing three or four titles a year, and he thought that $1 \times 1$ would work well in the new list. Cummings readily agreed, and by the time Connolly arrived in New York the final arrangements for publication were ready to be discussed.

Connolly's hotel was only a short walk from Patchin Place, the narrow street in Greenwich Village where Cummings lived with his wife Marion. The two men got on well from the start, and met socially on several occasions. They shared some French meals at the Hotel Lafayette in the Village, and one day Connolly introduced Cummings to another important poet in the neighbourhood – Auden. Later, Cummings wrote to his mother, 'Cyril Connolly, the editor of "Horizon" magazine (much the best periodical concerning socalled literature; & published in London) has been wining-and-dining Marion and me in celebration of a (let's trust) soon-forthcoming English edition of $1 \times 1$.'[12] The book did indeed come out on time, appearing in 1947 with two other titles: a collection of Goya's drawings and Philip Toynbee's novel *Tea with Mrs Goodman*. Meanwhile, in New York, Connolly collected first editions of Cummings's previous books, which were very difficult to find in England. (Before *Horizon* published Cummings's work, the only collection of his poetry printed in England had been a booklet in the 1930s, containing only twenty of his poems.) Connolly discovered some of the volumes he wanted while browsing at one o'clock in the morning in a secondhand bookshop, which was open all night. With the books tucked carefully under his arm, he walked back to his hotel in the cold December air watching the steam rise from the manholes on the empty streets. The urban night, punctuated by the sounds of tugboats in the distance, seemed perfect to him. In his diary he wrote, 'To buy [Cummings's] early books at 1AM, that is for me CIVILISATION.'[13]

One person Connolly did not see in New York was his ex-wife; she and Laurence Vail had left the previous summer and were living in France. At one of the several parties given for him, he did meet Clement Greenberg – Jean's lover in the early years of the war. He did not hold the affair against Greenberg; on the contrary, he was friendly and curious to learn more about Jean's years in New York. He even asked him to contribute an essay on American art for the proposed special issue, and the invitation was accepted. Later, Greenberg confided that he thought they were both lucky to be free of Jean. She was too good at mothering her lovers, he said, and in the long run her indulgence was destructive.

Wherever he went, Connolly found that people were anxious to please him and make him feel welcome. Greenberg described Connolly's stay in America as 'the most successful British visit to this country since Oscar Wilde's . . . so many parties for him, etc.'[14] Peter Watson was amazed to see the attention his friend was attracting, and in a letter to Brian Howard he reported, 'Cyril's triumphant progress here must be seen to be believed. The Director of the Metropolitan had us to lunch and gave us a personally conducted tour of the Museum, and everything else is rather on that level. It's much too much for me.'[15] After three weeks of interviews, parties, and meetings, Connolly too was beginning to find it 'too much'. He had become, as he later put it, 'a slave of my telephone and engagement book'.[16] By the time he was to leave for California (just before Christmas) he was grateful to have a break from the pace of New York life. Watson wanted to remain with his friends over the holidays, so Connolly went to the West Coast alone, travelling by plane to his first destination – San Francisco.

New York had the culture, but California had the climate that most appealed to him. He did not think much of the architecture in San Francisco, saying that the city had 'charming people and hideous buildings', but he was enchanted by the natural beauty and mild weather of the region, especially farther south along the coast at Monterey, Carmel, and Big Sur. A writer he particularly admired – Henry Miller – had settled in the area, and this was the reason for Connolly's journey from San Francisco.

Miller had a small house at Big Sur which was short on modern conveniences but surrounded by spectacular scenery: a long rugged coastline, mountains, and a towering redwood forest. Much to his delight, Connolly was invited to join the novelist there for a couple of days. Its beauty and isolation offered a tempting vision of the perfect life for a writer. It was cheap to live there – Miller's rent was six dollars a month – no telephone shrilled, and the only loud noise was the sound of the sea. Connolly concluded that Miller was 'one writer who has solved the problem of how to live happily in America.'[17] Whether he could have survived happily there for more than a few days is doubtful but, like many other writers, he always imagined that retreating to such a remote, inspirational spot would do wonders for his work. Miller had his own idea about the reason for Connolly's visit; after his guest had gone, he wrote to Lawrence Durrell: 'What [Connolly] really came for, I think, was to see the last of the lost race of otters, which are off this coast. But he saw none – and showed his disappointment keenly.'[18]

Connolly went next to southern California, which he did not like as well. 'On the whole those who have loved the Mediterranean will not be reconciled here,' he remarked, 'and those who care deeply for books can never settle down to the impermanent world of the cinema.'[19] It is not clear whether he met Christopher Isherwood, but he did spend time with Aldous Huxley, who had been living in California since the late Thirties.

In the Twenties and early Thirties his fiction had exercised a powerful influence on Connolly; in 1930, when Huxley was living in the South of France, Connolly had rented a furnished house a mile away from him, planning – as he put it later – 'to sit at the feet of my master'. The plan had failed: they made a bad start socially, and the young writer discovered that living near his idol was more intimidating than inspiring. 'I could not always follow his metaphysical flights and developed an inferiority complex which prevented me from writing myself for, as I sat exhausted by idleness in front of my desk, I could hear, in my imagination, the tapping of the typewriter of this most prolific of contemporary authors drumming out across the opaline sea-dazzle of the little Mediterranean bay. I became a kind of mental poor relation.'[20] Connolly's interest in Huxley faded and did not revive until near the end of the war, when he read *Time Must Have a Stop*. Reviewing it in the *New Statesman*, he wrote that it was 'Huxley's best novel for a very long time'; and a little while later the novelist repaid the compliment by telling him in a letter how much he had enjoyed *The Unquiet Grave*.[21] Connolly was delighted to receive this 'fan letter', as he liked to call it, and by the time he arrived in Los Angeles he was looking forward to meeting the 'master' once again.

He was not disappointed. The stylish author of *Antic Hay* and *Crome Yellow* had turned his back on the fashionable world of his early career to concentrate on philosophy, religion, and mysticism. Connolly was much taken with Huxley's 'strange new quality of sublimated sensuality, intellectual pity, spiritual grace'.[22] The awkwardness and tension which had characterised their meetings over a decade earlier were now absent. Their conversations were intense but pleasant. Instead of the 'clever' man of the Twenties, he found 'a man at peace with himself', and he said later that he had felt 'exquisitely refreshed' after his encounter with the 'new' Huxley.[23]

Connolly did not take mysticism seriously, but he respected the genuine nature of Huxley's conversion. Earlier in the year he had printed in *Horizon* a lengthy extract from Huxley's *Perennial Philosophy*, a collection of religious and mystical writings published in America in 1945. He had his doubts about the ultimate value of mysticism to Huxley's art, but what was most important to him was that he and the novelist-hero of his youth had made peace with each other. They could accept each other as they were, which was important to Connolly, who had never forgotten the sting of his failure to match talents with Huxley in the Thirties. That memory was made less painful, thanks to his success and Huxley's friendly reception.

Early in January Connolly went back to New York and stayed another week before returning home. Almost every writer who met him was invited to submit something for the American issue, but when he left he had very few contributions in hand. The deadline for submissions was later in the spring, and a number of people had promised that they would have work ready to send to London within the next month or two. The tentative plan was to bring out the special issue at the end of the summer as a double number consisting of 150 pages. Connolly would write a long 'Comment' for it, drawing some of his material from the diary he had kept during the trip. To ease the burden of dealing with contributors thousands of miles away, an American friend from pre-war days – Tony Bower – was appointed to serve as the magazine's 'resident agent, or prodder', in New York.[24] In addition, Watson decided to stay on in New York for another month, and hoped that more submissions would be ready to go back with him.

Before Connolly left, he confided to Cass Canfield that he had been thinking of 'discontinuing' his magazine at the close of 'the present decade'. In a letter written the next day, Canfield shared with Hamish Hamilton (an old friend) the details of Connolly's remarks. 'He feels that the job of editing a monthly takes up too much of his time and energy. Accordingly, his tentative idea is to switch from magazine to book editing. I gather in 1950 or thereabouts he will embark on a program of publishing eight or ten books a year. In this connection I don't believe he is in the least interested in the details of publishing outside of editorial work, and it is possible that you might wish to discuss in due course an arrangement like the one between Little Brown and The Atlantic Monthly Press, whereby Hamish Hamilton would produce the "Connolly Books", attend to sales and promotion and other details.'[25]

Just when *Horizon* was enjoying its greatest influence and prestige in America, Connolly was thinking ahead to the day when he could close it down. As always, it was easiest for him to be tempted away from something when it was most securely in his possession. And, as the Forties moved to their conclusion, he began to like more and more the notion of the magazine and the decade ending together. The proposed switch to the publication of 'Connolly Books' had great appeal, especially if he could continue to count on the help of Watson, Sonia, and Lys. He could concentrate on the fun part of editing – discussing a manuscript with E. E. Cummings, for example – and the rest of his time would be free for his own work. There would be no monthly 'Comment' hanging over him, and his name would be associated with half a dozen or more good books a year.

The idea that he might want to settle permanently in America had also tempted him, but only briefly. He liked Americans, and one region of the country – northern California – impressed him as a haven for a life devoted to beauty and art. But he needed the stimulation of a large city with a colourful and exciting literary life, and that could be found in America only in New York, three thousand miles from the shores of California. Other places closer to New York appealed to him – Cape Cod and Connecticut, for example – but they were too expensive for him. The idea of living in the city itself was rejected: in addition to being expensive, it was much too stimulating. Given his particular weaknesses, he knew that he would never get any meaningful work done in New York. After his visit he remarked, 'One thing only seems to me impossible in New York – to write well'; and he laid the blame on the city's 'glowing, blooming and stimulating material perfection', which 'over-excites the mind, causing it to precipitate into wit and conversation those ideas which might have set into literature. Wit and wisecrack, not art, are the thorny flowers on this rocky island, this concrete Capri.' What crippled his art in London would paralyse it in New York. The longer he stayed in New York the better London began to look: 'When "fabulous", "for Chris' sakes", "it stinks", "way off the beam" and "Bourbon over ice" roar off our lips, and when we begin to notice with distaste the Europeanism of others – it's time for flight, for dripping plane-trees, misty mornings, the grizzling circle of hypercritical friends, the fecund London inertia where nothing stirs but the soul.'[26]

## II

Unfortunately, the English climate Connolly returned to was much harsher than anyone could have expected. Heavy snow fell in London, and piled up in great drifts all over Britain. By the end of January the nation was almost at a standstill. High winds, sub-freezing temperatures, and a severe fuel shortage made life miserable. It was the worst winter for more than fifty years, and drastic restrictions had to be imposed on transport and electricity. Pressure in the gas mains was so weak that many people did not bother to light a fire.

In the *Daily Mail* Harold Nicolson commented on the novel sensation of having to wear gloves while working at the typewriter; in theatres the audiences sat bundled against the cold while the actors shivered; at night a partial blackout in the streets left pedestrians feeling as though the war years had not ended. In the middle of February the fuel crisis became so bad that the government decided to shut down the BBC's Third Programme and to suspend, for a fortnight, the production of all magazines – nearly 500 titles were covered by the order. Though this included such important national weeklies as the *New Statesman* and the *Spectator*, the government reasoned that the periodical press was a non-essential industry, and that even its relatively low consumption of power was unjustified in a national emergency. No exception was made, not even for small literary magazines; the March issue of *Horizon* had to be cancelled.

Nothing could have prevented the brutal winter weather, but many people were convinced that the nation's fuel problems were the fault of poor planning by the government. Throughout Britain, housing, food, and many other basic goods and materials were in short supply, yet all the Labour government seemed able to do was to impose tighter rationing and ask for further sacrifices. Wartime rationing had not ended; in 1947 almost all important food products were still rationed. Adults were allowed only one egg a week, and the weekly allowance of meat was a mere shilling's worth. Connolly had started out with great hopes for the new government, but his enthusiasm had begun to fade by 1946; after suffering through the winter of 1947, he lost all patience with Labour. His disenchantment was made clear in 'Comment' that summer. After expressing his opinion that 'the honeymoon between literature and action, once so promising, is over', he went on to criticise the government directly, pointing in particular to its lack of support for literature and art: 'The fact remains that a Socialist government, besides doing practically nothing to help artists and writers (unless the closing down of magazines during the fuel crisis can be interpreted as an aid to incubation), has also quite failed to stir up either intellect or imagination; the English renaissance, whose false dawn we have so enthusiastically greeted, is further away than ever.'[27]

There was also a personal sorrow associated with the winter crisis: his father died at the end of February. The major had turned seventy-five earlier that month, and had been in poor health since the previous autumn, when he had suffered a bad case of flu. When the snows and cold temperatures arrived in January, he was largely confined to his room at the Glendower Hotel in South Kensington, and during the worst weeks of the fuel shortages he did not use his gas fire because the pressure was so low. He died in his sleep on the night of 26 February, and his body was discovered the next morning when a young colleague from the Natural History Museum came to visit him. When Connolly later went to look over his father's belongings, he found the room painfully cold. He explained in a long letter to his mother in South Africa, 'I really think he was a victim of this endless cold spell and fuel shortage etc. as much as a bird that is frozen to death – at 75 and after his flu in the autumn I expect he had very little resistance.'[28]

Arrangements were made to bury him in Bath, the town of his birth, and on the day of the funeral there was a terrible snowstorm. The only people in attendance were Connolly, Lys, a young woman from the Museum, a curate, and a verger. 'The grave was so deep,' Connolly wrote to his mother, 'cut right through the Bath stone, and the coffin looked quite small at the bottom of it. It was like being left as a little boy at a new school. I thought – such a final hopeless parting.' After being outdoors in the storm, Connolly went down with a cold; as he suffered through the next several days, he thought a great deal about his father. The more he thought, the greater his sense of guilt became. He regretted that they had not been on closer terms, and he felt sorry that his father's life had been so 'dismal'. He told his mother, 'Of course his love for you was the great emotion of his life but I think he would have been happier without the conflict between his love of a living person and his hoarding, collecting, cataloguing passion for dead objects.'

When Connolly sent the news to Jean in France, she wrote immediately to give him her sympathy, but she also reminded him that his father had never been easy to get on with. 'Don't let the feelings of guilt you speak of increase your misery,' she wrote, 'after all, he was a sad and pathetic old man but he was often not v. nice, either to you or to your mother.'[29] Towards the end of his life, Connolly wrote about the 'chilling accuracy' of the major's scientific mind, and then, ironically, he went on to apply some of that same cold 'accuracy' to this simple descriptive fragment – 'A soldier and conchologist, whose voice I hear whenever I clear my throat.'[30]

One month before his father's death, Connolly heard that the French government would award him the Legion of Honour in the summer. Such recognition was gratifying and helped to lift his spirits during the gloomy winter. The French ambassador told him he was being given the decoration because of his 'services to French culture during the war'.[31] Connolly understood very well the irony that this recognition for wartime service came not from his own country but from a foreign power. Given the actions of the British government that winter, one could hardly expect medals to be handed out to a writer and editor in the 'expendable' periodical press. When the paper ration for magazines was cut by 10% in 1947, Connolly wondered whether the government had gone from neglecting culture to plotting an outright assault on it.

The Labour government's conduct inspired one of Connolly's best satires: a 'Comment', written late in 1947, which purports to be a public speech by a spokesman for the national 'offensive against Art'. The voice begins in a light and comic tone as he recounts the recent battles which have been successfully waged against 'the enemy' forces of art and literature – the 'daring fuel raid', for example, which 'put their dangerous radio station, Third Programme, out of action for a considerable period'.[32] His hopes for total victory are running high, but he cautions that no one should 'underestimate the foe', that it is still premature 'to talk of a break-through or to indulge in wishful thinking about a complete mopping-up of art and artists'. The speaker reminds his audience, however, that 'the morale of our enemy is sinking fast', and advises that the best strategy for the immediate future is to launch, with the help of the general public, a new round of psychological warfare. What is needed is a new 'hate' campaign directed against artists themselves. The public must rally behind the campaign and create a climate of hatred which will make cultural life intolerable. Connolly's satire becomes increasingly bitter:

I want to warn you against the Artist: I want you to learn to hate him like a whale. We've made short work of the whales lately (cheers); it's no secret that there soon won't be a whale left. (Loud cheers.) Radar, depth charges, blubber bombs – their number's up. Why is it that we all love a journalist, a civil servant, a Public Relations Officer, or a Member of Parliament when we see one? Yet we all hate instinctively an artist! I'm going to call them 'bats' to you, because they squeak, because they have no morals and hang upside down and stink and spend the day in a terrible fug and look revoltingly like human beings. (Laughter.) I'm going to appeal to you to rid our island workshop of our flitter-mice friends – every one of them . . .

The speaker's powerful tirade brings to mind the world of *Nineteen Eighty-Four*, the first draft of which Orwell was finishing at Jura when this 'Comment' appeared in *Horizon*. Working separately, hundreds of miles apart, the two writers had strikingly similar visions of a future plagued by demagogues and philistines. The speaker's attempt to portray artists as loathsome sub-human creatures and his efforts to whip up hatred against them have much in common with the 'Two Minutes Hate' in Orwell's work. Like Big Brother, Connolly's speaker favours censorship and the reduction of language to slogans and jargon. One of his slogans is 'Hatred begins in the home', and the speaker looks forward to the day when 'the book and periodical [are] entirely superseded by the bulletin and communique'. Smugly, he notes that his scheme is moving ahead quickly: 'And I'm glad to see that you're reading less. I'm told that books are getting nearly as hard to sell now as before the war.'

The regulations, shortages, and cuts of the post-war period took their toll on Connolly, making him increasingly reluctant to carry on with *Horizon*. The austerity of the times made it harder for him to write, or so he became convinced. In 1946 he had promised Cass Canfield and Hamish Hamilton that his book on Flaubert would soon be finished, but after his return from America he was unable to do much with it. Part of the problem was that he had changed the scope of the book, and was now intending to make it a study of Baudelaire as well as Flaubert. This plan not only created a great deal of new work for him but presented difficult and confusing organisational problems. He tended to play down these complications, attributing much of the blame for his slow progress to the privations and tensions of post-war life. To Canfield, he explained, 'For a European it is just as impossible to work now as it was at the time of Munich.'[33] Of course, bad times often produce great books, but he was in no mood to think philosophically about his problems. In his 'Comment' for April 1947, he stated his case against the Age of Austerity in practical terms. 'There is no deterrent to aesthetic adventure like a prolonged struggle with domestic difficulties, food shortages, cold, ill-health and money worries.' He was even more emphatic in a letter to his mother: 'Life is really too difficult – making money in London is like being a prisoner who can send out for meals.'[34]

### III

Peter Watson missed the worst of the English winter, because he stayed in New York until the end of February. He was happy during his long American visit, particularly in February, when he fell in love ten days before he was to leave. He was invited to dinner at the apartment of Parker Tyler's friend John Myers, who was an editorial assistant at *View*. Dining with them was Myers's room-mate, an aspiring poet of twenty-four named Waldemar Hansen. The attraction between Watson and Hansen proved irresistible, and by the end of the night they had become lovers.

The son of immigrant parents, Waldemar Hansen was born and grew up in a poor neighbourhood of Buffalo, in New York State. For a brief time he attended the University of Buffalo, but he moved to New York City in 1944, where he supported himself with a wartime job at a chemical plant. He was an avid reader of history and literature, and after the war he studied poetry writing in workshops at the Poetry Center of the YM & YWHA, on Lexington Avenue, making friends with several young writers there, including the poet James Merrill, then just beginning his career. Outgoing and confident, he made friends easily, and was a quick, enthusiastic conversationalist who enjoyed serious discussions about art and literature. He was drawn to Peter Watson from the moment they were introduced. As he recalled many years later, 'Peter had a wonderfully engaging way about him, a winsome way of smiling, a way of making people feel that he was absolutely on their wavelength. Early in our first evening together it was quite clear that something was transpiring between us. In the course of dinner we had both fallen quite silent, with John Myers doing all the talking, and Peter was simply looking at me mutely, and I was looking back at him. It really was love at first sight. Suffice it to say that Peter stayed the night.'[35]

Watson spent almost every moment in Hansen's company. The affair was intense on both sides, in part because so little time remained before Watson returned home. He asked Hansen to live with him in London, but the younger man was reluctant to accept the offer. He had never been abroad and was more than a little intimidated by the thought of going to live in a strange country, leaving behind his family and friends in America. He was also wary of becoming a rich man's 'kept boy'. When they first met, he knew nothing of Watson's wealth or social background, but he soon learned the relevant details, and this made him think twice about the position that he − a house painter's son from Buffalo − might occupy in the life of a wealthy Englishman, the younger son of a baronet. Watson put his offer another way: 'Then come stay with me at least for the summer,' he said. 'If you do only that, I will give you a summer that you will never forget.'[36] Hansen accepted and planned to join Watson in London during the second half of April.

Watson arrived in England early in March. During the next month, while he awaited the day Hansen would join him, he wrote almost daily letters to his new American love. For many of his casual friends in England, Watson was an enigmatic, elusive personality who guarded his privacy and took pains not to reveal his feelings; but in his early letters to Hansen, all of which have survived, he wrote with extraordinary candour about his emotional life. The circumstances of their relationship encouraged him to go into detail about his feelings: he was writing to someone thousands of miles away who lived in an entirely different world and knew relatively little about him. Many of his letters stress the difficulty of explaining his world to an American. By 1947 he had become as disenchanted with life in England as Connolly was, and in his first letter to Hansen, he wrote 'You do not know about the English problem and what a hell each return to this dying country means ... Some day I will explain.' (Later he remarked, 'There is some terrible psychological pain which gets me every time I get back to England. It goes back to the times when I used to race abroad to get away from my family I think.')[37]

Watson was in London for only a few days before he went to Paris 'to pack up' his belongings in the Rue du Bac apartment. He was giving up his lease there, under pressure from the landlord, who had been unable to persuade Denham Fouts to leave. Watson was not looking forward to confronting Fouts again, especially since he knew that he would have to tell him about his new lover. 'I am rather worried about his reactions,' he wrote to Hansen, 'as I must tell him everything, and he is still more attached to me than to anyone else and is likely to stay so.'[38] Watson did indeed tell 'everything', although it is doubtful that Fouts fully understood the news, so ravaged was his mind by drugs. On 28 March Watson wrote Hansen a remarkable account of his relationship with Fouts, going back to the time when they first met. It is worth quoting at length.

> Poor Denham. The situation is tragic. He senses that the worst for him has happened as I told him that I really cared about you. I have plenty of guilt about him, although it is not justified. I cannot love people I do not really respect, and I cannot respect the life he leads here. He still loves me, probably more than ever now since I have gone beyond his reach, and I suppose he will [go on loving me] until we have been completely separated for a year or so, which must happen I think now.
>
> I will tell you about him. We met in 1933, about, in a nightclub. He took me back to his hotel where he gave himself cocaine injections. He left for N.Y. on a tramp steamer, we corresponded and he came back to live with me in London. He had no confidence in anyone – this stimulated me and I thought if I took trouble he would [have confidence] in me. He was and is still terribly neurotic (his drawings are nightmares of frustrations and obscenities). We never shared any intellectual interests whatsoever and [he] always resented that side of me. Sexually he always liked and still likes boys about 14–16, which I could never understand and which horrifies me now. I became for him of course the responsible parent who just provided him with money. He never did and never has told me how he first came to Europe. Later I found he joined the Hitler Jugend in Germany and was a boy friend of Richtofen the Nazi ace. However, for better or worse there it was. We got thro' the years previous to the war somehow, he was still taking drugs and in 1940 left for U.S.A. . . . .
>
> When he came back to Paris I knew my feelings for him were dead altho' I will always feel affection for him in his way. He lapsed into a sort of pre-war cocktail haute pederaste life which still goes on in Paris . . . I have implored him to do something, appealed to his conscience, my wishes, everything, have done everything except stop him having money, as my god I do really believe in freedom and free decision. I am racked by wondering what I could have done that I didn't do. Of course I can [do] everything except love him, but when I did [love him] there was no empathy between us. Going to bed is a physical act with him, no more. He is stuck at 16 years old and resists any attempt to grow. And yet I feel it must be my fault, somehow.

There is an agonising sense of ambivalence in this letter. On the one hand, Watson wants to judge Fouts harshly and leave him alone – a free existential man – to suffer the consequences of his appalling behaviour. On the other, he is tempted to withhold judgment, even to show sympathy, and he cannot help feeling that it is he, not Fouts, who has failed.

Watson obviously thought that in Waldemar Hansen he had found a second chance, had discovered another young American to whom he could offer his affection and patronage; and this time there could be some real substance to the relationship: poetry, art, and ideas – all the things Fouts could not respond to.

Watson was in Paris for three weeks, and was able to remove most of his things from the Rue du Bac. Fouts had no intention of vacating the apartment, because he could not believe that Watson would have the willpower to force him out or that the lease would be terminated. On this last point, he was mistaken. Watson gave up the lease, and the problem of evicting Fouts was left to the hapless landlord. Several months later, after taking the matter through the French courts, the landlord regained possession of his apartment, and his unwanted tenant moved from Paris to Rome. One of the last people to stay with Fouts in the Rue du Bac was a young writer to whom he was briefly attached, a fellow Southerner visiting Paris for the first time – Truman Capote.

Watson's moods in his letters from Paris vacillate sharply. One moment deeply despondent and confused, his spirits suddenly lift, and he sounds bright and confident. 'I go up and down like a pre-penicillin pneumonia temperature chart,' he admitted to Hansen.[39] His troubles with Fouts left him feeling depressed about their past life together and uncertain about his chances of making a new life with Hansen. 'My idealism is so ridiculous and so strong,' he wrote, 'that when I see a possibility of realisation I get very scared. I give myself a certain amount of punishment, but I am only afraid of it from you in so far as I am progressively sensitive to you and therefore defenceless.'[40] In another letter he expressed his feelings like this: 'I get terrified by the thought of making a failure of any relationship as I can't bear the ensuing loneliness like I might have done once . . . I have perhaps become rather cynical but it is only then as a wildly struggling defence against protecting all I really believe in and hope for, for which I dare not risk any disappointment.' Ironically, immediately after giving this candid explanation of his deepest fears, Watson wrote, 'Forgive me talking about myself because I really hate myself so much and I rarely think about myself, but I wanted to explain a little to you.'[41]

In other letters he is overflowing with excitement and anticipation at the thought of greeting Hansen later in April. Writing to him on 1 April, he is playful and light-hearted. It is late at night, and he has just come back from the cinema:

How are you? I think of you with a real tenderness tonight and would so like to laugh and talk with you and put my fingers through your hair and kiss your toes, but I can't so it's no use worrying. Anyways it's not so long now. Perhaps you'll *hate* the old world – the wicked old world corrupts another fresh young American? I wonder. No, I *do not* find you vulgar but quite authentic from the top of your crew cut to the flat of your heels and almost upsettingly stimulating around the knees. Frivolous? Perhaps but it is fun to chuckle away by oneself for once. It is rare because I often feel so gloomy.

It was the 'fresh' American look which Watson found so irresistible. Even though Hansen was twenty-four at the time, he had the appearance of an eager young undergraduate at a typical American college – a vigorous, healthy look accentuated by his crew cut and casual American dress. That he came from Buffalo – an American city so far removed from the Old World – helped to complete the image of 'uncorrupted youth', at least in Watson's imagination. On the night of 1 April, he was so carried away by this image that he lost his English reserve and signed his letter, not with his usual 'Peter', but with the boyish (and very American) 'Pete'.

At the end of the first week in April, Watson returned to London. To reduce Hansen's travelling time, Watson had given him the money for a flight to Shannon in Ireland, and they planned to meet there before going to London together. Hansen's arrival in Ireland was set for 19 April, by which time the long winter was over. 'Spring has appeared to welcome you,' Watson wrote, 'in fact you will land on a carpet of primroses and a chorus of thrushes.' As the moment approached, he became more and more nervous, worrying that his young American would want to go straight back home at the first sight of London's shabby, darkened streets. He confessed in one letter, 'I am horrified by London,' and then added pessimistically, 'Perhaps it is a great mistake to get you here at all. You may identify me with this drab gloom. There isn't a single street lamp even guttering.'[42]

Hansen and Watson spent a few days together at a small hotel on the outskirts of Limerick before making the short flight from Dublin to London. By the end of April they were settled in Watson's flat in Palace Gate, and Hansen was trying to adjust to life in London. He was indeed appalled by the appearance of the city, writing to John Myers that it was 'monstrously Victorian', but he was happy living with Watson in their relatively modern flat, and he began to make new friends in London.[43] One was Lucian Freud, who took him to see the National Gallery. Hansen sent this description of a visit to Freud's studio: 'There is a zebra-head on the wall, an old fashioned phonograph with a huge horn, and a live falcon which swoops around the room and alights on the master's wrist! I think he is going to do a drawing of me, and I'm rather intrigued to see what I'll look like after going through that strange personal prism.'[44] (Freud completed the drawing later that autumn.)

Another person who was drawn to Hansen right from the start was Sonia. They visited the Gargoyle Club in Soho, and went to the cinema together – Sonia liked films, especially those starring Humphrey Bogart. Shortly after they met, Hansen showed her some of his poetry and, partly because she liked him, she responded sympathetically by accepting one of his poems for *Horizon*. Although it was a modest effort, Sonia told him that it was 'by far the best thing available in the office,' and she rushed to include it in the May number, where it was featured at the front of the magazine.[45] Connolly and Lys were on holiday in France and Sonia evidently felt free to make this editorial decision. Connolly never voiced any objection; he later commissioned Hansen, on two separate occasions, to review books for *Horizon* (the reviews, both concerned with American poetry, were published in September 1947 and January 1948). From time to time, Hansen also acted as an editorial reader at *Horizon*, at the invitation of both Connolly and Sonia. He was a capable writer, but his acceptance was undoubtedly helped by the fact that he was Peter Watson's lover, though Watson would never have asked for any special consideration.

As Watson had promised, the summer of 1947 was quite special for Hansen. Early in June the two men left London to tour the Continent, going first to Paris, where they spent two weeks. The weather was warm and dry, and Watson was feeling uncommonly energetic; he rented bicycles and they went out cycling in the streets of the city every day. They visited museums and Watson's favourite galleries, and in the evenings they almost always went out – to plays, nightclubs, or even the opera. They ate at the best restaurants, though Watson was careful to limit his intake of wine and to avoid rich foods. At the end of June they went to the South of France and spent July there, in Cannes, Nice, and Monte Carlo. August found them in Switzerland, visiting Zurich and St Moritz, then they moved south again to Milan, Florence, Rome, and Capri. Early in September they were back in Paris for several days, then returned to London, to be greeted by rain and fog. Their glorious summer was over, but the relationship continued, and Hansen decided to live with Watson in London. 'I haven't got much to say about love yet,' Hansen wrote at the end of a long letter to Myers in September. 'I'm too busy relaxing in it.'[46]

## IV

By September the problem of shortages in Britain took another turn for the worse, and the government decided to tighten controls yet again. Further cuts were made in the rations of meat and butter, the already meagre bacon ration was cut in half, the basic petrol ration was suspended, and stiff currency restrictions were imposed. Dining out was no great pleasure, because of a five-shilling limit on the price of a restaurant meal. Like many other people, Hansen and Watson supplemented their rations by asking friends in America to send food parcels. In October, John Myers sent them a large box of powdered milk, jam, cooking oil, fruit, rice, and tinned meat. At Sussex Place, Connolly received similar shipments, dispatched by sympathetic friends and admirers in both America and France. He was delighted with these gifts, exclaiming in one letter to his mother, 'Cheeses, butter, tongues, even avocado pears arrive from my American friends, *foie gras* from my French ones!'[47]

Many of Connolly's parcels came in response to an extraordinary full-page notice which appeared in the September number of *Horizon*. It was directed to American readers (the special American issue was due in October) and at the top of the page, in big bold letters, were the words 'Our American Begging Bowl'. It was an appeal for food parcels. Readers were told, 'If you have liked anything in *Horizon* this year, send the author a food parcel. Orange juice, tomato juice, butter, bacon, rice, tea, honey and tinned meats are all particularly acceptable to brain workers. They take two months to arrive so you could begin now.' Although he was quite serious about this proposal, Connolly also wanted to use it to poke fun at Labour bureaucrats and to cause the government a little embarrassment abroad. It was a small way to protest against the bureaucrats' determination to impose austerity on the nation. 'We English,' Connolly's notice began, 'are never so happy as with our backs to the wall, and an understanding Providence has ordained that we need seldom abandon our position.'

This was typical Connolly humour, dry and irreverent, but much to his surprise it brought him a stinging public rebuke from one of the nation's largest newspapers – the *News Chronicle*. On 26 September the paper told its one and a half million readers that Connolly's 'Begging Bowl' had compromised the dignity of the entire nation. Ignoring the fact that *Horizon* reached only a few thousand readers in America, the paper exaggerated the importance of the notice, and completely missed the tongue-in-cheek tone of the appeal. As far as the *News Chronicle* was concerned, Connolly was playing up to rich Americans and letting down his countrymen by appearing weak and supplicating in a national crisis. Moral outrage reached its peak when the paper accused Connolly of trying to 'barter the pride and honour of England for a tin of Spam'.

The paper obviously enjoyed making an example out of Connolly, and no doubt expected him to be intimidated by the attack. (For good measure, another blast appeared in the paper on 30 September.) Connolly did not back down. In December he printed another version of the announcement, and in the first sentence taunted his critics: 'The response to our American Begging Bowl (in spite of opposition from journalists and military men, whose moral indignation savours of the Fifth Form at St Dominic's) has been most favourable.' With that, he let the matter drop, but for months afterwards the food parcels continued to come to *Horizon*, many addressed to Connolly himself. A rumour soon spread that the epicurean editor was sampling items from tempting parcels addressed to other writers. Years later Edmund Wilson asked Peter Watson whether their friend had indeed taken food not intended for him. 'No,' Watson said cautiously, 'only the *foie gras*.'[48]

While the *News Chronicle* was denouncing Connolly's pursuit of Spam, *Horizon* published one of its most impressive issues in October: titled 'Art on the American *Horizon*'. At the time, it was difficult for both American and British readers to appreciate fully the excellence of this number, because several of the best contributions were from writers then relatively unknown or obscure. There was a brilliant article on 'American Advertising' by a young lecturer at the University of Toronto named Herbert Marshall McLuhan; a short story ('The Imaginary Jew') by an obscure poet named John Berryman; and an excerpt from the first chapter of a novel-in-progress called 'The Invisible Man', by a young black writer named Ralph Ellison. This was the first time any part of Ellison's great novel was published, either in America or Britain (the finished work did not come out in book form until 1952.) There was a magnificent long poem 'The Owl in the Sarcophagus' – Wallace Stevens's recently completed elegy for his friend, Henry Church; and an essay on American architecture by Philip Johnson, written two years before his 'Glass House' in New Canaan, Connecticut, began to win him fame, and important commissions, as a major American architect. More-established talents were also represented: poems by Auden ('Music Is International') and Cummings (the delightful 'to start, to hesitate; to stop'); four photographs of Chicago by Walker Evans; and an essay on Los Angeles by Christopher Isherwood. And there was Connolly's 'Comment', which described in detail his recent visit to America.

The issue was enthusiastically received in the United States. One of the few dissenting voices came from *Time*, which took exception to Connolly saying in 'Comment': 'The American way assumes a world without God, yet a world in which happiness is obtainable.' Positioned in the front line of the Cold War against godless Communism, *Time* could not let a statement like that go by without objecting that it was the distorted view of 'esthete Editor Cyril Connolly, peering beyond his ice-blue *Horizon*'.[49] *Time* also disapproved of the magazine's survey of contemporary American art. Clement Greenberg, author of the survey, had praised Jackson Pollock as the 'most powerful painter in America', but *Time* had great fun ridiculing this idea, and implied that 'Britain's highbrow magazine' had been duped into accepting a crank's view of American art.[50] So much for Connolly's 'brave little cultural candle', as *Time* had called *Horizon* at the end of the war. (Connolly later slipped into 'Comment' a satirical reference, recommending that weary travellers on long journeys pick up a 'copy of *Time* in case the sleeping pill doesn't work'.)[51]

A few days before the American issue came out, Evelyn Waugh offered *Horizon* the chance to publish *The Loved One*, his short novel about the mortuary business in southern California. Waugh had visited Los Angeles earlier in the year, not long after Connolly's stay there, and had been fascinated by the grotesque burial customs at Forest Lawn cemetery. When he returned to England, he constructed a story satirising the bizarre lives of the workers at Whispering Glades [Forest Lawn] and the Happier Hunting Ground, a pet cemetery. Connolly liked the work's 'Swiftian satire', and accepted Waugh's offer. They agreed that the story would appear as a separate number of *Horizon*, and Connolly suggested that the best time to publish it would be early in the coming year. 'I am keeping February for The Loved One,' he wrote to Waugh, 'as being likely to be the gloomiest month on the Horizon, though some find March worse.'[52]

While the manuscript was awaiting publication, Peter Watson read it and, although he did not usually contradict Connolly's editorial decisions, he reacted so strongly against Waugh's story that he wrote a harsh criticism of it. 'It just lacks all human feeling,' Watson explained. 'How [Waugh] hates everyone! I should not wish to be him. I just don't understand how he can be religious in any way. I am sorry a whole issue has to be devoted to it. It is just not on any one's side: certainly not God's! It's all so pointless. But there it is, I have to express my opinion and I reacted strongly with a horror which was certainly not the horror communicated as tragedy or as a work of art.'[53] This criticism upset Connolly, who wanted Watson's approval and who tried to explain to his friend why The Loved One worked as a satire. But Watson's mind was made up: 'I don't much like satire,' he said, 'because I think it is all too often used as a mask to cover an inner emptiness, and this is the reaction I have to the Waugh story.'[54]

This was one of the rare occasions when the views of the two editors were fundamentally opposed, but even in this instance, when his feelings were so strongly aroused, Watson did not pretend that he would have the final word on the subject. He wanted to make his views known, but was careful to remind Connolly, 'My opinion about something is not a prohibition.'[55] Accordingly, The Loved One appeared in Horizon in February 1948 as a complete issue, exactly as Waugh and Connolly had arranged. The number was well received, and Waugh was pleased with the result, boasting to Randolph Churchill that the story's appearance in Horizon had helped to raise his standing in London 'highbrow circles'.[56] In the magazine's introduction to the work Connolly called it 'one of the most perfect short novels of the last ten years'. Later, he qualified his praise a little. Writing to his friend Enid Bagnold, he remarked that The Loved One fell short of being a masterpiece because Waugh had failed to develop the love affair between Aimee – the Whispering Glades cosmetician – and Dennis – the expatriate Englishman employed at the Happier Hunting Ground. 'To be a masterpiece,' he observed, 'the love affair would have had to come to life in a desperate "Wuthering Heights" kind of way, but you can see that it is the cemetery with which Evelyn is in love and not the "loved ones".'[57]

# NINE

# GUILLOTINE WITH A CONSCIENCE
## 1947–1948

### I

Near the end of 1947 *Horizon* discovered a new writer, working in the magazine's Bloomsbury neighbourhood. His name was Angus Wilson. He was in his early thirties and firmly established in a job at the British Museum; except in school magazines, he had never had any work published. He had begun writing short stories the previous year, and by the autumn of 1947 had finished about a dozen. He thought of his writing as primarily a hobby, something to occupy the hours when he was not doing his 'real' work at the Museum. However, he allowed a friend, Robin Ironside, to show a few stories to Connolly and, to his surprise, *Horizon* accepted not one but two of them. The first – 'Mother's Sense of Fun' – appeared in November 1947, and the second – 'Crazy Crowd' – five months later. A publisher, Secker and Warburg, was soon asking to see more of his work. He submitted a collection and the firm published it in March 1949 as *The Wrong Set*. The book was so popular it had to be reprinted twice in the following three months.

Wilson went on to enjoy a very successful literary career, both as novelist and a writer of short stories. It could be argued that this career would have been launched without *Horizon*'s help, that even if Connolly had rejected his stories someone else would surely have 'discovered' him. But for many writers who encounter early rejection, there is no 'later on'. They give up, and turn to other things. In the post-war years, when there were so few outlets in England for good fiction, one or two rejections might well have persuaded Angus Wilson that his stories were only a diversion from the tedium of his 'safe' job at the British Museum. He has acknowledged that he would have been an easy prey to such thoughts. Many years after the appearance of his first story in *Horizon*, he wrote that he owed Connolly 'a great debt', explaining, 'If I had not been chosen by you for publication in *Horizon* it is almost certain that my writing would have petered out as the unfertilised hobby of a man who was looking for some means of self expression but never found it.'[1]

In the depressed literary and social climate of the late Forties, Connolly was not so sure that a young writer had much to gain from being discovered. In pessimistic moods he wondered why anyone would want to pursue a literary career in a country where the rewards were so few. His fictional creation of the period – the editor Brinkley in the unfinished novel 'Happy Deathbeds' – broods on 'the dismal and decorative decay of European culture', and questions whether a literary magazine can accomplish anything in such circumstances: 'Helping young writers? But to what did he help them? To jog on for a year or two in the vain hope that they were going to make an income by their writing while the opportunity for earning any other kind of living was inexorably withdrawn from them. J. Brinkley, BA, Instructor in creative writing. Candidates prepared for the British Council and the administrative departments of the BBC.'[2]

More and more writers were being pressed into the service of 'culture diffusion', which had claimed many names from *Horizon*'s list of English contributors; even one of the founding editors had succumbed to its charms. In the autumn of 1947 Stephen Spender went to serve for a year on the faculty of Sarah Lawrence College in New York. In 1948 Connolly wrote, 'Every writer I know under sixty (except one or two prosperous novelists) is ruining his talent through hack-work and part-time jobs: there is always a fistula through which the juices of genius are leaking away into some disgusting receptacle.'[3]

Young writers could bail out before it was too late, but what about the deserving man of letters who has pursued his career into middle age and discovered that it is too late to turn back? To comfort such people, Connolly included in the January 1948 *Horizon* a description of a new American foundation called the 'Society for the Redemption of Middle-aged Hacks'. The benefactor of this enlightened institution is one Filmore Van Rensselaer Crutch, a millionaire public-utilities baron who has decided that his charity dollars will bring the best return by investing them in grants to worthy middle-aged hacks. He will have nothing to do with the notion that his cash might be better spent on young writers. 'I'd rather pick an old car of a good make off the dump than buy a new Cheapie,' the practical Mr Crutch reasons. Once the foundation has found its men, twenty thousand dollars is spent to give each of them a year off. The wife and children are sent away; old bills, back taxes, and unearned publishers' advances are paid off; they are given new clothes, spending money, and are sent off to do nothing but relax and enjoy life in places like Paris and the Bahamas. This is a difficult period for the hacks, who have a hard time breaking with the routine of their old lives. 'But who'll review the gardening books for the *Financial Times*,' they are sometimes heard to protest.

After this year of rest, the hacks are given two more years in a sunny clime to write the books they have always promised to write. 'The Sicilian spring, the Alpine summer, the Venetian autumn pass in a flash! The book is finished, the publisher's crazy about it.' Although the scheme has not been in operation for long, it has enjoyed such success that several of its redeemed hacks have gone on to capture major literary prizes for their recent works. A modern patron, Mr Crutch asks for nothing in return except 'the satisfaction of a job well done – of seeing these poor human wrecks saved from their platitudes'.

Lacking the benefit of a three-year grant from an amiable Mr Crutch, Connolly spent the winter of 1947–1948 in sunless London, but his work at *Horizon* afforded him ample time to embark on his plan for his own literary 'redemption'. He abandoned his book on Flaubert and concentrated on writing his story about Brinkley, hoping to create a novel which would accomplish for him what *Brideshead Revisited* and *Animal Farm* had done for the careers of Waugh and Orwell. He had no trouble creating the mood of comic despair for the story and was able to write some excellent set pieces, but after about fifty pages the whole story began to break down. There was no coherent plot to connect the strands of Brinkley's complicated literary life and except for Brinkley himself there were no strong characters.

From the ruins of this fictional tale, Connolly might have been able to salvage enough material for a sequel to either *Enemies of Promise* or *The Unquiet Grave* – another freewheeling experiment in mixing auto-biography with meditations on literature and literary life. Instead, he kept on struggling to turn himself into a novelist, and the frustration of that effort made him more and more dissatisfied with himself, his career, and everything else in his life. His success in the first half of the Forties was not enough to satisfy him. What good was that previous success if he could not go on to become a real writer – by which he meant a novelist or poet – instead of the hybrid he had turned out to be: the celebrated man of letters? This feeling is reflected in a description of his fictional alter ego, Brinkley: 'Hating blame, he yet found praise all dust and ashes.'[4]

It was Connolly's nature, of course, to find fault with success and to seek out new sources of *angst*, but in this case the crisis was genuine.

He believed that he had to turn out a first-rate novel to prove himself as a writer. In a practical sense, he was right, because the prevailing standards of his day, and of ours, tend to rate the novelist higher than the gifted writer of 'creative' non-fiction. The cost of ignoring these standards was high: even if he went on refining the techniques of *Enemies of Promise* in half a dozen more books, he could not expect great fame as an artist unless he created a substantial work of fiction. It was beyond his powers to create such a work, but this failure was not in itself tragic. The tragedy was that he felt obliged to make the attempt; it was a waste of his talent, and his worst enemy of promise.

There were few indications in his public life that anything was amiss; he seemed to be making the most of his success. His publishers were enthusiastic about his work, *Horizon*'s reputation was higher than ever, and the circle of Connolly's friends and admirers was constantly growing. Sussex Place was the scene of one dazzling literary party after another: in the early spring of 1948 there was a large party for Auden, who had arrived from America on a brief visit. Among the guests were John Betjeman, Elizabeth Bowen, Lucian Freud, and Louis MacNeice. (The evening did not go entirely well. Auden's lover Chester Kallman was there, and Connolly indiscreetly asked him, 'How does it feel to be the male Alice B. Toklas?' Neither Kallman nor Auden appreciated the joke.) [5]

At the end of 1948 Connolly gave the grandest of all his parties at Sussex Place, inviting some seventy guests to celebrate T. S. Eliot's Nobel Prize. Since the end of the war Connolly's relations with Eliot had been good. He saw quite a lot of John Hayward, who shared a flat with the poet, and Hayward's good opinion had helped to raise his standing with Eliot. Everyone was in a particularly good mood on the night of the party. There was plenty of champagne, and by the end of the evening Connolly and Hayward were reciting 'Sweeney Agonistes' for Eliot, who surprised everyone when he responded with a song, a rendition of 'Under the Bamboo Tree'. (A few weeks after the party, Connolly wrote to his mother, 'I have so many friends here, it is like my last year at Eton, I am becoming a genial witch-doctor to the tribe.') [6]

As usual, it was Lys who did most of the work for these parties, planning the meals, doing the shopping, and preparing the food. She worked so hard that she was often too busy to see much of the guests, and her efforts did not always receive the attention or credit they deserved. Managing domestic and social life at Sussex Place was a demanding job, especially since she also had her work at *Horizon*. She did not expect much recognition for herself; she was content to remain in the background of Connolly's life. She was devoted to him, and wanted to do as much as she could to help both him and *Horizon*. But by the time she turned thirty (in late 1947) she was dissatisfied with simply being his companion, someone who shared his surname by deed poll but who lacked all the formal ties of marriage. However, Connolly had finally decided to begin divorce proceedings against Jean, and was again promising Lys that he would marry her as soon as he was free. Clement Greenberg and Laurence Vail were named as co-respondents in the divorce, and among the evidence was a letter from Greenberg, 'admitting his association with my wife', as Connolly described it.[7]

The case took several months to work towards a final settlement, while Lys continued to be a wife to Connolly in every sense but the legal one. She was indispensable in helping him through two major difficulties which arose in 1948. The first involved his health. At the beginning of February he began to feel listless and run-down; his vision was blurred, his teeth were bothering him, he was putting on too much weight, and his nerves were bad. At night he had terrible dreams, and during the day his struggles with his writing left him feeling irritable and depressed. When he had been in a similar condition during the war, Lys had learned of a health clinic at Tring, in Hertfordshire, and had persuaded him to go there for treatment. He had come back in excellent shape; once again she persuaded him to go to the clinic.

He needed persuasion because the regimen at Tring was far from pleasant. The 'cure' took about three weeks and involved massages and other stimulants, but the unpleasant part was the diet – one orange a day. For Connolly it was as close to hell as one could come in this life, but it produced results. By the end of February he had shed twenty-five pounds and was feeling much better. He told Lys, 'But for you, I would have no eyes and no teeth'; but he was relieved to be free of Tring.[8] He described his impressions of the place for Enid Bagnold, who was thinking of going there for treatment: 'About Tring, I would say that it most certainly was hell unless you went with a friend. It is not just the fasting, but the enormous length of the days and nights without any meals to break them. I say the nights because it is quite impossible to sleep while fasting ... The clientèle are not only uninteresting but positively repelling. It is best to go when the weather is nice as one can then get away from the building in the afternoons and consequently from the people.'[9]

Almost immediately after his return from Tring, another crisis broke out. This time it involved *Horizon*. Together with the food and fuel shortages plaguing England, there was a severe housing shortage, especially in London, where so many homes had been damaged or lost during the German bombing. In March the London County Council served notice that *Horizon*'s office in Stephen Spender's former flat was needed for housing, and that the magazine would have to move elsewhere. Lys took it upon herself to find new quarters and discovered a perfect place for the magazine in a familiar location – Bedford Square. At number 53, a corner house, an architectural firm occupied the ground floor and basement but was willing to let two large rooms on the floor above. Lys arranged for *Horizon* to take over this space.

The LCC almost managed to prevent the agreement, but they were persuaded to let it go through, accepting a compromise which left them in control of the top two floors. Connolly had many fond memories of life in Bedford Square, and enthusiastically gave his approval to Lys's choice. Sonia was happy with the new location because it was only a short walk away from her flat in Percy Street. And Watson was so pleased that he removed from storage some of the best paintings in his pre-war collection and placed them around the walls.

The move to new quarters coincided with *Horizon*'s 'centenary': the appearance of its one-hundredth issue. Initially, Connolly had big plans for marking the occasion; as he explained in 'Comment', he began by inviting 'six eminent poets' to contribute to the number, but the response was discouraging. Only one, Edith Sitwell, was able to send him something; the other five told him they had no poems ready. Instead of accepting this as a piece of bad luck, Connolly chose to see it as a sign of hard times in the literary world. He did not mention any of the five by name, but he described them as 'hard-working officials, publishers, teachers, etc.', which could mean only one thing: they were all 'culture diffusionists', and in Connolly's view that explained why none had submitted a poem. They were all too busy, he wrote bitterly, 'selling culture for a living like the Aga Khan his bath water'. Such criticism was completely unjustified; it was provoked not by facts but by his private fears and frustrations. As he later admitted, he was 'trying to externalise a guilty sterility on to the world . . . I seemed to be raising up dummies in order to transfix them with a toy sword which penetrated only myself.'[10] Whatever the reason, it was unwise to begin using 'culture diffusionist' as an insult to individual writers; if he chose to keep that up, he would soon have a long list of enemies.

One 'eminent' poet who was probably not among Connolly's mysterious group of five was W. H. Auden. In the late Forties there was no shortage of his poetry in *Horizon*. Between 1947 and 1949, nine of his poems appeared in the magazine. One month before the centenary issue, Connolly published his 'Lament for a Lawgiver', and four months later 'In Praise of Limestone', one of the genuine literary masterpieces of the 1940s. Humphrey Carpenter, Auden's biographer, has suggested that there was a falling-out between the poet and Connolly over the joke about Chester Kallman and Alice B. Toklas, and that this breach lasted until the 1950s. This hardly seems likely because Auden continued sending poems to *Horizon* up to the final months of the magazine's life. Indeed, his last contribution (in November 1949) was 'Memorial for the City'.

At that time no poet in Britain was doing work which could match the verse coming from Auden's pen, but the quantity of bad, or simply mediocre, poetry which flowed into *Horizon* day after day was unrelenting, and did not make easy the job of sorting the worthy from the second-rate. Connolly estimated that the 'poetry drawer' collected an average of eighty new submissions each week. Many came from amateur poets who had been sending material to *Horizon* regularly, without success, for years; not only their names but the look of their manuscripts had become well known in the office. One used only green paper, another wrote only in mauve ink. 'In the end,' Connolly remarked, 'one rejects them by texture, smell, paperweave – heartlessly – because within a month they all will be back.'[11]

The question of whether *Horizon* would be around to receive these submissions was raised by Connolly in the centenary number. In 1942 he had told readers that the magazine might not last beyond its fiftieth issue. That number had appealed to him as a stopping point, but the length of the war and the magazine's popularity had kept *Horizon* alive for twice that many issues. His future plans were still not established, but he still liked the idea he had shared with Cass Canfield in New York, and at the end of his 'Comment' for the centenary issue he put it to his readers: 'We would be rash to prophesy for *Horizon* a further existence of more than two years. This will enable us to have covered the whole of the forties and to have enslumbered the arts, like a skilled anaesthetist, into final oblivion.'

## II

Watson had his doubts that Connolly would be able to give up *Horizon* at the end of the decade. There had been talk in the past of closing the magazine, but after eight years it was still going strong. Watson did not want to see it close, and anyway he felt obligated to keep it going as long as Connolly wished. He knew that there was no point in trying to predict what Connolly would do and, typically, he did not want to force a decision or even discuss the question directly. As he saw it, he had to follow his editor's lead and hope for the best.

His activities as a patron of art had expanded in a new direction. In 1947 he had become a founding member of the Institute of Contemporary Arts, making an initial donation of five hundred pounds. In September of that year he placed a full-page notice in *Horizon* explaining the aims of the Institute and appealing for contributions to its Foundation Fund. He worked on the organising committee, and recruited Sonia as a temporary secretary. Its chairman was Herbert Read; other members included Frederick Ashton, Geoffrey Grigson, and Roland Penrose. According to an early prospectus, the ICA hoped 'to encourage collaboration between the various arts and to promote, by means of exhibitions, performances and discussions, the best modern and experimental work on a non-commercial basis'.

The ICA held two major exhibitions in London, in its first year, each of which drew over twenty thousand people. Watson helped to organise both events. When the first exhibition – '40 Years of Modern Art' – opened on 10 February 1948, it included three pieces on loan from Watson's private collection: Juan Gris's collage '*Le Journal*' (1914); Paul Klee's water-colour 'The Quaking Chapel' (1924); and Henry Moore's sculpture 'Family Group' (1945). The second exhibition, which opened on 20 December 1948, was an ambitious attempt to trace connections between modern and primitive art, and was given the amusing title, '40,000 Years of Modern Art'. Watson lent Wilfredo Lam's water-colour 'Annunciation' (1946), and Jacques Lipchitz's bronze sculpture 'Pegasus' (1946). The great attraction of the exhibition was a painting on loan from the Museum of Modern Art: Picasso's large masterpiece 'Les Demoiselles d'Avignon', which had not been shown in London before.

Like the other founders of the ICA, Watson hoped its activities would bring an international flavour to the English art scene, breaking down some of the traditional resistance to foreign influences, and making it easier for artists to absorb those influences without having to spend time and money abroad. (Writing in *Horizon* in March 1948, Geoffrey Grigson warned artists against the temptation to become 'either a little Englander or a larger Parisian', and he pointed to Henry Moore as one man who had established a successful career between the two extremes.) [12] Watson was encouraged by the success of the ICA's first exhibitions and tried to help with other events. He was an active supporter of its concerts and its evening discussions devoted to modern music. He sponsored contemporary chamber music concerts which featured works by Alban Berg and Stravinsky. According to Roland Penrose, Watson 'made it possible to organise musical events of an order rare in a London still suffering from its wartime isolation and pre-war indifference.'[13]

Britain's cultural isolation in the winter of 1947–1948 was in some ways worse than it had been during the war. To control the nation's dollar deficit, the government had made it impossible to import American films, and had placed a ban on the sale of foreign books and foreign art. (Connolly speculated that the real reason for the ban on foreign books had nothing to do with saving dollars. It was, he said, more likely that the government considered 'the margins immorally wide and the paper indecently thick'.)[14]

This isolation was especially hard on Waldemar Hansen, who was acutely aware of being cut off from home. 'London gets bleaker and bleaker,' he wrote to John Myers in December 1947. 'We all feel enclosed in a glass chrysalis, vacuum-sealed from everything which goes on outside this little jewel, this England.' His old way of life in New York seemed incredibly remote. He was finding it difficult to believe that he had once lived in a city where there were restaurants full of good food, shops without queues, and a night life which offered endless choice. A life of endless regulations and shortages had become the norm – 'Beaver meat is our latest import,' he wrote in a matter-of-fact tone, 'since whale steaks didn't go down so well' – and his visions of American life were turning into fantasy, as though that existence belonged to 'another planet, a cloud-cuckoo land'.[15]

Despite his unhappiness with London, Hansen remained happy in his relationship with Watson. There were occasional disagreements, but all were minor and short-lived. Life at Palace Gate was quiet and domestic. They entertained infrequently, and when they chose to go out in the evenings they kept things simple: a concert or play, or joining friends for dinner. Sonia was a favourite companion. Hansen had developed a solid friendship with her and felt that she was one of the few among Watson's English friends who accepted him for himself. 'The rest,' he complained, 'take the benevolent attitude towards a mistress, slightly condescending.'[16]

Watson usually went his own way during the day, on personal business or working for either the ICA or *Horizon*. Hansen did the shopping and cooked the evening meals. He also took French lessons, which he enjoyed immensely, and he went on writing poetry. In the middle of the winter he began sending his work to various magazines, and in the spring a poem was published in *Poetry* (Chicago), and another in *Poetry London*. By then he and Watson had made plans to get away from London for another long summer on the Continent. For Hansen it was a long overdue break. 'I thank my stars we are spending the summer in France,' he told Myers. 'Another couple of months in England would have finished me.'[17]

Connolly was also looking forward to spending the summer in France. During the winter Somerset Maugham had paid a visit to Sussex Place, and had been so pleased by the hospitality shown him that he had invited Connolly and Lys to be his guests in Cap Ferrat for a fortnight in June or July. The invitation was accepted, and Connolly began looking for ways to spend the whole summer travelling in France. He came up with an ambitious plan, one which required the help of his publishers. As he outlined it to Hamish Hamilton, the idea was that he would write 'a guide-book to S.W. France, Aquitaine: i.e., the country a hundred miles round Bordeaux (the valleys of the Charente, Dordogne, Lot, Tarn, Garonne, Adour)'. He wanted to pay homage to 'a very balmy and civilised region of France', and 'to celebrate all that is nicest about Europe and the *douceur de vivre*'. The finished work would be 'a hymn of gratitude with good maps . . . of practical use to the many and an aesthetic pleasure to the Few'.[18] What he lacked was the money for a long summer journey through the region, to make the notes for the book. He estimated the trip would take about two months, and would cost at least three hundred pounds. He proposed that Hamish Hamilton join with Harper's to advance him this amount and promised to deliver a manuscript of around 70,000 words by the following spring.

The two publishers had already advanced him three hundred pounds for his proposed book on Flaubert, which was now months overdue and still unfinished. But he told Hamish Hamilton that there was little chance of completing that work in the foreseeable future: 'As I explained the other evening, I feel I can't get on with the FLAUBERT at present. It is still the book I want most to write one day but I can't write and edit at the same time. My only chance is to get out of London for a bit, which is one reason why I want to do a travel book.'[19] This explanation was apparently sufficient, for he soon had the advance he had asked for; there was even an extra fifty pounds for a photographer to accompany him. From New York, Cass Canfield wrote enthusiastically: 'I can't tell you how pleased we are about this new project. To publish a book by you is an exciting event.'[20]

Early in June, Connolly used some of his advance to travel to France on his own, spending several days in Paris before visiting Bordeaux and the vineyards of the Médoc, and spending another week touring the villages along the Dordogne. In Bordeaux the centre of attraction for him was the Hotel-Restaurant Chapon Fin, where the wine list was a source of fascination and delight. On a postcard showing the restaurant's interior, he proclaimed, 'This is my spiritual home (last night it was Haut Brion '06). All the staff remember me as an undergraduate!'[21] Mouton Rothschild was another 'spiritual' experience; he toured the estate in a reverential mood, referring to the '*Grand Chai*' – the Great Storehouse – as a cathedral filled with 'pew-like rows of silent barrels'. On stationery headed '*Domaines de Mouton*' he wrote, 'Mouton was delicious and Philippe [Baron Philippe de Rothschild] was very sweet. We had five wines for dinner and wonderful crepes.'[22] At the end of June, Lys joined him in Paris, and they travelled to the South of France with Edward and Nika Hulton. They stayed at Maugham's villa for a fortnight, spending an evening in the company of the Duke and Duchess of Windsor, who had come to dinner. ('I liked her very much!' Connolly later exclaimed in a letter to his mother.)[23] After Cap Ferrat, they went to Cannes for a week.

This was the glamorous existence Connolly had been daydreaming about for months. Thanks to Maugham's generosity and the advance from Messrs Canfield and Hamilton, he spent the entire summer visiting his favorite haunts and indulging his appetite for the good life. And, as usual, Sonia was happy to take charge of the *Horizon* office; she even seemed to enjoy reporting the miseries of life at home, perhaps knowing that this would intensify his pleasure at being abroad. On 19 July she wrote that the weather had been dreary all month, and warned melodramatically, 'London is a death trap at the moment, and you must both have as much good food and air as you possibly can.'[24]

Her only good news concerned a new contribution from America, and her remarks provide insight into the way *Horizon* was run when its editor was away: 'Thurber has sent in his parody of H. James and I've laughed more than I can say. Now, he says that it is not going into any other magazine, but it is appearing in a book of his due out 23 September in which he has written in the acknowledgements that it was written for C. Connolly's *Horizon*. We have time to get it into the September number if you like it as much as I do, so would you like me to copy it and send it to you or have it set up and send you a proof? Please send me another nice p.c. with instructions.'

This was a piece that Connolly had long been hoping to receive, and it did indeed appear in the September issue. In America, he had learned that Thurber had been trying for many months to complete a parody of James, and he had asked permission to use it in *Horizon* as soon as it was ready. The finished piece – 'The Beast in the Dingle' – is a splendid pastiche of James's style. Connolly sent a note of thanks and a contributor's fee (probably about eighty dollars) to which Thurber made this memorable reply:

> I was delighted by the check which was larger than I had expected. Did I tell you the story of the Hollywood agent who flew east four years ago to offer me 3500 a week to write for Warner Bros? I told him I couldn't do it because I was engaged on a small pastiche of Henry James. He was bewildered but impressed. 'How much will you get for that?' he asked. I thought it over. 'Depending on what review I sell it to, anywhere from forty to ninety dollars.' He backed away from me as if I were insane, and happily dropped out of my life.[25]

At the beginning of August, Lys returned to London and Connolly headed back to Bordeaux. When he first negotiated his advance, he had told Hamish Hamilton that he wanted his old friend Dick Wyndham to take the photographs for his book, but Wyndham was working for the *Sunday Times*, covering the fighting between Jews and Arabs outside Jerusalem. He did not return from this assignment; in mid-May he was taking photographs from the Arab lines when bullets from a Jewish sniper struck him, killing him instantly. After hearing this grim news Connolly turned to another old friend, Joan Rayner (*Horizon* had published her photograph of the bomb-damaged Chelsea Old Church in June 1941). She agreed to be his photographer and joined him in France in August. In her mid-thirties at the time, she was – in Connolly's words – an 'old flame'. Their relationship went back to the years before the war, when she was Joan Eyres Monsell, daughter of Lord Monsell, First Lord of the Admiralty from 1931 to 1936. She had married John Rayner before the war, but was divorced in 1947.

Connolly and Joan spent almost all of August together. They travelled from the basin of Arcachon – in the southwest corner of Gironde – to La Rochelle – one hundred miles north of Bordeaux, and into the interior, as far as Toulouse and Albi. Nearly twenty years later Connolly recalled a memorable image of their tour: 'Climbing the Dune du Pyla, the highest in Europe . . . and looking down on that fantastic view of mile upon mile of green pine forest stretching towards Mimizan, the Atlantic breaking as far as the eye can see on an endless emptiness of golden beaches. We half ran, half tobogganed, down the hot precipice of sand into the woods underneath, where the sun streamed between the trunks and the undergrowth of arbutus.'[26] Much of their touring was done by taxi, so expenses mounted quickly. 'Money flows like water – on taxis,' Connolly wrote, adding, 'I think I shall write to H. H. [Hamish Hamilton] for £50 more.'[27] He did not receive any further money for his advance; indeed, Hamilton developed suspicions about the exact nature of Connolly's trip. Had he read the satire in *Horizon* about the 'Society for the Redemption of Middle-aged Hacks', he might have wondered whether he had been cast as Filmore Van Rensselaer Crutch. (When he found out, a few months before the manuscript was due, that very little work had been done on the book, the discovery was not a complete surprise.)

Hamilton was not the only one with doubts. Despite assurances from Connolly that his relationship with Joan was platonic, Lys was suspicious and anxious as she waited for him in London. To alleviate her fears, he emphasised that Joan was already attached to the writer Patrick ('Paddy') Leigh Fermor (who eventually married her – in 1968). 'Joan . . . is very much in love with Paddy,' he wrote. 'Their postal arrangements put ours to shame.'[28] But his feelings towards Joan were not platonic. Describing his summer to his mother, he wrote, 'I went off on a trip right across France with a friend who was to take photographs for my book, this was not too good as I chose an old flame of mine and fell very much in love with her.'[29]

At the end of August Connolly and Joan went their separate ways. He resumed his normal routine at Sussex Place with Lys, pretending that his feelings for her were unchanged. But they had changed. As he explained to his mother, his time with Joan had given him a new perspective. 'It made me realise that I could not marry Lys at present because I should only be unkind to her – she is so devoted to me and belongs to all the every-day part of my life – but Joan is like Jean, a very intelligent and remarkable person in her own right, an explorer, etc., and the one person who could have got me over Jean years earlier if we had had better luck.'[30]

He was once again caught up in dreams of what might have been and feeling inclined to cast off what was securely his to pursue something out of his reach. His relationship with Lys had been remarkably stable, but it had become too domestic, too tame. Her presence was inextricably connected with the cares and troubles of London life in the Forties. Although she had done so much to lighten those cares and troubles, he still associated them with her in his mind and could not see her in a romantic light. There was little mystery or glamour left, nothing forbidden or exotic. This was not new for him – he had thought it for many months – but the summer had made it more compelling. For his redemption the middle-aged man of letters now craved romantic adventures and an easy life in the sun.

Lys knew his feelings had changed, and she now had good reason to doubt his promise to marry her. His divorce from Jean had become final in June, but the summer had passed without any sign that he was ready to go ahead with the marriage. There were no excuses left, but he evaded the issue. The longer he did nothing, the more desperate he was to escape, and the more ashamed he felt. When he had been trying to write the story of his alter ego, Brinkley, earlier in the year, he had composed his most telling analysis of his character, explaining why he was forever being tempted into sabotaging his closest relationships. In the unfinished manuscript Brinkley awakens from a nightmare in which he has been tormented by memories of a dead father and of past lovers:

Owing to certain actions, certain lack of actions, since a very early age those who entrusted him with their happiness had been most basely betrayed and been driven to say intolerable things which he could never put out of his mind: 'Every grey hair your mother has, she owes to you.' 'Daddy!' 'You were my rock. For nine years I was faithful. I thought if I knew one man well enough I knew them all.' 'I am offering you the devotion of a lifetime.' 'You have the gift of destroying not only your happiness but the happiness of all who love you.' How well they expressed themselves! Picked it up from him . . . He knew he worked really hard to get people to love him to the point at which he could feel sure enough of them to hate them. His betrayals followed a seven-year cycle. He selected his victims and prepared them for sacrifice while pretending that they selected him. He was like a faulty machine which some malfunction led to the continual amputation of arms and legs in those who looked after it because all the time it really was a machine precisely for amputating arms and legs. A safety razor for cutting throats. But the razor was a man and one who wanted above all to be kind. The guillotine had a conscience . . .[31]

## III

Watson was also in France for the summer, but he saw little of Connolly. He was content to deal with *Horizon* business as Connolly did: through correspondence with Sonia. He spent a good deal of time in Paris, where he stayed at the Pont Royal Hotel, in the same area as his old apartment. He was there for a short time on his own in May, and back again in June, with Hansen, for a longer stay. (During his first visit he was entertained at a house where, several months earlier, Connolly had made an unflattering, though memorable, evaluation of the host. Watson reported, 'I went to dinner at the house of a wealthy Frenchman whom Cyril had dined with and in whose guestbook he had written, "Brief are the joys of little men," which hasn't gone down so well!')[32]

Watson and Hansen visited Switzerland and Italy at the end of the summer, and in mid-September they returned to London, a few days after Connolly. Their relationship had now reached a crucial point. After eighteen months together, they were faced with a long separation, because Hansen could not secure an extension of his visa beyond 1 October. He had no choice but to return to New York and stay until a new visa could be obtained. The two men worked out a plan: Hansen would spend the rest of the year in New York, and his companion would join him at the end of the year, after the opening of the ICA's '40,000 Years of Modern Art', which would claim most of Watson's attention during the autumn. The assumption seems to have been that they would stay in New York for at least three months.

When Hansen left at the beginning of October, Watson felt particularly anxious and lonely. 'Feel very uninspired and alone in this flat,' he wrote in mid-October, 'and only wish I could get away next month instead of the end of December.'[33] Another letter ended, 'Loneliness that natural state of man is the real torture,' and was signed, 'A rather sad, Peter'.[34] Watson's moodiness and depression were plaguing him again. Hansen had noticed signs of this problem much earlier, but had been at a loss to explain it, except to put it down to unease about post-war life in general. Writing from Paris in September, he tried to describe what he had observed:

He's so moody and strange a lot of the time, so depressed. Sometimes he doesn't want to eat dinner. He's pessimistic about a great many things (aren't we all), and just won't display any joie de vivre . . . I adore him and would do anything to make him happy, but he asks for nothing and doesn't even seem to want affection for weeks on end . . . I think he is terribly unhappy about the restrictions of his post-war life. Before the war he had an apartment in Paris with six servants, a house in London . . . And now, he's reduced to watching the lira in Italy, eating in cautious style, etc. He can't buy any more paintings because he hasn't got the money abroad, and England won't import. He loathes London and has to live there most of the time. He hasn't got a car, nor a house, nor an apartment in Paris. He watches the area of his life get smaller and smaller and smaller.[35]

In the early days of their relationship, when he had been the innocent young American dazzled by Watson's world, it had not been difficult for Hansen to lift his lover's spirits and charm him into a good mood; but living in London had made it harder to keep up his own spirits, much less Watson's. All he could do was to hope that a few months in America would dispel the gloom over Watson's life.

After Hansen's departure, Watson did find some cheer in thinking about a return visit to New York. At the beginning of November he wrote that he longed to be in an 'optimistic country' again. 'I feel very bored with life here,' he complained. 'The problem is how to make it more interesting but I don't see the way!'[36] He missed 'that toughness and self-assurance which always accompanies a system which still *works*'. However, that system did not always work for foreigners who wanted to make extended visits to America. 'Appalling difficulties for USA visitor's visa,' he wrote. 'I have to get a guarantee from a rich person describing his income, property, job, no. of shares, etc.'[37] To prove that he was capable of supporting himself during his visit, he asked the Hollywood director, George Cukor – one of his old friends from the Thirties – to vouch for him. This did the trick, but Watson found the paperwork a great nuisance, complaining to Hansen, 'Your country is far the most difficult to get into.'[38]

Autumn presented Watson with a number of troubling personal problems. There was the perennial difficulty of dealing with Brian Howard, who was drinking heavily again, and whose behaviour was distressing everyone around him. To avoid being a target of his drunken outbursts, Watson stayed out of the way, but Howard's crazy, and sometimes cruel, exploits were hard to ignore, as were his frequent letters and telephone calls, and assorted complaints about him from mutual friends. Another perennial source of trouble – Denham Fouts – was far away in Rome, but that did not stop him haunting Watson's life. He wrote desperate notes pleading for money, and made wild accusations, blaming Watson for a host of problems. In November Watson told Hansen, 'Denham wrote me a reproachful self-pitying letter from Rome saying that I had done nothing to help him! My

God, I have been paying for all his self-indulgent auto-destruction, besides his doctors and nursing homes . . . I can't understand what people *want* of me or expect me to do.'[39] But the feelings of guilt would not go away, no matter how logically he tried to dismiss them. 'Denham and what happened to him is the perfect example of someone evading every issue through someone else, and when he does have to stand on his own legs, they just aren't there. So he is forced to use everyone else as a prop to his own weakness. It is never anyone else's fault anymore than it is anyone's fault that Brian behaves as he does, but such people are diabolical in pinning the blame on to others.'[40]

Watson was so indulgent with his friends that some of them expected far too much from him. They were also quick to pass judgment on him when they felt he had let them down, and their judgments could be severe. In 1949, Cecil Beaton, whose friendship with Watson had cooled since the war, referred to him as a 'strange, warped individual'.[41] But anyone with a grievance against Watson, real or imagined, was not likely to force him into discussing it. His distaste for confrontation made it hard to pin him down, and the effect was that any misunderstanding or unhappiness tended to linger and end up being aired behind his back. He was convinced that he had always tried to avoid hurting anyone. 'Looking back over my life,' he wrote in November, 'I fail to see whom I have harmed deliberately or by accident . . . My only asset has been a certain amount of money and enthusiasm. Since the war both have considerably decreased, but I cannot see that I have used either to other people's disadvantage.'[42]

His work for the ICA and *Horizon* helped to take Watson's mind off his worries. But the lives of his friends at the magazine were also a source of concern. By the early autumn Lys's problems with Connolly were public, and the strain on her emotions was obvious to everyone. During a party at Sussex Place in October for Aldous and Maria Huxley, who had just arrived from the United States, Watson had noticed that Lys's composure was beginning to wear thin. She had been 'reduced to tears' after overhearing 'Maria Huxley saying how awful these sort of parties are . . . as usual [Lys] had slaved her guts out for everyone.'[43] By early November, Watson was reporting: 'Lys has been wildly hysterical and burst into tears twice coming into the office.'[44]

Sonia gave Hansen a more detailed picture: 'I expect Peter has told you all the HORIZON news – what there is of it which seems mostly to be private lives. I think we ought to drop all this nonsense about a Review of Literature and Art and call it straight out "Advice to the

Lovelorn". Cyril has settled into a routine of glamour and champagne which is all right for him, but everyone else has to pick up the pieces, which I confess is mostly Lys and manuscripts! Lys is more like a sad and bedraggled sparrow than ever, keeping up an unceasing chirping about "true love" while contemplating that ringless finger – and there's NOTHING one can do about it.' [45]

Lys was especially hurt by Connolly's decision in October to spend a fortnight in Paris without her. He tried to pretend that he was going over for business reasons, but once he was there he could not resist writing to say how much he was enjoying himself. 'It is terrible how well I take to a life of pure enjoyment. Seven women rang me up yesterday one after the other! The reward of chastity! I seem to do nothing but listen to their troubles.' Such words were hardly a comfort to Lys, especially since she knew that one of the seven women in Paris was Joan, and another was Jean, who had decided to meet Connolly again after more than eight years. So many friends from the Thirties were in Paris that it was as though the clock had been turned back ten years, and that Connolly and Jean had never been separated. He made no secret of the pleasure he took in seeing Jean again. 'The atmosphere here is so like before the war now that I can hardly believe it . . . Yesterday an old acquaintance of ten years ago walked into the bar of the Ritz where Jean and I were having a drink and said, "I hear you two are coming to Jamaica, you must stay with me!"' [46]

Lys's anxiety was made worse by a visit from, of all people, Brian Howard, who got drunk one evening and ended up at Sussex Place when Connolly was in Paris. Lys was alone in the house, cooking her dinner; while she worked, Howard taunted her with cruel remarks about her love for Connolly. According to Watson, Howard 'asked how she could possibly "love" such an unattractive man and told her Cyril had gone to Paris to meet another girl (Joan).' It was unforgivable and, of course, it came when Lys was most vulnerable. Sonia and Watson were outraged. Sonia wrote, 'Brian's fearful villainy [has] made me crosser than anything for ages'; and Watson declared, 'I am so furious, what has it to do with him and why try to make the innocent suffer?' [47]

Late in November, Lys went over to Paris, and Connolly hastened to restore himself to her good graces. They were reconciled and returned together to Sussex Place, but there was not much reason to expect that their troubles had ended. Lys was firmly fixed in Connolly's mind as a symbol of a past burdened by hardships and restrictions. He would want to break free again – it was only a matter of time. Piece by piece, the life he had built up during the Forties was disintegrating, and the cracks were noticeable even to those who knew little of his personal life.

The pages of *Horizon* showed that its editor was losing interest, and that his energies were being directed elsewhere. Few readers of *Horizon* in 1948 would have failed to notice that only a handful of issues contained a 'Comment' – only four of the twelve. The contrast with earlier years was striking, because 'Comment' had been eagerly awaited each month and it was rarely missing from its usual spot inside the front cover. To those who questioned the decline of 'Comment' as a regular feature, Connolly offered this cryptic answer early in 1949: 'Failing powers: militant reactionary decadence; bourgeois formalism. They all add up.'[48]

# TEN

# TWILIGHT
## 1949–1950

### I

On New Year's Day 1949 Peter Watson sailed to New York on the *Queen Mary*. The journey was a sad one because he spent much of his time brooding over a message which had reached him some days earlier. He had received a cable from Rome telling him that Denham Fouts had suffered a fatal heart attack. Fouts had collapsed in a lavatory of the small hotel where he had been staying with an English friend, and had died before help could be summoned. He was thirty-four but, given the way he had chosen to live, it was inevitable that he would die young. His drug habit had severely weakened his heart, which long before had revealed a dangerous murmur. When Fouts left the Rue du Bac, Watson had resigned himself to the fact that death might soon claim his former lover, but the event was still difficult to accept, not least because Watson had experienced so much guilt over their estrangement. When the news reached him, he wrote to Hansen, 'My own feelings are so mixed that I can not begin to express them in a letter.' Eight days later, as he was preparing to leave for America, he confessed, 'Denham's death has affected me rather deeply,' and he warned, 'Please be very patient with me because I shall arrive in a very depressed condition.' [1]

During his lonely voyage, Watson's depression grew, and he was in an extremely agitated mood by the time he arrived in New York. Hansen met him and they went to the Hotel Weylin, on Madison Avenue, where a double room was reserved for them. Hansen could see that Watson was deeply troubled, but he was not prepared for the revelation which came shortly afterwards. Watson announced abruptly that he no longer felt comfortable in their relationship, and that he wanted to be on his own in America while he tried to sort out his feelings. Hansen was shocked and pressed for an explanation; he was surprised to learn that another man was involved, one whom Watson had not seen for two years. Like Fouts and Hansen, he was a young American; his name was Norman Fowler.

Hansen knew the name well – he and Norman Fowler had once been lovers. The story is full of coincidences, but it can be understood without going too far back. Early in 1946, a year before he met Peter Watson, Hansen had become involved with Fowler. They met quite by accident outside a theatre in New York, where there was a production of *Swan Lake*. When Hansen arrived, the performance was sold out. As he prepared to leave, a man on the sidewalk announced that he had two tickets to give away. Hansen quickly stepped forward to take one, and a voice from behind said, 'I'll take the other.' Turning around, he discovered that the voice belonged to a young sailor. Their seats were next to each other and they struck up a conversation, which they continued when the ballet was over.

The sailor was Norman Fowler, then only nineteen. Stationed at a naval base in Virginia, he went to New York whenever he was granted a short leave. He had to return to his base the day after he met Hansen, but they kept up their acquaintance by correspondence, and on Fowler's next visit they became lovers. They were still seeing each other a year later when Peter Watson visited New York in 1946–1947. On New Year's Eve 1947, Hansen, Fowler, and John Myers, went on the town together to several parties, one of which was at Tchelitchew's apartment. Watson was there but did not meet Hansen, who was ill from too much drink and went home early. He was introduced to Fowler, who was his lover for a single night. An affair might have developed, but Fowler had to go back to his base the next day, and did not return for several weeks. By that time Watson had met Hansen, and Fowler was out of the picture.

Watson never hid from Hansen the fact that he had once been involved with Fowler, but he was not forthright about the lingering influence of that brief encounter. Fowler had no special artistic talent and he was not particularly intelligent or witty, but he had a magnetic quality, a strange seductive charm which reminded Watson of Denham Fouts at his best. Although he had not seen Fowler for two years, Watson had not forgotten the excitement he had felt during their short time together, and he was now determined to see him again. No doubt Fouts's recent death played a part in his decision. He had sought an escape from Fouts's self-destructive passions with Hansen, but he now saw a chance to recapture some of those passions without the poisoning influence of drugs.

Hansen doubted whether Watson understood what he was getting into. There may not have been drugs in Fowler's life, but there was a dark, irrational side to his character just as disturbing as anything in Fouts's personality. Hansen had not regretted the end of his relationship with Fowler, because he had seen enough of that side to know that something was seriously amiss. In his words, 'Norman was a very strange person. He would have moments – in fact, occasionally, it happened right in front of my eyes – when he would have something, not exactly like a catatonic seizure, but he would space-out in rather peculiar ways. In fact, once I had to slap him to bring him to.'[2] Hansen hoped that Watson would return to him once the extent of Fowler's strange personality had revealed itself.

It was not at all certain that Watson could arrange a meeting with Fowler, who had left the navy and was living in Los Angeles. Hansen decided not to interfere with Watson's plans and left New York. With money provided by Watson, he went to Jamaica, where he established himself in a small hotel and settled in for the winter, concentrating on his writing. Watson wrote to him, and at the end of February a letter arrived with the return address, 'Hotel Montecito, Franklin Avenue, Hollywood'. Hansen found the contents depressing, if not surprising. Watson wrote: 'Norman met me. How to explain what has happened? We just seemed to take up where we left off. I don't know what to say as there is no rational way of explaining such a thing . . . Of course I feel guilty although I know I have not really done harm to you. I am most attached to you and will always be, I think. I am most grateful for the consideration you have always shown me. What the future can bring I don't know, but at the moment I must tell you that my deepest emotions are involved and that this is really important to me.'

It sounded as though he had closed the door on Hansen, but he left a chink. Not everything was going as he had hoped. He did not want to stay in California ('Hollywood is awful and I hate it,' he complained. 'It has the kiss of death on it and I couldn't bear to live here'), but Fowler was unwilling to go anywhere else, at least for the time being. So he wrote, 'As to the immediate future I want to stay until about March 6th, then I'll go on to New Orleans and I suppose fly to Jamaica from there about March 10th. If you are still there and want to see me, I would be very pleased in a rather different relationship.'[3] Although deeply disappointed by the turn of events, Hansen met Watson in Jamaica, and agreed not only to remain his friend but to continue living with him temporarily. They went back to New York and returned to London late in April. As long as Fowler remained in California, there was hope for Hansen. Fowler might turn up in London or

Watson might go racing back to Hollywood, but Hansen tried to remain patient, telling John Myers, 'I think it best to let the hawk fly high until he decides to do what he wants to do.'[4]

During his stay of nearly four months in America, Watson had little contact with *Horizon*. He kept an eye out for new material, but the magazine did not really need more contributors from America. As Connolly noted in 'Comment' for March 1949: 'Many of the unknown and original contributors to this magazine are now American. In the last year we have published nineteen American authors in fourteen numbers, and they would seem especially to excel in poetry and the short story. And in much that we do not print, the American talent seems superior; the stories which are not quite good enough will be more original, fresh and vigorous, the poems will be modern – never that stream of Victorian cliché which continues to pour from so many aspiring hearts nearer home.'

*Horizon* became the first magazine in England to publish a story by Truman Capote ('Master Misery') in January 1949 and the next month an entire issue was devoted to Mary McCarthy's *The Oasis*, winner of *Horizon*'s first – and last – contest for the best short novel submitted to the magazine (the competition had attracted more than a hundred entries). Watson had read the manuscript in November and pronounced it 'very good', observing that its appeal was centred in 'its Americanism'.[5] It tells of a small band of American intellectuals struggling to establish a utopian community – a mountaintop 'oasis' in New England – but their struggle is largely a dramatisation of conflicts within the stormy intellectual circle of the *Partisan Review*. Some of its principal members are thinly disguised as characters in the story: Macdougal Macdermott (Dwight Macdonald) and Will Taub (Philip Rahv). (Mary McCarthy had lived with Rahv in the late Thirties, when she was the *Partisan Review*'s drama editor.) When Connolly published *The Oasis*, he warned English readers that they might have difficulty sorting out the analysis of the 'intelligentsia of New York'; and perhaps because he felt defensive about awarding the *Horizon* prize to such a thoroughly American story, he made an awkward effort to place its author in an English tradition: 'The mind and style of Mary McCarthy, though so American, derive partly from the world of Congreve and Constant, of Elizabeth Bowen and Compton Burnett or the Cambridge period of Virginia Woolf.'

*The Oasis* contains some lively descriptions of individual characters but, as Connolly admitted, the work 'lacks narrative power'.[6] There is plenty of philosophical baggage for the characters to drag around, but not much of a story. The work caught Connolly's interest because, among other things, its description of the *Partisan Review* crowd must have reminded him of his efforts to portray life at *Horizon* through the eyes of his fictional creation, Brinkley. He no doubt derived vicarious pleasure from publishing her finished work, especially since its sharp character portraits were likely to spark controversy among American intellectuals. *The Oasis* issue quickly sold out and received widespread attention in New York, where the rumour spread that Philip Rahv was thinking of suing Mary McCarthy. The interest shown helped to keep *Horizon*, and its editor, prominent on the American literary scene. An ironic twist was that Connolly's major literary contributions in 1949 (other than to *Horizon*) went to the *Partisan Review*. They were two instalments of a 'London Letter', both of which appeared after the publication of *The Oasis*.

According to the contract he had signed with Hamish Hamilton and Harper's, Connolly's major publication of 1949 should have been his travel book on the southwest region of France. At the beginning of the year Hamish Hamilton discovered that his author had not got beyond the note-taking stage, and Connolly told him that the idea of doing a guide book had lost its appeal. He was now considering writing a novel about a writer who was touring France on an assignment to write a travel book. He described it vaguely as 'a novel which is not a novel and may contain some illustrations'. But Hamilton dismissed this: 'My own interpretation,' he told Cass Canfield, 'is that it is largely an attempt to waste more time in discussing the form of the book.' He said he had asked Connolly for a sample of the manuscript. 'I happen to know that he has not written a line,' he explained, 'so that this should flick him on the raw.' His hope was that by 'keeping after him persistently for the next few months', some acceptable manuscript might emerge. 'If it turns out to be a series of episodes with some connecting thread like "Ashenden" and "Hecate County" it should be an attractive piece of work, though no doubt it will occur to you, as it has to me, that it could have been written just as well if we had not financed the trip to France.'[7]

Connolly might have known from the beginning that the travel book was an ill-conceived idea, but it had taken him to France, which was all that mattered at the time. Canfield and Hamilton seem to have convinced themselves that it was a sham from beginning to end and that their author never intended to write the book described in his contract. Connolly did eventually use his notes to write a long travel essay on Bordeaux and the Dordogne, which he published in his 1953 collection *Ideas and Places*. It is a rather conventional piece, evidence enough that he would have been wasting his time if he had tried to write a full-scale book on the region.

Despite prodding from his publishers, he never completed a manuscript for his travel contract. The advance had given him an eventful summer in France, but had not provided the literary inspiration that he had hoped. There had been no magical release of creativity, no outpouring of energy to dash off the travel book and perhaps a new novel as well. He continued struggling with problems of the past, spinning his wheels as the old excuses came back to him. If only he had more time and money . . . If only the right woman were beside him . . . If only London were not so cold and depressing . . . If only he could finish one book before going on to another . . .

He had gambled that he could make his summer in France pay, but by the following spring he saw that the gamble was lost. He was forced to admit to Hamish Hamilton that he had no manuscript, and was not likely to have one for the foreseeable future. When he had failed to finish work in the past, he had been able to keep it to himself, but now his publishers shared the disappointment and a significant financial loss. They decided not to demand immediate repayment of the advance, choosing instead to withhold royalties on *The Unquiet Grave*. (The modest income from this book did not cut the deficit by much. Harper's had advanced him one thousand dollars for the Flaubert book and the travel book; as late as 1953 he still owed them $943.49.) He tried to shrug off this failure and insist that he would soon have a novel to give his publishers, but his new promises did not make up for his failure to meet existing obligations.

Canfield tried to sound encouraging but his words seem merely perfunctory, with more than a hint of scepticism: 'I hope that the tide is in flood again and that you now feel the impulse to write a novel about your experience of setting out to write a travel book.'[8] Canfield was not surprised when this also came to nothing; though Harper's published two more books by Connolly – *Ideas and Places* and *Previous Convictions* (the latter was also published by Hamish Hamilton in Britain) – the aborted travel book was an embarrassment which would not soon be forgotten. It meant that Connolly could no longer hope to give up magazine editing and become an editor of books published by Canfield and Hamilton. Neither would now be likely to enter into a business arrangement with him. How could he be trusted to edit half a dozen 'Connolly Books' in a year when he could not complete a single book of his own? However, it was difficult to hold a grudge against the

author, despite his failings. Several years later, when Connolly tried
to persuade Harper's to give him another advance for an unfinished
novel, Canfield remarked, 'I give Connolly full credit for being one of
the most charmingly devious literary gentlemen not actually behind
bars.'[9]

## II

Connolly's social life was so busy during the winter and spring of 1949
that it is no wonder he had little time available for writing. There
seemed to be a party at Sussex Place nearly every week, and the guest
list grew ever larger and more distinguished. One night there was even
a film star in attendance. ('I met Joseph Cotten at Cyril's the other
night,' Sonia wrote to Hansen in March, 'and thought he was the
stupidest man I'd ever met.')[10]

Connolly was also spending much time in the Gargoyle Club, often
with a new young friend named Anne Dunn. The youngest daughter
of the millionaire banker Sir James Dunn, Anne was an aspiring
painter whose good looks and social background had attracted Connolly's interest. She was sophisticated but only nineteen; Connolly fell
hopelessly in love with her. This proved to be more than Lys could
tolerate. She left Connolly, travelled to Florence, and stayed away from
Sussex Place for more than a month. The big parties ended, the house
grew quiet, and Connolly struggled once more with the common pre-
dicament of his love life. 'My id is furious with you,' he wrote to Lys,
'I wish you wouldn't play about with my desertion complex – it really
is dangerous – it (the id) is smouldering with rage and doesn't know
whether to pay you out by dying of pneumonia before you come back
or going somewhere nicer and further with someone else . . . I miss
you so abominably but I feel so angry at the same time, I know it is
unreasonable but there you are.'[11]

He began to pine after Lys and weave romantic plots around her.
Early in June he wrote, 'I feel terribly depressed today and imagine
you casting me off like an old shoe and marrying a rich American or
an Italian count – oh dear, I do hope you are behaving.' As for his
own behaviour, he maintained that he had been doing his best to stay
out of trouble: 'I have been completely chaste and am getting very
randy.' Although he admitted that he was seeing 'a great deal' of Anne
Dunn, he claimed that his romantic interest in her was dead. 'I have
let her paint in the spare room. She is starting on a portrait of me and
is doing the drawings – she obviously adores painting and it keeps her

very quiet, she is no longer in the least sexy, at any rate with me, and I get nothing but lectures: I am afraid I am doomed to uncle-dom.' He complained bitterly of the dreariness of his days alone at Sussex Place, telling Lys that since her departure he had been unable to do any work at all. 'I miss you terribly in every way and I'm quite helpless without you. I really can't bear living alone, except in hotels – I can't be *bothered* to do anything, and the rock of despair shows above the water. It makes me go to bed drunk and fritter the morning away. The house is very strange . . . a peculiar empty atmosphere like a school in the holidays.' But Connolly vowed to stay put in Sussex Place: 'I am not planning any brilliant getaway and shall await your return with pained dignity.'[12]

To keep him company, Nicky – Janetta's six-year-old daughter – would have a late breakfast with him, and he entertained her with wild stories and comic impressions. He liked to tease her, but she teased him back, often with unexpected results. As a mimic, she was every bit his match. 'When people telephone she mimics everything I say like a fantastic echo. I don't know what they think is happening.' On one occasion her innocent humour was revealing and, though the joke was at Connolly's expense, he reported the details with obvious delight: 'Today Nicky said, "Now I'm going to be Lys." I said, "Go ahead," rather wondering if some Freudian drama would come out. She tried to mimic your voice, pursed her lips and shrilled, "Get up Cyril and go to your office. You're lazy. Now come along to the office with me."'[13]

Connolly went into *Horizon* very rarely. He kept in touch with Sonia, who telephoned almost every day and went regularly to see him at Sussex Place. She tried to persuade him to complete a 'Comment' for each issue and during the first half of 1949 he did produce one each month, though of a quality far below his editorials of the war years. The style is lacklustre, the subject matter uninspired, and in most cases the 'Comment' is very short, and it is clear that his heart was not in the work. Good material continued to come into the magazine, much of it concerned with the world outside Britain: Dwight Macdonald's 'The Waldorf Conference' (May); Jacob Weinshall's 'A Crank in Israel' (June; translated by Arthur Koestler); Michel Leiris's 'Thoughts Around Alberto Giacometti' (June); Lawrence Durrell's 'Henry Miller' (July); Lionel Trilling's short story 'The Lesson and the Secret' (August); and Auden's 'The Ironic Hero: Some Reflections on Don Quixote' (August). One of the few important British contributions, 'A Fragment of Life Story' (September), was the work of a writer who had died almost a year earlier – Denton Welch. From the vantage point of *Horizon*, the British literary scene was not promising.

Peter Watson was in London during most of May and June, but saw very little of Connolly. The Institute of Contemporary Arts claimed more of his attention than *Horizon*, and its future was beginning to look more interesting than the magazine's. The ICA's effort to build up an endowment from private funds was going well, and the Arts Council was providing it with some financial support. Plans were made to acquire a permanent exhibition hall, and Watson was looking forward to the work of organising future art exhibitions. He wanted to put more money into the ICA, but did not have funds to spare as long as *Horizon* was dependent on his financial help. The magazine had never been truly self-supporting, although Connolly later remarked that 'there were several years when solvency reared its ugly head.'[14]

Watson was willing to underwrite the magazine as long as Connolly was committed to editing it, but that commitment was in question by the summer of 1949. If Connolly was not putting much effort into editing, Watson felt that there was little reason to keep the magazine alive. He tried to find out what his friend's plans were, but it was impossible to get a definite answer. By the end of July, he was so frustrated by Connolly's evasiveness that he told Hansen, 'A rather terrible showdown with Cyril is about to happen. Either the magazine will end in November or continue under very different auspices. He has behaved with shattering cynicism and it has upset me so much.'[15]

Sonia was the only one who still seemed to enjoy work at *Horizon*. She liked the independence and she knew how to get on with both Watson and Connolly. Both men took pains to please her, and to some extent her commitment to *Horizon* made it difficult for Watson or Connolly to be decisive about closing the magazine. But she could hardly ignore the signs that *Horizon*'s days were numbered; she knew she would have to make provision for her future, and that she would have to do it soon. That summer a serious opportunity presented itself to create a different life, because George Orwell was once again proposing marriage, and this time his offer was difficult to refuse.

Early in June the first copies of *Nineteen Eighty-Four* had gone on sale; within a few days it was clear that the book would be an enormous success, financially and critically. In its first year over 400,000 copies were sold in Britain and America. A few weeks before the British edition appeared, the Book-of-the-Month Club selected the novel, and this alone meant that Orwell would earn at least forty thousand pounds from American sales. This was an embarrassment of riches for a writer who three years earlier had suggested in *Horizon*'s 'The Cost of Letters' that a thousand pounds a year would be the ideal literary income. If Sonia were to marry him they could live comfortably, but the most pressing question for Orwell was not whether he could live comfortably but whether he could go on living at all. Since the beginning of the year he had been seriously ill with tuberculosis in a sanatorium in Gloucestershire. 'Ghastly' was his favourite adjective for describing the state of his health in 1949, but he told Fredric Warburg, his British publisher, that he was determined to recover his health, and that marrying Sonia might help him pull through. 'Apart from other considerations,' he remarked, 'I really think I should stay alive longer if I were married.'[16]

Orwell's case was not hopeless. After visiting him in June, Warburg estimated that 'at worst' there was 'a 50/50 chance' that his author would fail to recover.[17] Sonia knew that if she married Orwell she might soon be a widow, but she also appreciated that he might live for quite a few years. He was, after all, only forty-six and, if his health improved, it was conceivable that he might live to write several more books, with Sonia at his side to help him. She could make use of the practical skills that she had developed at *Horizon*: type his manuscripts, correct his proofs, sort out his business affairs, handle his routine correspondence, and give him editorial opinions on work in progress. (She would no longer need to be a mother to his adopted son, who was being brought up by Orwell's sister.) Orwell needed someone to cut the drudgery and loneliness his work had imposed; and after *Nineteen Eighty-Four* he was a worthy candidate for the devoted attention Sonia had always wanted to lavish on the right 'great man'.

That summer, however, there was another 'great man' in Sonia's life. He was the French philosopher, Maurice Merleau-Ponty, then forty-one and an editorial associate of Sartre's at *Les Temps Modernes*. In 1947, on a visit to France with Peter Watson, Sonia had met Merleau-Ponty and fallen in love with him. They had a brief affair but had seen little of each other after Sonia's return to England. In July 1949 Watson invited Sonia to accompany him on another visit to France, and she quickly accepted because she apparently wanted to see Merleau-Ponty once more before giving a final answer to Orwell's proposal. Although little is known about their reunion in Paris, it appears that they quarrelled and parted on unhappy terms. When she arrived back in London, she was ready to say yes to Orwell. By the end of August she and Orwell had announced that they were planning to marry, and near the end of a long letter to John Myers, Waldemar Hansen wrote: 'I almost forgot, Sonia is going to marry George Orwell next week ... Nobody seems to really approve, since they all feel she is doing it as a Florence Nightingale gesture. There is some truth in that, but the real truth is that she doesn't love M. P. [Merleau-Ponty] any more.'[18]

The marriage did not take place until October, and in the meantime Orwell was moved from the sanatorium to a private room at University College Hospital in Bloomsbury. The hospital was close to Sonia's small flat in Percy Street and to *Horizon*'s office in Bedford Square, so she could be with Orwell frequently. His health remained unpredictable, but he and Sonia decided to have a bedside wedding in his small hospital room. A chaplain married them on 13 October in a brief ceremony, so as not to place too great a strain on Orwell's delicate condition. David Astor and Janetta were the witnesses. Orwell wore a smart new smoking jacket, and David Astor took Sonia for lunch at the Ritz Hotel.

News of Sonia's intention to marry Orwell was slow to reach Peter Watson. He had not seen her since she had accompanied him to Paris; after their arrival he had gone his own way and spent the rest of the summer travelling on the Continent. Late in September he wrote from Paris to Hansen, who was staying in London: 'And Sonia's engagement? It's all a shock to me. This week's *Time* reports it in the People section under the heading "That Old Feeling". Mmm – I'm not so sure.'[19] (On 26 September *Time* noted that Orwell was to marry 'Sonia Brownell, 30 [she was, in fact, thirty-one], assistant editor of the highbrow *Horizon*'.) Although Watson doubted whether love had much to do with Sonia's decision, he was not in a position to know what was happening in her life or in the affairs of *Horizon*. His threatened 'showdown' with Connolly appears not to have taken place, because by the end of the summer nothing had been resolved about the magazine's future. Watson seems to have wanted to remain out of touch with what was going on in London, preferring to put his worries behind him and enjoy his summer on the Continent. He was content to let *Horizon* take care of itself.

Much of his time was spent with Norman Fowler. Waldemar Hansen had feared that Fowler would show up before long, and had learned that Watson was expecting him at the end of July. Hansen had finally been forced to accept that his relationship with Watson had reached 'the end of the end'.[20] In the middle of June they had agreed to spend the rest of the summer apart, but both seemed to regard the separation as final. Hansen went to France for several weeks, and in September he lived at Palace Gate while Watson and Fowler were abroad. Watson was mostly in Italy and Switzerland, absorbed again in the excitement of sharing his favourite European retreats with a young, uninhibited American lover.

Hansen moved out of Palace Gate at the end of September and took ship for New York. It was hard for him to let go of a love which had once seemed full of promise. Earlier in the summer he had received a letter from Watson with an apology for the way things had turned out: 'I am very melancholic and sad and have been thinking a lot. I have come to the conclusion that I was very stupid and have acted badly.' But Watson quickly added a few words in his own defence: 'Whatever I am doing or not doing I am being honest to myself and therefore to everyone else.'[21] Many years later Hansen tried to analyse what had gone wrong, and concluded that the dark side of Watson's character had made their life together impossible: 'Peter was, on one level, a very involved masochist, and he really wanted to be tormented. He wanted to be punished in some way. Denham Fouts was a past master at that. Peter had mistaken a certain kind of melodramatic ardour on my part as an indirect hint that I also was going to lead him into some kind of emotional apache dance ... As time wore on and as I refused to play this involved, subtle game of sado-masochism, he lost interest.'[22]

Norman Fowler did not have any trouble keeping Watson's interest. When they came back from their two-month stay on the Continent, Watson was as deeply attracted to him as before; indeed, he was obsessed with Fowler in the same way he had been obsessed with Denham Fouts in the Thirties. And his new relationship soon began to take on some bizarre twists not unlike those which had characterised his long affair with Fouts. Immediately after returning to London with Watson, Fowler abruptly left Europe far behind and went off to a job as a bookshop clerk in a most unlikely spot: Rio de Janeiro. If this strange move was meant to unsettle Watson, it worked. Fowler left for Brazil on 6 October, and Watson immediately began planning his own trip to South America, hoping to meet his lover there within a few months and persuade him to return to England.

Shortly after Fowler left for Brazil, Watson finally met Connolly to settle the question of *Horizon*'s future. There was no need for a 'showdown'; both men were ready for an agreement. It was now obvious that there was not much room for *Horizon* in the lives of any of the people running it. Watson and Connolly gave some consideration to keeping the magazine alive for a little longer. Connolly suggested that the magazine might be sold to a new patron/publisher who would retain him to edit it as a quarterly. Watson considered having Stephen Spender return to edit the magazine, if only as a way of keeping it going, but this was just talk: *Horizon*'s demise was inevitable. To flourish again, it would need an editor with the wit and inspiration Connolly had shown during the magazine's best years, but by 1949 the splendour of those years was past recapture.

The first sentence of the November 'Comment' gave readers the bad news: *Horizon* would close at the end of 1949. This announcement probably did not surprise too many readers and was softened by Connolly's remark that it might reappear in a year's time. Such a possibility was remote, but there was always the chance that Connolly might have a change of heart, so he kept open the option of reviving the magazine. He was candid about wanting at least a year to forget about editing and do more of his own writing, admitting that as an editor and a writer he was suffering from a 'temporary staleness'.

He had other, less personal reasons for closing the magazine, some of which he had been complaining about in 'Comment' for many months. He spoke out against the malaise which infected life in post-war London, calling the metropolis 'a particularly disheartening centre from which to operate', and making it clear that he longed to escape from its 'sterile' atmosphere. He brought up the problem of finding good contributors from the ranks of young British writers. He lamented the increasingly high costs of producing a literary review of quality, and castigated British readers for not subscribing to *Horizon* in greater numbers. He claimed that the only thing which had prevented a sharp decline in circulation over the previous three years was the steady rise of the magazine's American readership. He fulminated against the 'apathy' of British readers, declaring bitterly that 'a decade ... is quite enough to devote to a lost cause such as the pursuit and marketing of quality in contemporary writing.' (Connolly's complaint was not unfounded. The British circulation of *Horizon*'s principal rival – *Penguin New Writing* – had also suffered a major decline after 1947; in 1950 it too went out of business. There was general agreement that the reading public's interest in serious literature had fallen sharply since the middle years of the decade.)

During the war *Horizon*'s purpose had been clear. Every issue had been a reaffirmation of the importance of culture in wartime; and the enemies of that culture had been easy to spot and to criticise. But in the post-war period those enemies were more difficult to define, the battle lines were more loosely drawn, and the purpose of the struggle was much less certain. *Horizon*'s historical moment had come and gone; never again would one small independent magazine assume such an important place in the cultural life of the nation, attracting so many important writers without cash, political interest or a new literary movement as bait. Watson and Connolly had seized the moment and made the most of it; the decline of their extraordinary partnership was unavoidable.

'A magazine should be the reflection of its time,' the very first 'Comment' had declared, 'and one that ceases to reflect this should come to an end.' Perhaps the greatest thing about *Horizon* was that during its decade of life it captured so brilliantly the spirit of the time. The cultural life of the period comes alive in all its diversity and richness. During his best years at the magazine – as an editor and as the author of 'Comment' – Connolly surveyed the world of literature and art with a discerning eye and was quick to note new developments and react intelligently. The part he played best was that of the affable but eccentric guide, taking readers on a tour through the cultural landscape, pointing out the good as well as the bad features – approaching the job as though he were taking friends on a tour of one of his favourite towns in the South of France. He knows all the monuments, the old palaces and churches, the public squares and gardens, the best hotels and restaurants. He lectures, tells funny stories, argues with the natives, condemns signs of neglect, recalls fond memories, and occasionally mumbles something about his own life. He is not the best guide – he has a tendency to stray from his subject and is moody and disorganised. But no guide could be more entertaining, more intriguing, more perceptive, more appreciative of the fine scenery.

## III

Connolly wanted to believe that an escape from *Horizon* would unclutter his life and give him the freedom to be a 'real' writer again, but *Horizon* had not been much of a burden on either his time or his energy. By the end of the Forties he spent no more than a few hours each week on editorial business, leaving more than enough time to attend to his own writing. It was easy to place some of the blame for his problems on the magazine, and to forget how much its success had boosted his reputation. It was still 'only' a magazine, and he feared that as long as he stayed with it he would be regarded as 'only' a man of letters. Sink or swim, he had to 'walk the plank', as he put it, to prove that his talent was 'creative' by writing a book which resembled the literary form so highly prized by the reading public and men of letters: the novel.[23]

There was every reason to doubt that Connolly would settle down quietly and begin working diligently on a new book. To do that, he would need stability and tranquillity in his life, a rather unlikely event as long as he thought he could find literary inspiration in non-stop romantic adventures. Lys had returned to live with him at Sussex Place, but by the autumn their relationship was again on the point of collapse.

Connolly was now pursuing a stunningly attractive woman who had been a favourite companion of King Farouk. Her name was Barbara Skelton and although Connolly had known her during the war it was only at the end of the Forties – when she was approaching her mid-thirties – that he became involved with her. He found her sexual appeal irresistible, describing her once as a sensuous 'lioness – her silvery hair and her greenish and feline eyes'.[24] She was also a moody, difficult woman who was Connolly's match when arguments flared up, which was frequently. 'A destructive and empty girl, mischievous but not ever lethal on any very big scale', Edmund Wilson said of her.[25] The tough, combative side of Barbara had its appeal for Connolly: she was fully up to the job of filling his emotional life with complications. He once called her 'a good companion for the desperate', and remarked that being alone with her for any time made him feel as though he 'had been to a Tring for the emotion instead of the body'. Trying to explain his involvement with Barbara, he wrote, 'B. is certainly unhappy but she is tough and she is so horrible to me most of the time that I don't feel guilt about her.'[26]

Despite all their troubles, Lys stayed with Connolly through *Horizon*'s final days, helping to bring out the last issue and oversee the tedious work of closing down the magazine's business affairs. *Horizon*'s tradition of eclecticism was carried through to the final number: three short poems by Octavio Paz and C. Day Lewis's long poem 'Flight to Italy'; a short story by a new American writer, James Lord; an essay on the Marquis de Sade by Maurice Blanchot; Geoffrey Gorer's 'Some Notes on the British Character'; and Robert Melville's essay on Francis Bacon's paintings, which was illustrated by a reproduction of the profoundly disturbing 'Three Studies for Figures at the Base of a Crucifixion' – an apocalyptic vision which suited the occasion of *Horizon*'s death. Connolly's final 'Comment' had an apocalyptic touch, too. He cast an eye towards the future and found no sign of promise on the horizon, declaring in the last sentence: 'It is closing time in the gardens of the West and from now on an artist will be judged only by the resonance of his solitude or the quality of his despair.'

This last pronouncement has become the most famous of the sentences Connolly wrote for *Horizon*, but it appears at the end of an editorial which is perhaps one of his dullest and most predictable. The sentence is the only jewel; the rest is a summary of the issue's contents, with a single paragraph in the middle providing some random reflections on the magazine's ten years. Weary and distracted, Connolly goes through the motions of evaluating *Horizon*'s record, writing in a flat, understated way about its achievements. 'We have always believed,' he says, 'that the real vocation of this magazine was to feel its way to what is, in the best sense of the word, contemporary, to print what many years hence will be recognised as alive and original.' This is true enough, but it lacks the forceful tone of conviction it deserves, and which Connolly in earlier times would have given it.

To find his best words on the magazine's life-and-times one must go to the introductions of the two books issued in 1953: *Ideas and Places*, his second book of essays, which includes many of his postwar editorials from *Horizon*; and *The Golden Horizon*, his personal anthology of material from the magazine. In the latter he writes engagingly about the challenges of editorial work, recalling the experience of 'being given once a month the opportunity to produce a perfect number and every month failing, and just when despair sets in, being presented with one more chance. Plop! The afternoon post falls on the carpet, the letter-box becomes a periscope on the outside world, encouragement arrives and fat subscriptions, notices in other magazines, letters from California and Brazil, contributions from all over the world, one of which may have been long awaited and another be totally unexpected and yet just as good.'

The announcement of *Horizon*'s closing brought Connolly letters from friends and admirers who were distressed that the magazine would no longer occupy a place in their lives. One of the most interesting came from Augustus John, whose autobiography was featured as a long serial in *Horizon*, at irregular intervals between 1941 and 1949. Like many other admirers, he felt there was 'nothing to take the place of *Horizon*'. He remarked: 'Our civilisation grows more and more to resemble a mixture of a concentration and a Butlin camp and without your unique magazine there won't be much of a view left or means to escape to open country.'[27]

By the end of the year the office was empty. 'We closed the long windows over Bedford Square,' Connolly wrote later, 'the telephone was taken, the furniture stored, the back numbers went to their cellar, the files rotted in the dust. Only contributions continued to be delivered, like a suicide's milk.'[28] Peter Watson was conspicuously absent during *Horizon*'s last days. Even before the final issue had appeared, he had gone to visit Norman Fowler in Rio de Janeiro, and he did not return until February 1950. He was determined to spend more time with Fowler despite the enormous distance that separated them and, as usual, he was happy to have an excuse for escaping the winter gloom of London which the death of *Horizon* would make even more depressing. Very little news reached him in Brazil; he did not even see a copy of *Horizon*'s last issue until late in January, when he passed through Jamaica on the way back to England. He read it in Kingston, thousands of miles from home and ten years after he had first held a copy in his hands.

Back in England, Sonia was helping Orwell in his last illness. His condition had worsened, and he was weak and painfully thin, joking feebly that he was 'just like a skeleton'.[29] The doctors had warned against his remaining in London for the winter, suggesting that the higher altitude of a Swiss or French sanatorium might prove beneficial, perhaps reducing some of the pressure on his lungs. He and Sonia approved, and made plans to move to a Swiss clinic at the end of January, chartering a plane to get there. Despite his appearance and the pain he suffered, Orwell refused to give up hope. Among the belongings he wanted Sonia to pack for their trip was a fishing-rod, which he looked forward to using after his recovery, perhaps in the spring. He did not recover. Within the space of a month, literature lost not only *Horizon* but *Horizon*'s greatest contributor. On 21 January 1950 Orwell's lung haemorrhaged, and he died during the night.

Many years after his friend's death, Connolly lamented that success had come too late for Orwell: 'He had fame and was too ill to leave his room, money and nothing to spend it on, love in which he could not participate: he tasted the bitterness of dying.'[30] But, as Connolly was well aware, Orwell never cared much for fame or money. He preferred to live modestly and did not expect that his last two novels would do so well. But his love for Sonia did matter; regardless of what anyone thought, he regarded her as a fantasy come to life and, if he did recognise at the end that she would never be fully his, indeed he must have felt keenly 'the bitterness of dying'. He gave Sonia all that could be left behind of his fame and fortune. There was a large insurance policy to benefit his adopted son, but the rest of his estate went to Sonia, who would achieve a certain fame as the widow of the 'great man'.

## IV

'G. Orwell is dead and Mrs Orwell presumably a rich widow,' Evelyn Waugh wrote to Nancy Mitford, adding maliciously: 'Will Cyril marry her? He is said to be consorting with Miss Skelton.'[31] It might have delighted Waugh to contemplate Connolly pursuing Sonia, but it was a product of his imagination. He was, however, right about Barbara Skelton; Connolly was spending more and more time with her, and it was clear that his life with Lys was almost at an end.

She moved out of Sussex Place early in the summer, and although she saw Connolly from time to time during the next few months she considered their relationship over. But he could not walk away from any romance, no matter how troubled. 'A well-tried love like ours is the most valuable thing two people can have,' he wrote, 'it has nothing to do with sex or marriage.'[32] He admitted that he had behaved badly over the past two years, but he also thought that she had failed him. 'If you had understood me better you would have realised that I loved you and needed you but that I was in despair at the emptiness of my London existence ... It was not you but my own life I was fed up with – the Etoile, the Gargoyle, *Horizon* etc. I don't know what you could have done for it or me, but at least you need not have left me.'[33]

Such rationalisations did not change Lys's mind. After nearly a decade of living and working in the background to Connolly, she set out to establish a separate existence, and before the summer was out had made a good beginning, as an assistant in the London office of the *New Yorker*.

Connolly's fascination with Barbara lost none of its intensity. When she travelled to France to spend a few weeks with King Farouk, Connolly followed her, remaining at a distance but taking every opportunity to see her alone. According to Peter Watson, 'While the Royal party was at Biarritz gambling through the night Cyril was waiting at St Jean de Luz for Barbara on her days-off.'[34] To the amazement of many of their friends, Connolly and Barbara were married shortly afterwards in a civil ceremony in Kent. They quarrelled on their way to the ceremony and they quarrelled on their way back. Within days Connolly was complaining that he had not meant to get married again, and that he wanted to go back to Lys. But Lys would not have him, and there was nowhere else for him to go. Sussex Place was put up for sale, and he moved to Oak Cottage, Barbara's four-roomed house in Kent. The newlyweds led a stormy life there, each apparently determined to use their marriage as a form of punishment for the frustrations and failings in their lives. Barbara has described this period vividly, portraying it as an exercise in verbal warfare punctuated by periods of uneasy silence when Connolly would assume a dark expression, 'brooding like a furious fallen emperor'.[35]

At the end of 1950, Lys announced that she was leaving England and settling permanently in America. She was taking a job in New York as an assistant editor at Doubleday. Despite his marriage, Connolly was writing her long, agonised letters explaining how much he wanted to have her back, but her decision made it clear that there was no room left for him in her life. That America was her destination was a painfully ironic reminder of the way Jean had left him in 1940. 'Your departure is so like Jean's,' he wrote to Lys, 'that it reopens all the agony and confuses it so that I feel my heart is breaking.'[36] His first wife was very much in his thoughts at this time. Earlier in the summer a telegram from Jean's sister contained the news that Jean had died at the age of thirty-nine. She had suffered a stroke while on a visit to Paris with Laurence Vail, and had not recovered.

Just as Jean's departure had signalled the end of his 'Condemned Playground' days, so Lys's departure was a reminder that his *Horizon* years were over. The finality of that fact did not sit comfortably because his 'sabbatical' had run out and he had nothing to show for the year which had passed. He was short of money, his marriage was filled with turmoil, his plans to write a new book had not worked, he had no permanent job, and there was no hope of reviving *Horizon*. He was bitter and missing the life he had so deliberately put aside at the close of the Forties. 'Really, I think life is awful everywhere for almost everyone,' he observed of English life in a letter to Lys shortly after she had settled in America, 'it's only because of Peter's Bounty that we didn't find it out ourselves before!'[37]

He began writing more reviews to earn money, and gradually found himself slipping back into literary journalism. He was offered a permanent position with the *Sunday Times*, and though he considered the job to be 'glorified hack-work' he took it.[38] He went on trying to write fiction; his efforts to complete a novel did not succeed, but part of an unfinished novel – 'Shade Those Laurels' – found its way into print as a magazine feature in 1956. The accomplishments of his *Horizon* years faded quickly into the past, and the best years of his career were behind him. In 1953 he wrote to Lys,

I don't know if I will ever finish a novel or indeed anything – so much of the time I feel my life is over and I am just 'waiting for death' as my father used to say – or rather preparing for it like an examination and having to give up many activities because they interfere with the examination, but I have no thoughts of God or spiritual illumination, only extraordinarily vivid dreams of you and Jean – and when it comes it will be death by boredom. (He 'literally' bored himself to death, poor Cyril.) It is not an inner boredom so much as an ever increasing death-wish as if one was following a beautiful woman. The other night I had a sudden vision of you walking towards me along the edge of the pavement in the brown coat I bought you with the velvet collar.and a yellow scarf round your head – it was not a dream but like a shot in a film-sequence. Ever since I have tried to start this film going again but with no success.[39]

# EPILOGUE

Connolly, Watson, and Sonia Orwell continued to see one another fairly often in London in the early 1950s, keeping their old friendships alive long after the death of *Horizon*. Lys remained in New York; she prospered in her job at Doubleday and developed a large circle of American friends, which included Edmund Wilson and the *New Yorker* cartoonist Charles Addams. For a time she was also close to Waldemar Hansen, who had kept up his interests in writing: he served as a ghost writer for Cecil Beaton in the Fifties and later published a book of his own – *The Peacock Throne*, a history of the Moghuls in India. In 1955 Lys married Sigmund Koch, a young psychologist, and eventually she and her new husband settled in North Carolina, where he became a distinguished professor at Duke University.

Sonia became an editor at Weidenfeld and Nicolson, and in 1953 helped to oversee that firm's publication of *The Golden Horizon*, which Connolly dedicated to her. In the 1960s she co-edited *Art and Literature*, a small review based in Paris, and in 1968 she was the co-editor of the four-volume *Collected Essays, Journalism and Letters of George Orwell*, a magnificent work which testifies to her late husband's genius. Twelve years later, near the end of 1980, she died at the age of sixty-two.

Connolly divorced Barbara Skelton in 1956, and in 1959 he married Deirdre Craig, a young woman half his age. In 1960, when he was in his late fifties, Connolly became a father for the first time. Deirdre bore him a daughter, Cressida, and later a son, Matthew, named after Major Connolly. He and his family settled in East Sussex, and in the last few years of his life his home was in Eastbourne, not far from the site of St Cyprian's, his old prep school. He kept his position with the *Sunday Times*, commuting to London, and in 1963 he put together the first collection of his newspaper reviews, publishing them under the title *Previous Convictions*. This was followed in 1973 by a second, and final, collection – *The Evening Colonnade*. There are a number of superb prose passages in each of these books, and scattered among them are many bits and pieces of autobiographical detail, some of which have been referred to in this book.

Unable to make any progress with longer forms, he exercised his talent for autobiography in the short bursts his reviews sometimes allowed him. Part of the pleasure of reading *Previous Convictions* and *The Evening Colonnade* comes from following the intricate process by which both books build up a portrait of the critic as a man and an artist. It is a delicate pattern which weaves its way through the sturdy fabric of his literary journalism. Although made up of fragments which suggest only vaguely the outlines of a larger, unified work, the beauty and wit of those fragments should not be undervalued. In 1960, when Connolly brought out a special American edition of *Enemies of Promise* which included a short collection of his literary journalism, he told his readers, 'Do not despise the scrappiness of my book. I work best in scraps and, besides, a little of me goes a long way.'

Watson stayed active in the ICA in the post-*Horizon* years. In 1950 he helped to organise two important exhibitions – 'London/Paris: New Trends in Painting and Sculpture' (Bacon, Craxton, and Freud were among the English artists represented); and '1950: Aspects of British Art' (Watson wrote the exhibition pamphlet and Graham Sutherland designed the poster). Also in 1950, Norman Fowler returned to England to live with Watson. Shortly afterwards, Fowler developed an ambition to be a sculptor, so Watson looked for a place in the country where his young lover could work quietly and where they could enjoy refuge from the cares of the busy world outside. After so many years of living in his cramped quarters at Palace Gate, Watson was ready for a change. He wrote of his house-hunting efforts: 'I am very choosy and want something small but terribly grand and aristocratic. No cottages please – however cunningly converted. When the hydrogen bomb bursts I want to disintegrate in ... dust made up of Renaissance plaster-work, William Kent tables, Picassos, brandy and Alban Berg records.'[1]

He looked at house after house, but he was never able to locate just the right one. When he and Fowler moved from Palace Gate, early in 1956, it was to go to another flat not far away, at 53 Rutland Gate. Watson told friends that he was pleased with the new place, which he described as 'spacious, quiet and warm, in fact quite unusual for London.'[2] Just before making the move, he had been ill, suffering from anaemia during the coldest weeks of the winter, but his health improved in the spring, and he was in a bright mood, working enthusiastically on a new ICA exhibition. Lunching with him one day in April, Cecil Beaton was impressed by Watson's improved spirit, noting that he seemed lively and self-assured, 'a completely fulfilled, integrated person; someone who has been through many vicissitudes and has now discovered himself.'[3] But, tragically, there was not much time left him. On 3 May his life was cut short; he was found dead in the bathroom of his new flat, having mysteriously drowned in his bath.

It was a sad and curious end to a life so unselfishly devoted to art and beauty. The *New Statesman* published a notice of his death written by Stephen Spender, who had become the co-editor of *Encounter*, a small magazine which events would prove was sponsored by the Central Intelligence Agency. Although Spender says that he was unaware of the CIA's involvement until much later, his remarks about his old patron at *Horizon* make an interesting contrast with the nature of the patronage at *Encounter*. 'No other patron,' he wrote of Watson 'was so individual, so non-institutional: even the word "patron" seems wrong for him – perhaps a better word would be friend.'[4]

Watson was not alone in the flat at the time of his death. Norman Fowler was there, and the young American soon fell under police suspicion. His version of events was that he had fallen asleep in the bedroom while Watson was in the bathroom, and that he had called to his friend when he woke but had received no response. Finding the bathroom door locked and water flowing underneath it, he ran out to the street and found a policeman, who had broken down the door. They found the taps still running and Watson's body slumped down in the overflowing bath, with his nose and mouth under water. At the inquest Fowler admitted that he had quarrelled with Watson just hours before. Watson had returned from a short visit to friends in the country, and when Fowler had asked questions about the visit, demanding to know the names of the friends, an argument had broken out. It ended when Watson disappeared abruptly into the bathroom, announcing that he had no more to say and was going to prepare a hot bath for himself. A short time later he was dead.

No case was ever brought against Fowler: murder and suicide were both ruled out at the inquest. The final verdict was that the death was accidental. One assumption seems to have been that he had suffered a fainting fit, and drowned; another, less convincing, was that he had fallen into a deep sleep before drowning. There was no evidence of heart failure, and the fact that the door had been locked from the inside convinced the authorities that there was no foul play. But the idea that a man in his forties, with a healthy heart, who was over six feet tall, could drown in his bath is difficult to accept. It is impossible to say now whether the evidence of the locked door is proof enough that Fowler did not have any part in Watson's death. The body was cremated and Fowler is now dead. However, Fowler was a strange, deeply disturbed young man whose surviving letters reveal an intense fascination with death, especially violent death. One letter, written to Waldemar Hansen in 1952, describes a long dream about death. It is a confused, frightening vision in which a nameless, bloody form pursues Fowler along a rocky seashore:

> The figure stood on a sheer precipice which dropped to a series of three ledges each only a few feet wide. Below was the sea. It lept. It landed with an ungodly agonizing groan. Badly hurt, with bits of flesh torn from his body. I realized with horror the intention. It raised itself, cutting its hands . . . tearing strips of flesh off. It fell to the second ledge. The same. The third, the same. By this time it was unrecognizable, a formless bloody pulp. A streaming path of flesh and blood from the first ledge to the last. The last struggle was one of nerve and torn tissue, into the sea. The sea was immediately rendered from red and grey into bloody red. The sea the sky me and me all blood.[5]

Fowler inherited most of Watson's estate, which included considerable cash and several impressive works of art – pieces by Braque, Giacometti, Juan Gris, Henry Moore, Rodin, and even an early oil by Poussin. (Two thousand pounds was left to Sonia, and one thousand went to Connolly.) Not long after Watson's death Fowler went to live in the British Virgin Islands, where he spent a good deal of time sailing and fishing. Eventually he bought a small resort hotel on the island of Nevis, called the Bath Hotel, because there were a number of large hot water baths where the weary tourist could soak away the cares of life.

On 23 March 1971, a few weeks before the fifteenth anniversary of Watson's death, Norman Fowler died. He was forty-four. There was some suspicion that he had been murdered, but the local investigation into the circumstances of his death turned up no evidence to support a murder charge. On his death certificate, there is this simple notation for the cause of death: 'Coroner's inquest subsequently held verdict death by drowning in hot water bath at Bath Hotel.'

# NOTES

On the first citation of a book, full publication information is provided. A shortened form is used for subsequent references. The Select Bibliography has a list of sources consulted in the writing of this book.

The following shortened terms are used in the Notes:

Beaton Papers   Letters from Peter Watson to Cecil Beaton, in the possession of the Beaton estate

Columbia   Butler Library, Columbia University

Craxton Papers Letters from Peter Watson to John Craxton, in the possession of John Craxton

Eton   Eton College Library

HP   Letters from Peter Watson to Waldemar Hansen, and other personal papers, in the possession of Waldemar Hansen

Harvard   Houghton Library, Harvard University

Lilly   Lilly Library, Indiana University

Northwestern   Special Collections, Northwestern University Library, Evanston

Orwell Archive Orwell Archive, University College, London

Princeton   Rare Books and Manuscripts, Princeton University Library

Texas   Harry Ransom Humanities Research Center, University of Texas

Tulsa   McFarlin Library, University of Tulsa

Victoria   University of Victoria Library, British Columbia

Washington   University of Washington Library, Seattle

Yale   Manuscripts and Archives, Yale University Library

## INTRODUCTION

1 David Pryce-Jones, *Cyril Connolly: Journal and Memoir* (London: Collins, 1983) 244.

2 Roland Penrose, 'Cyril and Peter: Complementary Opposites', *Adam*, Nos. 385–390 (1974–75).

3 'Comment', *Horizon* July 1942.

4 'Comment', *Horizon* April 1940 [reprinted in *The Condemned Playground* 267].

5 Stephen Spender, *The Thirties and After: Poetry, Politics, People, 1939–1970* (New York: Random House, 1978) 66.

6 Raymond Mortimer, 'Books in General', *New Statesman* 30 December 1944; Edmund Wilson, 'Books', *New Yorker* 27 October 1945.

7 'Comment', *Horizon* November 1949 [reprinted in *Ideas and Places* 211–14].

8 *The Evening Colonnade* (London: David Bruce and Watson, 1973) 423.

9 'Literary Outlook', *Times Literary Supplement* 1 January 1954.

## CHAPTER ONE

1 Matthew Connolly to Cyril Connolly, 23 August [1940] (Tulsa).

2 *The Evening Colonnade* 499.

3 *Previous Convictions* (London: Hamish Hamilton, 1963) 402.

4 Quoted in Pryce-Jones, *Cyril Connolly* 29.

5 Quotations describing Connolly's time at Eton are taken from 'A Georgian Boyhood', *Enemies of Promise* (London: Routledge, 1938; revised edition, 1949).

6 *The Evening Colonnade* (New York: Harcourt Brace, 1975) 10. There are essays in the American edition that are not in the British edition and vice versa, so the notes hereafter will indicate which edition is being cited. In cases where the same essay is included in both editions, the reference will be to the British one.

7 Ibid.

8 Quoted in John Russell, Introduction, *A Chime of Words: The Letters of Logan Pearsall Smith*, ed. Edwin Tribble (New York: Ticknor and Fields, 1984).

9 *A Romantic Friendship: Cyril Connolly's Letters to Noel Blakiston*, ed. Noel Blakiston (London: Constable, 1975) 161.

10 See Daniel Halpern, 'Interview with Cyril Connolly,' *Antaeus* Winter 1971.

11 Ibid.

12 Pryce-Jones, *Cyril Connolly* 202, 215, 216.

13 *A Romantic Friendship* 330.

14 Ibid. 332.

15 See Introduction, *The Condemned Playground: Essays, 1927–1944* (London: Routledge, 1945).

16 Cyril Connolly to Sylvia Beach, n.d. [early 1935] (Princeton).

17 Ibid.

18 Cyril Connolly wrote to George Orwell in the spring of 1936 (Orwell Archive). The long sentence that is so critical of London publishers is taken from the Preface, *The Rock Pool* (New York: Scribner's, 1936).

19 Quoted in Cyril Connolly, 'Some Memories', *W. H. Auden: A Tribute*, ed. Stephen Spender (New York: Macmillan, 1975) 72.

20 See Pryce-Jones, *Cyril Connolly* 246.

21 At her request, Diana is referred to in this book by her first name only.

22 Cyril Connolly to Jean Connolly, n.d. [9 July 1939, and 10 July 1939] (Tulsa).

23 Cyril Connolly to Jean Connolly, n.d. [4 July 1939 and 10 July 1939] (Tulsa).

24 Cyril Connolly to Jean Connolly, n.d. [late July 1939] (Tulsa).

25 'The Movies', *New Statesman* 12 August 1939.

26 Cyril Connolly to Jean Connolly, n.d. [22 August 1939] (Tulsa).

27 Peter Watson to Cyril Connolly, 17 August [1939] (Tulsa).

28 'Horizon' typescript, n.d. [March 1940] (Tulsa).

29 Cyril Connolly to Jean Connolly, n.d. [6 September 1939] (Tulsa).

## CHAPTER TWO

1 Stephen Spender to author, March 1984.

2 'Horizon' typescript, n.d. [March 1940] (Tulsa).

3 Stephen Spender, Unpublished journal, 1956 (Tulsa).

4 Ibid.

5 Stephen Spender to author, March 1984.

6 'Great Anarchs', *New Statesman* 4 May 1935.

7 Stephen Spender, *Journals: 1939–1983*, ed. John Goldsmith (London: Faber, 1985) 23.

8 T. S. Eliot to Stephen Spender, 5 October 1939 (Northwestern).

9 Virginia Woolf, *The Diary of Virginia Woolf*, ed. Anne Olivier Bell, 5 volumes (London: Hogarth Press, 1977–1984) 5: 251.

10 John Lehmann, *In My Own Time: Memoirs of a Literary Life* (Boston: Atlantic-Little, Brown, 1969) 247.

11 Virginia Woolf, *The Letters of Virginia Woolf*, ed. Nigel Nicolson and Joanne Troutmann, 6 volumes (London: Hogarth Press, 1975–1980) 6: 364.

12 Spender, *Journals* 22.

13 Woolf, *Diary* 5: 247.

14 Unsigned letter, 23 October 1939 (Tulsa).

15 Stephen Spender, *World Within World* (London: Hamish Hamilton, 1951) 296.

16 *The Evening Colonnade* (British edition) 425.

17 Diana to author, July 1985.

18 Written on the back of unsigned letter, 23 October 1939 (Tulsa).

19 Cyril Connolly to Maud Connolly, n.d. [14 October 1939] (Tulsa).

20 Ibid.

21 Peter Watson to Parker Tyler, 18 October [1939] (Texas).

22 Edouard Roditi to author, 12 February 1985.
23 Diana to author, July 1985.
24 Peter Watson to Cecil Beaton, 12 December 1939 (Beaton Papers).
25 Peter Watson to Parker Tyler, 28 November [1939] (Texas).
26 *New Statesman*, 16 December 1939.
27 Cyril Connolly to Diana, n.d. [late 1939] (private collection).
28 Peter Watson to Parker Tyler, 7 January 1940 (Texas).
29 Quoted in Humphrey Carpenter, *W. H. Auden: A Biography* (Boston: Houghton Mifflin, 1981) 291.
30 George Orwell, *The Collected Essays, Journalism and Letters of George Orwell*, ed. Sonia Orwell and Ian Angus, 4 volumes (1968; Harmondsworth: Penguin Books, 1980) 4: 378.
31 Spender, *World Within World* 293–5.
32 Quoted in J. Maclaren-Ross, *Memoirs of the Forties* (1965; Harmondsworth: Penguin Books, 1984) 78.
33 Spender, *The Thirties and After* 215–16.
34 Jean Connolly to Cyril Connolly, n.d. [29 February 1940] (Tulsa).
35 Jean Connolly to Cyril Connolly, n.d. [26 March 1940] (Tulsa).
36 Jean Connolly to Cyril Connolly, n.d. [10 June 1940] (Tulsa).

## CHAPTER THREE

1 Spender, *Journals* 57.
2 Diana to author, July 1985.
3 Cyril Connolly to Tony Witherby, n.d. [early August 1940] (private collection).
4 Diana to author, July 1985.
5 Ibid.
6 Peter Watson to Waldemar Hansen, 28 March [1947] (HP).
7 Truman Capote, 'Unspoiled Monsters', *Esquire* May 1976.
8 Ricki Riker to author, January 1985.
9 See 'Some Memories', *W. H. Auden: A Tribute* 70.
10 Jean Connolly to Cyril Connolly, 16 November 1945 (Tulsa).
11 Cyril Connolly to Jean Connolly, n.d. (Tulsa).
12 Cancelled passage from corrected proofs of *The Unquiet Grave* (Lilly).
13 'What Will *He* Do Next?' is reprinted in *The Condemned Playground*.
14 Orwell, *Collected Essays, Journalism, and Letters* 2: 444.
15 'Comment', *Horizon* December 1940.
16 Peter Quennell to author, June 1985.
17 Harold Nicolson, *The War Years: 1939–1945, Volume Two of Diaries and Letters*, ed. Nigel Nicolson (New York: Atheneum, 1967) 388.
18 Peter Watson to Cecil Beaton, n.d. [autumn 1940] (Beaton Papers).
19 Peter Watson to Parker Tyler, 26 May [1940] (Texas).
20 Peter Watson to Cecil Beaton, n.d. [autumn 1940] (Beaton Papers).
21 Spender, *World Within World* 292.

22 Quoted by Connolly in the Introduction to *The Golden Horizon* (London: Weidenfeld and Nicolson, 1953).
23 Quoted in John Pikoulis, *Alun Lewis: A Life* (Bridgend: Poetry Wales Press, 1984) 126–7.
24 Diana to author, June 1987.
25 Diana to author, August 1985.
26 Peter Quennell, *The Wanton Chase: An Autobiography from 1939* (London: Collins, 1980) 16.
27 Lys Koch to author, October 1984.
28 Ibid.
29 Information provided to author by Lady Caroline Lowell, July 1985.
30 Lys Koch to author, October 1984.
31 Quennell, *The Wanton Chase* 21–2.
32 Elizabeth Bowen to Cyril Connolly, 10 May 1945 (Tulsa).

## CHAPTER FOUR

1 Spender, *Journals* 433.
2 Sonia Brownell to Stephen Spender, 4 March 1940 (Tulsa).
3 Cyril Connolly to Anne Dunn, n.d. (Tulsa).
4 The manuscript of Connolly's unfinished novel is located at the McFarlin Library (Tulsa).
5 See Stephen Wadhams, *Remembering Orwell* (Harmondsworth: Penguin Books, 1984) 213.
6 Quoted in Spender, *Journals* 435.
7 Wadhams, *Remembering Orwell* 213.
8 Ibid.
9 Spender, *Journals* 434.
10 Cyril Connolly to Diana, n.d. [early 1941] (private collection).
11 Peter Watson to Brian Howard, n.d. [1944?] (Eton).
12 Information provided to author by John Craxton, July 1985.
13 See the pamphlet *John Craxton: An Exhibition of Paintings and Drawings, 1980–85* (London: Christopher Hull Gallery, 1985) 21.
14 See the pamphlet *John Craxton: Paintings and Drawings, 1941–1966* (London: Whitechapel Art Gallery, 1967) 9.
15 Peter Watson to John Craxton, n.d. [1941?] (Craxton Papers).
16 Priaulx Rainier, 'Personal Recollections', *Adam* Nos. 385–390 (1974–75).
17 Dylan Thomas, *The Collected Letters of Dylan Thomas*, ed. Paul Ferris (London: Dent, 1985) 452.
18 Ibid. 471–3.
19 See interview with Stephen Spender, *Writers at Work: The Paris Review Interview*, 6th series, ed. George Plimpton (New York: Viking, 1984) 45.
20 Quoted in Constance FitzGibbon, *The Life of Dylan Thomas* (London: Dent, 1965) 303.
21 Thomas, *Collected Letters* 575.

22 'Comment', *Horizon* February 1943.
23 Quoted in Iain Hamilton, *Koestler* (New York: Macmillan, 1982) 76.
24 Lys Koch to author, 8 November 1984.
25 Quennell, *The Wanton Chase* 21.
26 Harold Nicolson to Cyril Connolly, 21 July 1941 (Tulsa).
27 'Comment', *Horizon* December 1941.
28 S. Lawford Childs to Klaus Mann, 3 April 1941 (Yale).
29 'Highbrows' *Horizon*', *Time* 25 March 1946.
30 Cyril Connolly to Klaus Mann, 3 April 1941 (Yale).
31 '*Horizon*'s Questionnaire', *Horizon* April 1941.
32 T. S. Eliot to Stephen Spender, 3 February 1941 (Northwestern).
33 T. S. Eliot to Cyril Connolly, 10 May 1941 (Northwestern).
34 William Makins to Stephen Spender, n.d. (Northwestern).
35 Cyril Connolly to Herbert Read, 26 November 1941 (Victoria).
36 Cyril Connolly to Herbert Read, 5 December 1941 (Victoria).
37 Unpublished manuscript, 'Dialogue between Ego and Superego' (Tulsa).
38 Stephen Spender to author, March 1984.
39 Quoted in Wadhams, *Remembering Orwell* 142.
40 Lehmann, *In My Own Time* 277.
41 Introduction, *The Golden Horizon*.
42 Connolly's talk was later printed in *Talking to India: A Selection of English Language Broadcasts to India*, ed. George Orwell (London: Allen and Unwin, 1943).
43 Quoted in Spender, *The Thirties and After* 67.
44 Diana to her brother, 1 May 1942 (private collection).
45 Peter Watson to John Craxton, n.d. [1942] (Craxton Papers).

## CHAPTER FIVE

1 Evelyn Waugh, *The Letters of Evelyn Waugh*, ed. Mark Amory (1980; Harmondsworth: Penguin Books, 1982) 182.
2 Ibid. 579.
3 Evelyn Waugh, *The Diaries of Evelyn Waugh*, ed. Michael Davie (1976; Harmondsworth: Penguin Books, 1982) 451.
4 Waugh, *Letters* 578, 137.
5 *The Evening Colonnade* (American edition) 8.
6 Christopher Sykes, *Evelyn Waugh: A Biography* (1975; Harmondsworth: Penguin Books, 1978) 542–3.
7 Waugh, *Letters* 578.
8 Quoted in Ann Fleming, *The Letters of Ann Fleming*, ed. Mark Amory (London: Collins Harvill, 1985) 295.
9 Waugh, *Letters* 578.
10 Janetta Parladé to author, March 1984. Janetta's brother was the pilot Rollo Woolley, who contributed a story to *Horizon* before he was shot down over North Africa.
11 Waugh, *Letters* 346–8.

12  Ibid. 375.

13  Spender, *The Thirties and After* 215.

14  Cancelled passage from corrected proofs of *The Unquiet Grave* (Lilly).

15  'Sotheby's as an Education', *Sotheby's 217th Season* (London: Sotheby, 1960).

16  Draft letter, n.d. [1944] (Tulsa).

17  Peter Watson to Cyril Connolly, n.d. (Tulsa).

18  Quoted in Clive Jordan, 'Among the Lost Things', *Daily Telegraph Magazine* 25 February 1972.

19  Quoted in Wadhams, *Remembering Orwell* 143.

20  Eric Blair [George Orwell] to Cyril Connolly, n.d. [1942] (Orwell Archive).

21  David Astor to Cyril Connolly, 20 August 1943 (Tulsa).

22  David Astor to Peter Quennell, 21 August 1943 (Tulsa).

23  Draft letter, n.d. [1943] (Tulsa).

24  Lord Astor to Cyril Connolly, 7 September 1943 (Tulsa).

25  Interview Notes, Cyril Connolly to John Pearson, 11 March 1965 (Lilly).

26  Cyril Connolly to Lys, n.d. [18 May 1943] (Lilly).

27  Brian Howard to Cyril Connolly, 9 June 1942 (Tulsa). Connolly wrote his own description of this incident on the back of the envelope containing Howard's letter.

28  Foreword, *Enemies of Promise and Other Essays: An Autobiography of Ideas* (Garden City: Anchor Books, 1960).

29  Introduction, *Previous Convictions*.

30  Introduction, *The Unquiet Grave: A Word Cycle by Palinurus* (1944; 2nd revised edition, London: Hamish Hamilton, 1951).

31  Connolly's term 'erotic nostalgia' can be found in *The Evening Colonnade* (British edition) 183.

32  Evelyn Waugh, 'A Pilot All at Sea', *Tablet* 10 November 1945.

33  Quoted in Wendy Baron, *Miss Ethel Sands and Her Circle* (London: Peter Owen, 1977) 253.

34  Jean Connolly to Cyril Connolly, 10 December 1945 (Tulsa).

35  'Letter from a Civilian', *Horizon* September 1944 (reprinted in *Ideas and Places* 2–6).

36  Ibid.

37  Ibid.

38  Peter Watson to Brian Howard, 11 January [1943] (Eton).

39  Peter Watson to Brian Howard, n.d. [July 1943] (Eton).

40  Peter Watson to Brian Howard, n.d. [December 1947] (Eton).

41  Rainier, 'Personal Recollections'.

42  Peter Watson to John Craxton, n.d. [1944] (Craxton Papers).

43  Lys Koch to author, December 1984.

44  'Letter from a Civilian', *Horizon* September 1944.

45  Matthew Connolly to Cyril Connolly, 29 June 1944 (Tulsa).

46  'Some Memories', *W. H. Auden: A Tribute* 71.

47  Matthew Connolly to Cyril Connolly, 15 June 1941 (Tulsa).

48 Quoted in Frederic Prokosch, *Voices: A Memoir* (New York: Farrar Straus, 1983) 169.
49 Ernest Hemingway to Cyril Connolly, 15 March 1948 (Tulsa).

# CHAPTER SIX

1 Cyril Connolly to Lys, n.d. [January 1945] (Lilly).
2 Ibid.
3 'Comment', *Horizon* May 1945 (reprinted in *Ideas and Places* 11–25).
4 Quoted in Herbert R. Lottman, *The Left Bank: Writers, Artists, and Politics from the Popular Front to the Cold War* (Boston: Houghton Mifflin, 1982) 198.
5 'Comment', *Horizon* May 1945.
6 Ibid.
7 Ibid.
8 'Comment', *Horizon* January 1946 (reprinted in *Ideas and Places* 52–5).
9 Edmund Wilson, 'Books', *New Yorker* 27 October 1945.
10 Ibid.
11 Edmund Wilson, *Classics and Commercials* (New York: Farrar, Straus, 1950) 285.
12 'Edmund Wilson: An Appreciation', *Sunday Times* 18 June 1972.
13 Waugh, *Diaries* 625.
14 Lehmann, *In My Own Time* 387–8.
15 Quennell, *The Wanton Chase* 44.
16 Edmund Wilson, *Europe Without Baedeker* (1947; New York: Farrar, Straus, 1966) 15.
17 'Edmund Wilson: An Appreciation', *Sunday Times*, 18 June 1972.
18 'Comment', *Horizon* April 1947 (reprinted in *Ideas and Places* 142–6).
19 Wilson, 'Books', *New Yorker* 27 October 1945.
20 Quoted in 'Highbrows' *Horizon*', *Time* 25 March 1946.
21 Waugh, *Diaries* 628.
22 Matthew Connolly to Cyril Connolly, 2 April 1945 (Tulsa).
23 Peter Watson to John Craxton, 19 July 1945 (Craxton Papers).
24 Peter Watson to Cecil Beaton, 13 October [1945] (Beaton Papers).
25 Ibid.
26 Cyril Connolly to Lys, n.d. [14 July 1945] (Lilly).
27 All quotations in these two paragraphs are taken from two letters: Cyril Connolly to Lys, n.d. [14 July 1945] and Cyril Connolly to Lys, n.d. [17 July 1945] (Lilly).
28 'Comment', *Horizon* September 1945 (reprinted in *Ideas and Places* 28–33).
29 Cyril Connolly to Lys, n.d. [14 July 1945] (Lilly).
30 Cyril Connolly to Lys, n.d. [22 July 1945] (Lilly).
31 Quotations in this paragraph are taken from 'Comment', *Horizon* February

1946 (reprinted in *Ideas and Places* 55–66), and from Peter Watson to John Craxton, 19 July 1945 (Craxton Papers).

32 Cyril Connolly to Lys, n.d. [22 July 1945] (Lilly).
33 'Comment', *Horizon* February 1946.
34 Cyril Connolly to Lys, n.d. [29 July 1945] (Lilly).
35 Cyril Connolly to Lys, n.d. [22 July 1945] (Lilly).
36 'Comment', *Horizon* February 1946.
37 Cyril Connolly to Lys, n.d. [29 July 1945] (Lilly).
38 Ibid.
39 Elizabeth Bowen, *Tatler* 23 January 1946.
40 *Listener*, 12 July 1945.
41 Peter Watson to Cyril Connolly, 2 September [1945] and 8 September [1945] (Tulsa).
42 Peter Watson to Cyril Connolly, 16 September 1945 (Tulsa).
43 Ibid.
44 Peter Watson to Cyril Connolly, 10 October [1945] (Tulsa).
45 Peter Watson to Cyril Connolly, 5 October [1945] (Tulsa).
46 Peter Watson to Cyril Connolly, 19 October [1945] (Tulsa).
47 Peter Watson to Cecil Beaton, 13 October [1945] (Beaton).
48 Peter Watson to Cyril Connolly, 5 October [1945] (Tulsa).
49 Peter Watson to Cyril Connolly, 19 October [1945] (Tulsa).
50 Ibid.
51 Ibid.
52 Peter Watson to Cyril Connolly, 26 October [1945] (Tulsa).
53 Peter Watson to Cyril Connolly, 28 November [1945] (Tulsa).
54 Lys Koch to author, March 1984.

## CHAPTER SEVEN

1 Jean Connolly to Cyril Connolly, 18 October 1945 (Tulsa).
2 Draft letter, n.d. [written on back of 18 October 1945 letter from Jean to Connolly] (Tulsa).
3 Jean Connolly to Cyril Connolly, 20 November 1945 (Tulsa).
4 *Ideas and Places* 232.
5 Cyril Connolly to Robert Gathorne-Hardy, n.d. [9 March 1946] (Lilly).
6 *Ideas and Places* 232.
7 Cyril Connolly to Robert Gathorne-Hardy, 8 September 1948 (Lilly).
8 The quotations in this paragraph are taken from *Ideas and Places* 228, and from Cyril Connolly to Robert Gathorne-Hardy, n.d. [9 March 1946] (Lilly).
9 Theodore Roethke to Cyril Connolly, 15 April 1946 (Washington).
10 Sonia Brownell to Theodore Roethke, 4 July 1946 (Washington).
11 Quoted in Allan Seager, *The Glass House: The Life of Theodore Roethke* (New York: McGraw-Hill, 1968) 152.
12 'Comment', *Horizon* April 1947 (reprinted in *Ideas and Places* 142–6).
13 *The Evening Colonnade* (British edition) 300.

14 Notes of conversations, Sonia Orwell to Ian Angus, 25 April 1967, and 4 June 1963. Quoted in Ian Angus to author, 30 July 1985.
15 Ibid.
16 Orwell, *Collected Essays, Journalism and Letters* 4: 374–7.
17 Sonia Brownell to Cyril Connolly, 9 April 1946 (Tulsa).
18 Sonia Brownell to Cyril Connolly, 1 August 1946 (Tulsa).
19 Ibid.
20 Peter Watson to Cyril Connolly, 17 July [1946] (Tulsa).
21 Memorandum, Cass Canfield to Mr Allen, 4 December 1946 (Princeton).
22 Hamish Hamilton to Cass Canfield, 7 August 1946 (Princeton).

## CHAPTER EIGHT

1 'USA 1946' diary (Tulsa).
2 'Comment', *Horizon* October 1947 (reprinted in *Ideas and Places* 166–82).
3 'USA 1946' diary (Tulsa).
4 'Comment', *Horizon* October 1947.
5 Charles Henri Ford to author, 17 February 1985.
6 Cass Canfield, 'Memorandum on talk with Connolly', 3 December 1946 (Princeton).
7 'Comment', *Horizon* October 1947.
8 'State of Art', *New Yorker* 14 December 1947.
9 The source of this story is to be found in *Selected Letters of E. E. Cummings*, ed. F. W. Dupee and George Stade (London: Deutsch, 1972) 172.
10 *The Evening Colonnade* (British edition) 326.
11 Cyril Connolly to E. E. Cummings, 1 February 1946 (Harvard).
12 Cummings, *Selected Letters* 171–2.
13 'USA 1946' diary (Tulsa).
14 Clement Greenberg to author, 29 April 1987.
15 Peter Watson to Brian Howard, n.d. [January 1947] (Eton).
16 'Comment', *Horizon* October 1947.
17 Ibid.
18 *Lawrence Durrell and Henry Miller: A Private Correspondence*, ed. George Wickes (New York: Dutton, 1963) 235.
19 'Comment', *Horizon* October 1947.
20 'How Aldous Huxley Sees It Now', *Picture Post* 6 November 1948.
21 *New Statesman* 7 April 1945.
22 *Picture Post* 6 November 1948.
23 'Comment', *Horizon* October 1947.
24 Cyril Connolly to Jacques Barzun, 9 March 1947 (Columbia).
25 Cass Canfield to Hamish Hamilton, 23 December 1946 (Princeton).
26 'Comment', *Horizon* October 1947.
27 'Comment', *Horizon* July 1947 (reprinted in *Ideas and Places* 158–60).
28 Cyril Connolly to Maud Connolly, n.d. [March 1947] (Tulsa). Also see the notice of Major Connolly's death in *Nature* 19 April 1947.
29 Jean Connolly to Cyril Connolly, 6 March 1947 (Tulsa).

30 Introduction, *The Evening Colonnade* (American edition).
31 Quoted in Cyril Connolly to Matthew Connolly, n.d. [1 February 1947] (Tulsa).
32 'Comment', *Horizon* November 1947 (reprinted in *Ideas and Places* 182–5).
33 Cyril Connolly to Cass Canfield, 18 July 1947 (Princeton).
34 Cyril Connolly to Maud Connolly, n.d. [March 1947] (Tulsa).
35 Waldemar Hansen to author, August 1984.
36 Ibid.
37 Peter Watson to Waldemar Hansen, n.d. [17 March 1947] and n.d. [18 March 1947] (HP).
38 Peter Watson to Waldemar Hansen, n.d. [17 March 1947] (HP).
39 Peter Watson to Waldemar Hansen, 21 March [1947] (HP).
40 Peter Watson to Waldemar Hansen, first of two letters from 28 March [1947] (HP).
41 Peter Watson to Waldemar Hansen, second of two letters from 28 March [1947] (HP).
42 Peter Watson to Waldemar Hansen, n.d. [11 April 1947] (HP).
43 Waldemar Hansen to John Myers, 30 April 1947 (HP).
44 Waldemar Hansen to John Myers, 4 May 1947 (HP).
45 Waldemar Hansen to John Myers, 30 April 1947 (HP).
46 Waldemar Hansen to John Myers, 20 September 1947 (HP).
47 Cyril Connolly to Maud Connolly, n.d. [11 January 1949] (Tulsa).
48 Quoted in Edmund Wilson, *The Fifties*, ed. Leon Edel (New York: Farrar, Straus, 1986) 107.
49 'Reflections', *Time* 29 November 1948.
50 'The Best?' *Time* 1 December 1947.
51 'Comment', *Horizon* June 1949.
52 Cyril Connolly to Evelyn Waugh, n.d. [late 1947] (Texas).
53 Peter Watson to Cyril Connolly, n.d. [5 October 1947] (Tulsa).
54 Peter Watson to Cyril Connolly, n.d. [7 or 14 October 1947] (Tulsa).
55 Ibid.
56 Waugh, *Letters* 268.
57 Cyril Connolly to Enid Bagnold, 1 March 1948 (Tulsa).

## CHAPTER NINE

1 Angus Wilson to Cyril Connolly, 6 September 1973 (Tulsa).
2 Unpublished manuscript (Tulsa).
3 'Comment', *Horizon* April 1948 (reprinted in *Ideas and Places* 192–5).
4 Unpublished manuscript (Tulsa).
5 Quoted in Waldemar Hansen to John Myers, 6 May 1948 (HP).
6 Cyril Connolly to Maud Connolly, n.d. [11 January 1949] (Tulsa).
7 Cyril Connolly's divorce deposition, 22 October 1947 (Tulsa).
8 Lys Koch to author, October 1984.
9 Cyril Connolly to Enid Bagnold, 1 March 1948 (Tulsa).

10 Introduction, *Ideas and Places*.

11 'Comment', *Horizon* December 1949 (reprinted in *Ideas and Places* 214–19).

12 Geoffrey Grigson, 'Authentic and False in The New "Romanticism"', *Horizon* March 1948.

13 Roland Penrose, *Scrap Book: 1900–1981* (New York: Rizzoli, 1981) 144.

14 'Comment', *Horizon* November 1947.

15 Waldemar Hansen to John Myers, 14 December 1947, and 13 June 1948 (HP).

16 Waldemar Hansen to John Myers, 9 November 1947 (HP).

17 Waldemar Hansen to John Myers, 13 June 1948 (HP).

18. Cyril Connolly to Hamish Hamilton, 21 April 1948 (Princeton).

19. Ibid.

20 Cass Canfield to Cyril Connolly, 4 May 1948 (Princeton).

21 Cyril Connolly to Lys, n.d. [22 June 1948] (Lilly).

22 Cyril Connolly to Lys, n.d. [June 1948] (Lilly).

23 Cyril Connolly to Maud Connolly, n.d. [11 January 1949] (Tulsa).

24 Sonia Brownell to Cyril Connolly, 19 July 1948 (Tulsa).

25 Quoted in Burton Bernstein, *Thurber: A Biography* (New York: Dodd, Mead, 1975) 372.

26 '"Les Soirs Sont Plus Humains": Olivier Larronde,' *Art and Literature* Autumn 1966.

27 Cyril Connolly to Lys, n.d. [8 August 1948] (Lilly).

28 Cyril Connolly to Lys, n.d. [August 1948] (Lilly).

29 Cyril Connolly to Maud Connolly, n.d. [11 January 1949] (Tulsa).

30 Ibid.

31 Unpublished manuscript (Tulsa).

32 Peter Watson to Waldemar Hansen, n.d. [May 1948] (HP).

33 Peter Watson to Waldemar Hansen, 14 October [1948] (HP).

34 Peter Watson to Waldemar Hansen, 28 December [1948] (HP).

35 Waldemar Hansen to John Myers, 11 September [1948] (HP).

36 Peter Watson to Waldemar Hansen, 1 November [1948] (HP).

37 Peter Watson to Waldemar Hansen, 14 October [1948] (HP).

38 Peter Watson to Waldemar Hansen, n.d. [27 October 1948] (HP).

39 Peter Watson to Waldemar Hansen, 30 November [1948] (HP).

40 Peter Watson to Waldemar Hansen, 20 October [1948] (HP).

41 Quoted in Hugo Vickers, *Cecil Beaton: The Authorized Biography* (London: Weidenfeld and Nicolson, 1985) 341.

42 Peter Watson to Waldemar Hansen, 22 November 1948 (HP).

43 Peter Watson to Waldemar Hansen, 14 October [1948] (HP).

44 Peter Watson to Waldemar Hansen, 9 November [1948] (HP).

45 Sonia Brownell to Waldemar Hansen, 27 December 1948 (HP).

46 Cyril Connolly to Lys, n.d. [November 1948] (Lilly).

47 Peter Watson to Waldemar Hansen, 9 November [1948], and Sonia Brownell to Waldemar Hansen, 27 December 1948 (HP).

48 'Comment', *Horizon* April 1949.

## CHAPTER TEN

1 Peter Watson to Waldemar Hansen, 20 December [1948], and Peter Watson to Waldemar Hansen, 28 December [1948] (HP).
2 Waldemar Hansen to author, August 1984.
3 Peter Watson to Waldemar Hansen, 27 February [1949] (HP).
4 Waldemar Hansen to John Myers, 5 May 1949 (HP).
5 Peter Watson to Waldemar Hansen, n.d. [11 November 1948] (HP).
6 Introduction to *The Oasis*, *Horizon* February 1949.
7 Hamish Hamilton to Cass Canfield, 8 July 1949 (Princeton).
8 Cass Canfield to Cyril Connolly, 8 July 1949 (Princeton).
9 Cass Canfield to S. M. Bessie, 13 March 1953 (Princeton).
10 Sonia Brownell to Waldemar Hansen, 1 March 1949 (HP).
11 Cyril Connolly to Lys, n.d. [May 1949] (Lilly).
12 Cyril Connolly to Lys, n.d. [4 June 1949] (Lilly).
13 Ibid.
14 Introduction, *Ideas and Places*.
15 Peter Watson to Waldemar Hansen, 27 July [1949] (HP).
16 Orwell, *Collected Essays, Journalism and Letters* 4:568.
17 Quoted in Bernard Crick, *George Orwell: A Life* (1980; Harmondsworth: Penguin Books, 1982) 563.
18 Waldemar Hansen to John Myers, 6 September 1949 (HP).
19 Peter Watson to Waldemar Hansen, 24 September [1949] (HP).
20 Waldemar Hansen to John Myers, 3 July 1949 (HP).
21 Peter Watson to Waldemar Hansen, n.d. [28 June 1949] (HP).
22 Waldemar Hansen to author, August 1984.
23 'Comment', *Horizon* November 1949 (reprinted in *Ideas and Places* 211–14).
24 Quoted in Wilson, *The Fifties* 373.
25 Ibid. 375.
26 Cyril Connolly to Lys, n.d. [15 January 1951]; n.d. [May 1950]; n.d. [Autumn 1950] (Lilly).
27 Augustus John to Cyril Connolly, 25 November 1949 (Tulsa).
28 Introduction, *Ideas and Places*.
29 Quoted in Wadhams, *Remembering Orwell* 215.
30 *The Evening Colonnade* (British edition) 377.
31 Waugh, *Letters* 320.
32 Cyril Connolly to Lys, n.d. [early 1951] (Lilly).
33 Cyril Connolly to Lys, 16 June [1952] (Lilly).
34 Peter Watson to Waldemar Hansen, 14 October [1950] (HP).
35 Barbara Skelton, *Tears Before Bedtime* (London: Hamish Hamilton, 1987) 105.
36 Cyril Connolly to Lys, n.d. [early 1951] (Lilly).
37 Cyril Connolly to Lys, 3 March [1951] (Lilly).
38 Cyril Connolly to Lys, n.d. [1955] (Lilly).
39 Cyril Connolly to Lys, n.d. [early Spring 1953] (Lilly).

# EPILOGUE

1 Peter Watson to Brian Howard, n.d. [March 1950] (Eton).
2 Peter Watson to Lys, 10 April [1956] (Lilly).
3 Cecil Beaton, *Self Portrait with Friends: The Selected Diaries of Cecil Beaton, 1926–1974*, ed. Richard Buckle (London: Weidenfeld and Nicolson, 1979) 304.
4 'Peter Watson', *New Statesman* 12 May 1956.
5 Norman Fowler to Waldemar Hansen, 25 March 1952 (HP).

# SELECT BIBLIOGRAPHY

Ackroyd, Peter. *T. S. Eliot: A Life*. London: Hamish Hamilton, 1984.

*Age of Austerity: 1945–1951*. Ed. Michael Sissons and Philip French. London: Hodder and Stoughton, 1963.

Baron, Wendy. *Miss Ethel Sands and Her Circle*. London: Peter Owen, 1977.

Beaton, Cecil. *Self Portrait with Friends: The Selected Diaries of Cecil Beaton, 1926–1974*. Ed. Richard Buckle. London: Weidenfeld and Nicolson, 1979.

Bernstein, Burton. *Thurber: A Biography*. New York: Dodd, Mead, 1975.

Berthoud, Roger. *Graham Sutherland*. London: Faber, 1982.

Calder, Angus. *The People's War: Britain 1939–1945*. London: Jonathan Cape, 1969.

Carpenter, Humphrey, *W. H. Auden: A Biography*. London: Allen and Unwin, 1981.

Connolly, Cyril. *The Rock Pool*. Paris: Obelisk Press, 1936; New York: Scribner's, 1936; London: Hamish Hamilton, 1947.

——. *Enemies of Promise*. London: Routledge, 1938; Boston: Little, Brown, 1939. Rev. ed. New York: Macmillan, 1948; London: Routledge, 1949.

——. *The Unquiet Grave: A Word Cycle*, by 'Palinurus'. London: Horizon, 1944. Rev. ed. London: Hamish Hamilton, 1945; New York: Harper, 1945.

——. *The Condemned Playground: Essays, 1927–1944*. London: Routledge, 1945; New York: Macmillan, 1946.

——. *Ideas and Places*. London: Weidenfeld and Nicolson, 1953; New York: Harper, 1953.

——. *Previous Convictions*. London: Hamish Hamilton, 1963; New York: Harper, 1963.

——. *The Evening Colonnade*. London: David Bruce and Watson, 1973; New York: Harcourt, 1975.

——. *A Romantic Friendship: Cyril Connolly's Letters to Noel Blakiston*. Ed. Noel Blakiston. London: Constable, 1975.

Crick, Bernard. *George Orwell: A Life*. Rev. ed. London: Secker and Warburg, 1981.

Cummings, E. E. *Selected Letters of E. E. Cummings*. Ed. F. W. Dupee and George Stade. New York: Harcourt Brace, 1969.

De-la-Noy, Michael. *Denton Welch: The Making of a Writer*. Harmondsworth: Viking, 1984.

Finney, Brian. *Christopher Isherwood: A Critical Biography*. London: Faber, 1979.

FitzGibbon, Constance. *The Life of Dylan Thomas*. London: Dent, 1965.

Fleming, Ann. *The Letters of Ann Fleming*. Ed. Mark Amory. London: Collins Harvill, 1985.

Gathorne-Hardy, Robert. *Recollections of Logan Pearsall Smith: The Story of a Friendship*. London: Constable, 1949.

Glendinning, Victoria. *Edith Sitwell: A Unicorn Among Lions*. London: Weidenfeld and Nicolson, 1981.

——. *Elizabeth Bowen: Portrait of a Writer*. London: Weidenfeld and Nicolson, 1977.

*The Golden Horizon*. Ed. Cyril Connolly. London: Weidenfeld and Nicolson, 1953.

Goodman, Celia. *Living with Koestler*. London: Weidenfeld and Nicolson, 1985.

Gowing, Lawrence. *Lucian Freud*. London: Thames and Hudson, 1982.

Green, Martin. *Children of the Sun: A Narrative of 'Decadence' in England after 1918*. London: Constable, 1977.

Gross, John. *The Rise and Fall of the Man of Letters*. London: Weidenfeld and Nicolson, 1969.

Hamilton, Iain. *Koestler*. London: Secker and Warburg, 1982.

Harries, Meirion, and Susie Harries. *The War Artists: British Official War Art of the Twentieth Century*. London: Michael Joseph, 1983.

Hewison, Robert. *Under Siege: Literary Life in London, 1939–1945*. London: Weidenfeld and Nicolson, 1977.

——. *In Anger: Culture in the Cold War, 1945–1960*. London: Weidenfeld and Nicolson, 1981.

Isherwood, Christopher. *Down There on a Visit*. London: Methuen, 1962.

Lancaster, Marie-Jacqueline. *Brian Howard: Portrait of a Failure*. London: Blond, 1968.

Lehmann, John. *In My Own Time: Memoirs of a Literary Life*. Boston: Little, Brown, 1969.

Lottman, Herbert R. *The Left Bank: Writers, Artists, and Politics from the Popular Front to the Cold War*. Boston: Houghton Mifflin, 1982.

Maclaren-Ross, J. *Memoirs of the Forties*. London: Alan Ross, 1965.

Mitford, Nancy. *The Blessing*. London: Hamish Hamilton, 1951.

Myers, John Bernard. *Tracking the Marvelous: A Life in the New York Art World*. New York: Random House, 1983.

Orwell, George. *Collected Essays, Journalism and Letters of George Orwell*. Ed. Sonia Orwell and Ian Angus. 4 volumes. London: Secker and Warburg, 1968.

Partridge, Frances, *Everything to Lose: Diaries 1945–1960*. London: Gollancz, 1985.

Pearson, John. *The Life of Ian Fleming*. London: Jonathan Cape, 1966.

Penrose, Roland. *Scrap Book, 1900–1981*. New York: Rizzoli, 1981.

Pikoulis, John. *Alun Lewis: A Life*. Bridgend: Poetry Wales Press, 1984.

Plante, David. *Difficult Women: A Memoir of Three*. London: Gollancz, 1983.

Powell, Anthony. *To Keep the Ball Rolling: The Memoirs of Anthony Powell*. Harmondsworth: Penguin Books, 1983.

Prokosch, Frederic. *Voices: A Memoir*. New York: Farrar, Straus, 1983.

Pryce-Jones, David. *Cyril Connolly: Journal and Memoir*. London: Collins, 1983.

Quennell, Peter. *The Wanton Chase: An Autobiography from 1939*. London: Collins, 1980.

Simon, Oliver. *Printer and Playground: An Autobiography*. London: Faber, 1956.

Spender, Stephen. *World Within World*. London: Hamish Hamilton, 1951.

——. *The Thirties and After: Poetry, Politics, People, 1939–1970*. New York: Random House, 1978.

——. *Journals: 1939–1983*. Ed. John Goldsmith. London: Faber, 1985.

Sykes, Christopher. *Evelyn Waugh: A Biography*. London: Collins, 1975.

Thomas, Dylan. *The Collected Letters of Dylan Thomas*. Ed. Paul Ferris. London: Dent, 1985.

Vickers, Hugo. *Cecil Beaton: The Authorized Biography*. London: Weidenfeld and Nicolson, 1985.

Wadhams, Stephen. *Remembering Orwell*. Harmondsworth: Penguin Books, 1984.

Waugh, Evelyn. *Unconditional Surrender*. London: Chapman and Hall, 1961.

——. *The Diaries of Evelyn Waugh*. Ed. Michael Davie. London: Weidenfeld and Nicolson, 1976.

——. *The Letters of Evelyn Waugh*. Ed. Mark Amory. London: Weidenfeld and Nicolson, 1980.

White, Antonia. *Frost in May*. London: Desmond Harmsworth, 1933.

Wilson, Edmund. *Europe Without Baedeker*. New York: Farrar, Straus, 1947.

——. *Classics and Commercials*. New York: Farrar, Straus, 1950.

Wishart, Michael. *High Diver*. London: Blond and Briggs, 1977.

Woolf, Virginia. *The Letters of Virginia Woolf*. Ed. Nigel Nicolson and Joanne Trautmann. 6 volumes. London: Hogarth Press, 1975–1980.

——. *The Diary of Virginia Woolf*. Ed. Anne Olivier Bell. 5 volumes. London: Hogarth Press, 1977–1984.

Ziegler, Philip. *Diana Cooper*. London: Hamish Hamilton, 1981.

# INDEX

Acton, Harold, 3, 16
Astor, David, 93, 104–6, 218
Astor, Lord, 6, 104, 106
Auden, W. H., 1, 23, 45, 167, 192
    contributions to *Horizon*, 6, 44,
      47, 157, 187, 194–5, 215
Ayer, A. J., 124

Bacon, Francis, 71, 80, 161–2
Bakewell, Jean *see* Connolly
Barzun, Jacques, 163
Bates, H. E., 1
Beaton, Cecil, 27, 64, 80, 125, 144,
    205, 230
Beauvoir, Simone de, 123–4
Berryman, John, 186
Betjeman, John, 1, 44, 47,
    152–3
Blair, Eric *see* Orwell
Blanchot, Maurice, 222
Bowen, Elizabeth, 1, 72, 130, 140,
    152–3
Bower, Tony, 173
Bowra, Maurice, 98, 126
Brown, Ivor, 104–5
Brownell, Sonia, 73–8, 205–6,
    214, 228
    and Hansen, 184, 197
    and Orwell, 78, 159–60, 216–
      18, 224

work for *Horizon*, 75, 155–6,
    160–1, 184, 199, 215, 216
Burgess, Guy, 72

Canfield, Cass, 164, 168, 173–4,
    198, 212–14
Capote, Truman, 57, 182, 211
Clark, Kenneth, 16, 49, 79–80, 85,
    87–8, 157
Colquhoun, Robert, 79, 80
Connolly, Barbara (Skelton)
    (second wife), 222, 225–6,
    228
Connolly, Cyril Vernon
    ambivalence towards women,
      24, 111, 148, 201–2, 206–
      7
    aphorisms, 14, 15, 23, 64, 92,
      179, 186, 216
    awareness of his weaknesses, 9,
      19, 31, 50, 110, 150, 152,
      169, 202, 213
    *The Condemned Playground*
      (1945), 7, 140–3, 163
    'Connolly Books', 164, 170,
      174, 213
    difficulty with literary form, 9,
      22, 191
    on editing a magazine, 86, 92,
      173–4